Global Basic Rights

Global Basic Rights

Edited by
Charles R. Beitz and Robert E. Goodin

OXFORD
UNIVERSITY PRESS

OXFORD
UNIVERSITY PRESS

Great Clarendon Street, Oxford OX2 6DP

Oxford University Press is a department of the University of Oxford.
It furthers the University's objective of excellence in research, scholarship,
and education by publishing worldwide in

Oxford New York

Auckland   Cape Town Dar es Salaam Hong Kong Karachi
Kuala Lumpur Madrid Melbourne Mexico City Nairobi
New Delhi Shanghai Taipei Toronto
With offices in
Argentina Austria Brazil Chile Czech Republic France Greece
Guatemala Hungary Italy Japan South Korea Poland Portugal
Singapore Switzerland Thailand Turkey Ukraine Vietnam

Oxford is a registered trade mark of Oxford University Press
in the UK and in certain other countries

Published in the United States
by Oxford University Press Inc., New York

The editors and contributors have donated their royalties and
other income from the sale of this book to Oxfam GB.

ISBN 978-0-19-960438-8

Printed in the United Kingdom by
the MPG Books Group Ltd

For Henry Shue

Contents

Notes on Contributors

Elizabeth Ashford is Lecturer in Philosophy, University of St Andrews. Her primary research interests are in moral and political philosophy. Her publications include "Utilitarianism, Integrity and Partiality," *Journal of Philosophy* (2000) and "The Demandingness of Scanlon's Contractualism," *Ethics* (2003).

Charles R. Beitz is Edwards S. Sanford Professor of Politics at Princeton University. He teaches and writes about topics in global political philosophy and democratic theory and is the author, most recently, of *The Idea of Human Rights* (2009). He edits *Philosophy & Public Affairs*.

Simon Caney is Fellow and Tutor in Politics, Magdalen College, Oxford University. He is the author of *Justice Beyond Borders* (2005). His current research interests focus on topics in global political philosophy, and particularly the ethical issues surrounding global climate change.

Neta C. Crawford is Professor of Political Science and African American Studies, Boston University. Her research interests include ethics of war and ethical argument. She is the author of *Argument and Change in World Politics: Ethics, Decolonization and Humanitarian Intervention* and co-editor of *How Sanctions Work: Lessons From South Africa*.

Robert E. Goodin is Distinguished Professor of Philosophy and of Social and Political Theory, Research School of Social Sciences, Australian National University. He is the founding editor of *The Journal of Political Philosophy*, General Editor of the ten-volume series of *Oxford Handbooks of Political Science*, and author, most recently, of *Innovating Democracy* (2008).

Andrew Hurrell is Montague Burton Professor of International Relations at Oxford University and a Fellow of Balliol College, Oxford. He recently published *On Global Order: Power, Values and the Constitution of International Society* (2007). His research interests cover theories of international relations, with particular reference to international law and institutions;

theories of global and regional governance; and the history of thought on international relations.

Judith Lichtenberg is Professor of Philosophy, Georgetown University. She is author, with Robert Fullinwider, of *Leveling the Playing Field: Justice, Politics, and College Admissions*. She has written articles on war and global justice, and is currently at work on a book, *Charity, Its Scope and Limits*.

David Luban is University Professor and Professor of Law and Philosophy, Georgetown University. His research interests center around individual responsibility in organizational settings. His most recent books are *Legal Ethics and Human Dignity* (2007) and the forthcoming *International and Transnational Criminal Law* (with Julie O'Sullivan and David P. Stewart).

Richard W. Miller is Professor of Philosophy, Cornell University. His writings include *Analyzing Marx* (1984), *Fact and Method* (1987), *Moral Differences* (1992), many articles in political philosophy, ethics, epistemology, and the philosophy of science, and *Globalizing Justice: The Ethics of Poverty and Power* (forthcoming).

Thomas Pogge is Leitner Professor of Philosophy and International Affairs, Yale University, and Research Director at the Oslo University Centre for the Study of Mind in Nature. He has published widely on Kant and in moral and political philosophy, including various books on Rawls and global justice. He is editor for social and political philosophy for the Stanford Encyclopedia of Philosophy and a member of the Norwegian Academy of Science. With support from the European Commission (7th Framework), he currently heads a team effort toward developing a complement to the pharmaceutical patent regime that would improve access to advanced medicines for the poor worldwide.

Christian Reus-Smit is Professor of International Politics, Australian National University. He is author of *American Power and World Order* (2004) and *The Moral Purpose of the State* (1999), co-author of *Theories of International Politics* (4th edn., 2008), editor of *The Politics of International Law* (2004), and co-editor of *The Oxford Handbook of International Relations* (2008), *Resolving International Crises of Legitimacy* (Special Issue, *International Politics* 2007), and *Between Sovereignty and Global Governance* (1998).

Jeremy Waldron is University Professor, New York University (School of Law). He teaches and writes in the areas of political theory and legal philosophy. He is the author of *Law and Disagreement* (1999) and *God, Locke and Equality* (2002).

1

Introduction: *Basic Rights* and Beyond

Charles R. Beitz and Robert E. Goodin

In *The Law of Peoples* John Rawls observes that the post-World War II settlement contained two revolutionary elements: the lawful purposes of war were restricted to self-defense and protecting international security, and the traditional prerogatives of sovereignty were limited by an international doctrine of human rights.[1] However improbable the second of these initiatives might have appeared in the aftermath of the war, today there is no question that human rights have attained the status of a *lingua franca* of global moral discourse. And it is also clear that, among the works of political philosophy stimulated by and contributing to this development, none has proved more seminal than Henry Shue's *Basic Rights*.[2]

Shue wrote during the presidential term of Jimmy Carter, the first American president to make the protection of human rights an explicit priority of foreign policy. There was disagreement at that time about the proper scope of such a commitment—in particular, whether a "human rights foreign policy" should concentrate on protecting against threats to personal security from authoritarian regimes, or whether it should engage with the broader evils associated with material deprivation. Shue's well-known central argument—that what he called "subsistence rights" are as "basic" as are rights to personal security—was thus an intervention in an intensely practical dispute.[3] Regarded as a matter of U.S. public political disagreement, this dispute was fairly short lived. The Reagan Administration was interested only in pressing civil and political rights as a ploy in Helsinki arms

---

[1] John Rawls, *The Law of Peoples* (Cambridge, Mass.: Harvard University Press, 1999), p. 79.
[2] Henry Shue, *Basic Rights: Subsistence, Affluence and U.S. Foreign Policy*, 2nd edn. (Princeton, N.J.: Princeton University Press, 1996). The first edition was published in 1980.
[3] This is clearer in the first edition than in the 1996 revision, in which the original final chapter, devoted to policy implications, has been replaced by a new Afterword.

control negotiations with the USSR.[4] There was no realistic prospect of it pressing "subsistence rights" as well. There was, however, plenty of room for influence in the international arena, where Shue's arguments in *Basic Rights* had profound impact upon foundational UN documents on, for example, international rights to food and health.[5]

Why should a book whose immediate aim was to influence a passing U.S. foreign policy dispute continue to be read today, thirty years later? The answer will be obvious to anyone who reads the philosophical literature or follows international human rights developments that it helps to shape. Although the U.S. foreign policy disputes of the 1970s and 1980s were mainly political and ideological, they nonetheless had important philosophical dimensions. Some of these represent longstanding puzzles in the theory of rights: about the nature of rights and their relationship to social institutions; the social conditions necessary for the enjoyment of rights; the implications of rights for those in a position to respect and protect them; the significance of the distinction between "negative" duties to forbear and "positive" duties to contribute; the association of security rights with "negative" duties and of welfare rights with "positive" ones; and the force of claims of right lodged within versus outside one's own society.

In order to address the political questions of its time, *Basic Rights* had to engage with all these philosophical problems. In doing so, it gave shape to the subject of human rights as a coherent preoccupation of political philosophy. Not only does the book have interesting things to say about all of the puzzles just listed (and various others). About some of them— particularly those concerning the duties associated with basic rights—it advances positions which, although heretical when the book was first published, have since become close to philosophical orthodoxy. Both for its intellectual architecture and for its contributions to the theory of human rights, Shue's book remains a landmark that repays multiple rereadings.

---

[4] Daniel C. Thomas, *The Helsinki Effect: International Norms, Human Rights and the Demise of Communism* (Princeton, N.J.: Princeton University Press, 2001).

[5] As further discussed in Andrew Hurrell's contribution to this volume. Thomas Pogge, in footnote 11 of his chapter in this volume, traces Shue's impact on "the right to adequate food" as elaborated by the UN Committee on Economic, Social and Cultural Rights in its 1999 General Comment No. 12. Shue's influence can be seen even more clearly in the opening words of that Committee's 2000 General Comment No. 14 which read: "Health is a fundamental human right indispensable for the exercise of other human rights"; see "The Right to the Highest Attainable Standard of Health, E/C.12/2000/4," available at <http://www.unhchr.ch/tbs/doc.nsf/(symbol)/E.C.12.2000.4.En>. Describing the importance of this document, the UN Rapporteur responsible for this area writes: "Not until 2000 did an authoritative understanding of the right emerge—when the UN Committee . . . , in close collaboration with WHO and many others, adopted General Comment 14"; Paul Hunt, "Right to the Highest Attainable Standard of Health," *The Lancet*, 370 (Aug. 4, 2007), 369–71 at pp. 369–70.

Basic Rights is also provocative, in the most constructive sense. It is hard to imagine how anybody with an interest in human rights could read this book without being forced to think more deeply about his or her own views. And since it is a book that engages a range of empirical concerns in order to make sense of human rights, this is as true for those whose interests are essentially practical or political as it is for those whose interests are more purely philosophical. That is also as true for ideas at one remove from the book's explicit concerns as it is for those that are its main preoccupations.

As the chapters that follow abundantly illustrate, *Basic Rights* generated fruitful research agendas for both normative theorists and empirically minded students of global politics. The aim of this volume is to explore its ramifications in both domains. As background, this chapter characterizes the important central argument of the book and poses some preliminary questions about both its persuasiveness and its implications. These questions situate the research agenda launched by *Basic Rights*, which each of the following chapters assess and further extend.

1. The Central Thesis

The central thesis of Shue's book is that everyone has "basic rights" to "security" and "subsistence." The case for this thesis has two main branches. The first is an argument that both security and subsistence bear the same relation to other rights; in a sense we shall define, they are equally "basic." Call this the "Basic Rights Argument." The second is an argument that the duties that flow from each of those basic rights have a parallel, complex structure; both rights serve as grounds for duties that require both forbearance and active contribution. Call this the "Correlative Duties Argument." The conclusion is that whether we consider matters from the point of view of the potential beneficiary of basic rights or from that of potential holders of the duties associated with these rights, there is no systematic distinction to be drawn between security and subsistence. Both are basic rights. And so too, we suggest later in this chapter, might be some others.

1.1. The Basic Rights Argument

We shall set out the two main branches of Shue's argument separately, beginning with the Basic Rights Argument. This argument has two steps, the first definitional and the second normative. First, Shue defines "basic rights" as rights whose "enjoyment is essential to the enjoyment of all other rights" (p. 19).[6] That is *not* to say that basic rights are either more valuable or more satisfying than other rights. A non-basic right such as freedom of expression might contribute more to one's capacity to achieve what one deems to be important in life, and its exercise might generate more satisfaction, than "basic rights" to security and subsistence.[7] A right is "basic" in Shue's sense only if, for any other right (whatever our other rights turn out to be), the non-basic right cannot be enjoyed unless the basic right is in place.

Now, of course, one might accept this definition of "basic rights" but deny that there are any rights that satisfy the definition. Perhaps there is no right such that its enjoyment is essential for the enjoyment of all other rights. So the second step of the argument—showing that rights to security and subsistence are each "basic" in the sense called for by that definition— is essential. Shue's basic strategy is to argue as follows: "Take any right you believe yourself to have. Call this right R. Now consider the background conditions that would have to be satisfied in order for you to enjoy R. You will find on reflection that these conditions include guarantees of security and subsistence. Without these guarantees, you could not enjoy R."[8]

First, Shue argues that "if there are any rights (basic or not basic) at all, there are basic rights to physical security" (p. 21). He argues that threats to our physical security are, by their nature, "among the most serious and—in much of the world—the most widespread hindrances to the enjoyment of any right" (ibid.). Without protection against these threats, we could not enjoy any other right. This would be straightforwardly true if we were to be victims of such a threat. But it would also be true if we were somehow to escape being victimized, since we would still be forced to devote ourselves to our own self-protection. Either way, we could not enjoy any other right.

Most people probably would regard the argument thus far as pretty uncontroversial.[9] Indeed, it seems to reformulate a commonsense thought

---

[6] We give page references to *Basic Rights* in the text.

[7] In a direct sense. Of course, indirectly basic rights can be credited with all the value or satisfaction which they are necessary preconditions for attaining through free expression, etc.

[8] Courts sometimes deploy similar strategies in declaring rights nowhere mentioned in the constitution to be implied or presupposed by things that are explicitly stated there. The High Court of Australia, for example, declared that although a "right to free political speech" is not explicitly stated in the Constitution, it "is necessarily implied" by the references to "representative government" that are in the Constitution; *ACT TV Ltd v Commonwealth*, 177 *Commonwealth Law Reports* 106 (1972), at p. 141.

[9] Although the "right to security," understood as an absolute right, has become more controversial in light of the excesses of the war on terror, as Jeremy Waldron and David Luban argue in their chapters in this volume.

about the value of personal security—namely, that its importance is at least partly instrumental, deriving from its role as a necessary condition for our accomplishment of any of a very wide range of possible ends. Part of the importance of Shue's thesis is to recognize that the same commonsense thought applies to our subsistence interests (e.g., in adequate food, clothing, shelter, and health care). The satisfaction of these interests seems to bear precisely the same relationship to our various possible ends as the satisfaction of our interest in personal security. In both cases, if the "basic" interests are not satisfied, then it will be either impossible or infeasible to achieve our ends, whatever, within reason, they turn out to be. Subsistence is just as "basic" as security.

This reasoning recalls an argument made by H. L. A. Hart for his claim that "there is at least one natural right, the equal right of all men to be free."[10] Hart's famous argument was couched in a conditional form. His claim was that if we have any rights at all, then we must have at least this one "natural right," since without such a principle in the background no assertion of right, whether "general" or "special," would make any sense. Rights, as Hart understands them, are special warrants for interfering with another person's liberty; and you simply would not need a special warrant unless there was a background presumption (his "one natural right") to be free of interference without one.[11] For Hart this conclusion is virtually a necessary truth, but it is clearly a conditional one. The argument leaves open the possibility that we might not have any rights at all. Perhaps that possibility is difficult to conceive, but if it were the case, then we would not be entitled (by Hart's argument, anyway) to believe that there is a natural right to equal freedom.

Shue's argument resembles Hart's in both respects just mentioned. It is conditional in form, and it seeks to invest its conclusion with a status close to that of a necessary truth. It is worth noting, however, that the "near necessity" claimed by Shue's argument differs importantly from that of Hart's. In Hart's argument, the necessity in view derives from a fact about the meaning of the notion of a "right," which is that it offers a reason to justify an interference with a person's liberties: we would have no need for rights without a background presupposition that interferences with freedom require justification. Shue's position turns, instead, on an inference from the most general and (he believes) uncontroversial facts about the needs and vulnerabilities of human beings. It is a claim about the social conditions required for what he calls the "enjoyment" of a right. To

---

[10] H. L. A. Hart, "Are There Any Natural Rights?" *Philosophical Review*, 64 (1955), 175–91 at p. 175.

[11] The argument is set forth in section III of "Are There Any Natural Rights?" pp. 188–91.

continue with the example of physical security, he argues that "no rights other than physical security can *in fact* be enjoyed if a right to physical security is not protected" (p. 21, our emphasis).

It is important to recall that, for Shue, a right (and *a fortiori* a basic right) is an ambitious thing. A right "provides (1) the rational basis for a justified demand (2) that the actual enjoyment of a substance be (3) socially guaranteed against standard threats" (p. 13). Here we draw particular attention to the ideas of "actual enjoyment" and "social guarantee" as they apply to "basic" rights. The force of these ideas can be brought out by comparing Shue's analysis of the concept of a right with what we might call the "simple" conception. According to the simple conception, A has a right to X if there is someone, B, who is under a duty not to interfere with A's attempts to have or to do X. If A tries to X and B interferes, then A has a claim against B—perhaps that B desist from the interference or make good the damage done by it.

The idea that the "actual enjoyment of a substance" should be "socially guaranteed against standard threats" elaborates the simple conception in two ways. In holding that a right must guarantee "the actual enjoyment of a substance," Shue means to deny that it would be proper to say that A has a right to X if a society's laws or conventions were simply to *declare* that "A has a right to X" while leaving A vulnerable *in fact* to various kinds of ("standard") threats to his having or doing X. "A right does not ... demand that it should be *said* that people are entitled to enjoy something, or that people should be *promised* that they will enjoy something. A proclamation of a right is not the fulfillment of a right, any more than an airplane schedule is a flight" (p. 15, our emphasis). Proclamation is not fulfillment. To think otherwise involves such an empty, formal conception of rights that it is hard to see why anyone should care about them.[12] But what, exactly, is missing from this "formal" conception of rights? The idea of "enjoyment of a substance" suggests a reply: what is missing is some assurance that a person said to "have" the right will in fact be in a position to enjoy the advantage that having the right is supposed to secure. If public officials proclaim that everybody has a right to X, but then do nothing to ensure that people can in fact have or do X if they so wish, then the

---

[12] One reason might be suggested by Joel Feinberg's remarks about "manifesto rights" in "Nature and Value of Rights," *Rights, Justice and the Bounds of Liberty* (Princeton, N.J.: Princeton University Press, 1980), pp. 143–58. In his view, "manifesto rights" are rights that cannot be correlated with another's duty (presumably including duties to establish a "social guarantee"). He regards claims based on such rights as a "valid exercise of rhetorical license" serving to call attention to values that states should recognize as "determinants of *present* aspirations and guides to *present* policies" (p. 153, emphasis in original).

so-called "right" can hardly have much value; indeed, people then can hardly be said to "have" the right at all.

It is easy to take this line of thought too far, however. One might be tempted to equate "enjoying the substance" of a right with success in attaining some end toward which the right is directed. For example, we might think that a person "enjoys the substance" of the right to free speech only if she succeeds in getting her ideas heard by an audience. But this can't be correct. We ordinarily think of rights as freedoms, not achievements: they protect us against interference in our efforts to seek various ends; they give us reasonable opportunities to pursue those ends; but they do not guarantee that we will actually achieve the ends we seek.[13] The right to free speech does not guarantee an attentive audience. Shue himself does not adopt this position: his official account of "enjoyment of a substance" of a right is more circumscribed.[14] It must be conceded, however, that occasionally the language of *Basic Rights* is sometimes ambiguous on this point.[15] Indeed, the word "enjoyment" itself might seem to invite the temptation to misunderstanding we have described.

A familiar and quite general problem lurks beyond this ambiguity. Suppose we say that an agent has a right if she enjoys some kind of protection against a set of actual or potential obstacles ("standard threats") that could block some type(s) of action that might otherwise be open to her. To characterize any particular right completely, we would then have to identify (1) the agent or class of agents that has the right, (2) the kinds of obstacles protected against, and (3) the types of action protected. This gives us a three-part analysis of the idea of a right.[16] The familiar problem is that it is not always clear how the second and third of these parts should be filled in. It can be particularly controversial whether the obstacles protected against should be limited to physical or legal obstructions (e.g., in the case of free speech, prior restraint of publication by law) or should also include any of various kinds of deprivations that could make it more difficult to perform the protected types of action (e.g., lack of resources to buy television time or newspaper advertisements).

---

[13] As Jeremy Waldron puts it, "we may not infer from the right to emigrate a requirement that society subsidize trips abroad for anyone who wants them." "Liberal Rights: Two Sides of the Coin," in *Liberal Rights: Collected Papers 1981–1991* (Cambridge, Mass.: Cambridge University Press, 1993), pp. 1–34 at p. 9.

[14] For example, he writes that the substance of a right to liberty is liberty, and when we enjoy the right, it is liberty we enjoy, not the ends we might attain by exercising it (p. 15).

[15] For example: "if people have rights to free association, they ought not merely to 'have' the rights to free association but also to enjoy their free association itself" (p. 20).

[16] This formulation adapts G. C. MacCallum's triadic account of the idea of a liberty: "Negative and Positive Freedom," *Philosophical Review*, 76 (1967), 312–34 at p. 314.

Philosophers have addressed this problem in several ways. John Rawls, for example, distinguishes between liberty and the worth of liberty: a liberty is a socially protected option, while its worth is the value that a person is in a position to derive from the exercise of this option, given the person's material and other circumstances.[17] Amartya Sen similarly distinguishes between two aspects of freedom: "procedural power" (a matter of formal legal protections) versus "effective control" over outcomes (which is a matter of having command over sufficient resources to achieve one's ends).[18] The point of noticing these distinctions is to suggest that there is no single, pre-theoretically correct way of specifying what we commit ourselves to when we make claims to the effect that "A has a right to (or should be free to) have or do X." In working out the details of any proposed "right," one quickly finds oneself embroiled in an argument about the importance of various kinds of barriers to action and the responsibilities it is proper to place on other people for their removal. These arguments are normative, not analytical. In the framework of *Basic Rights*, they take place in the context of reasoning about the duties associated with each basic right, a topic to which we turn in a moment.

The second noteworthy element in Shue's account of a right is the idea that A has a right to X only when A is in a position to demand that his or her enjoyment of a substance be "socially guaranteed against standard threats." He writes: "that a right involves a rationally justified demand for social guarantees against standard threats means, in effect, that the relevant other people have a duty to create, if they do not exist, or if they do, to preserve effective institutions for the enjoyment of what people have rights to enjoy" (p. 17).[19] Of course, the thought that rights should be enforceable is not new. Mill discusses this idea at some length in the final chapter of his *Utilitarianism* (though the idea was not new with him, either[20]). There, Mill famously observes, "To have a right ... is ... to have something which society ought to defend me in the possession of."[21] Mill was clear

---

[17] In Rawls' system, the distribution of liberties is controlled by the first principle of justice, while the distribution of the material means required to derive value from the exercise of liberties is controlled by the second. John Rawls, *A Theory of Justice*, rev. edn. (Cambridge, Mass.: Harvard University Press, 1999), p. 179. (Political liberty is an exception; cf. pp. 197–9.)

[18] Amartya Sen, "Well-Being, Agency, and Freedom: The Dewey Lectures 1984," *Journal of Philosophy*, 82 (1985), 169–221 at pp. 208–12; see similarly his "Elements of a Theory of Human Rights," *Philosophy and Public Affairs*, 32 (2004), 315–56 at pp. 330–8.

[19] We say more below about the importance of institutions.

[20] The idea that there is an analytical connection between the idea of a right (actually a "perfect" right, or a right, strictly so called) and enforcement can be traced at least to Grotius and arguably to Duns Scotus or even Seneca; see J. B. Schneewind, *The Invention of Autonomy* (Cambridge, Mass.: Cambridge University Press, 1998), pp. 78–81.

[21] J. S. Mill, *Utilitarianism*, ch. 5, para. 25; in *The Collected Works of John Stuart Mill*, ed. J. M. Robson (Toronto: University of Toronto Press, 1985), vol. X, p. 250.

that "society" can "defend me" in more than one way: some rights are suitable to be enforced with the state's police power, whereas others are more suitably enforced by means of social disapproval. Shue's contribution is to generalize the idea of enforcement even further, and to relativize the idea of enforcement in any particular case to the kinds of threats at which enforcement should be directed. We comment briefly about each aspect in turn.

Shue emphasizes that what is important about a right—its "single most important aspect" (p. 16)—is its role in justifying a person in demanding that others "make some arrangements" that will guarantee that the person can enjoy the substance of the right. Conceding that the term "arrangements" is vague, Shue explains that the aim is to recognize both that different rights are susceptible to different kinds of "arrangements" for their enjoyment and that different kinds of "arrangements" may be appropriate in different settings.[22] One of the larger lacunae in Shue's theory is why we should think that giving people *rights* to the background conditions necessary for the enjoyment of their other rights is necessarily the best way to guarantee that those background conditions are in place. Someone might wonder, for example, why "basic rights" rather than "basic duties," the performance of which is "socially guaranteed" in some other possibly more effective way, should be the preferred "arrangement."

The main point is clear enough, however. When we think about protecting any particular right as a problem for whole societies, rather than as a problem for individuals taken one by one, any effective solution will involve establishing institutions with whatever capacities are necessary to ensure that individuals will actually be able to enjoy the substance of the right—which is to say, to enable people to do that which the right protects, without fear of interference. Moreover, the institutional steps called for in connection with any particular right will depend on the nature of the right—in particular, on the range of threats it is standardly supposed to protect against (a subject we turn to next). The result of this is that what a right requires of institutions may be more complicated than Mill's idea of "enforcement" suggests. Indeed, the most important requirements of some rights may seem to have little in common with what we normally think of as "enforcement" (consider, for example, rights to subsistence). We shall see some implications of this when we come to the question of correlative duties.

---

[22] "From no theory like the present one is it possible to deduce precisely what sort of institutions are needed, and I have no reason to think that the same institutions would be most effective in all places and at all times," as Shue says (p. 17).

Now consider the idea of "standard threats." Here we shift focus to part (2) of our tripartite analysis of a right: (1) an agent is protected against (2) certain kinds of interference in performing (3) certain types of actions. It is conceivable that a right could protect an agent against *all* conceivable kinds of interference in performing certain types of actions. Most rights are not like that, however, and for good reason. There are simply too many conceivable but highly improbable ways in which the actual enjoyment of some right might be threatened to expect society to expend scarce resources to protect against all of them. It is conceivable that someone might invent a highly discriminating device that turns the broadcast speeches of environmentalists, but only environmentalists, into white noise. But at this point, such a device is just barely conceivable. We would not expect society to invest any substantial resources in protecting people against this threat to their free speech, until the technology in question is much nearer fruition and the threat is more a "standard" rather than "extraordinary" one.

The idea of rights only protecting against "standard threats" is difficult to state precisely—more so, perhaps, than Shue himself may recognize. Still, as a start, we might say that "standard threats" are those "ordinary and serious but remediable" potential interferences that can reasonably be expected to arise in the normal circumstances of human social life (p. 32).[23] The significance of this is to register a kind of non-arbitrary variability within the concept of a basic right: what counts as an "ordinary and serious" potential interference to any particular type of action may be different in one society or at one historical moment rather than another. As a result, basic rights may have different institutional requirements in different social contexts. In view of the tendency of discourse about rights to fix on particular institutional solutions to relatively abstract problems, this is a particularly important recognition.

1.2. The Correlative Duties Argument

As Thomas Pogge observes at the beginning of Chapter 6 below, *Basic Rights* recast philosophical argument about responses to global poverty out of a language of beneficence and into a language of rights. It did so in two ways. The first we have already mentioned: it argues, in effect, that security and subsistence are equally necessary for effective human agency. The second main dimension of Shue's thesis has been at least as influential, not only in

---

[23] For a similar idea, see T. M. Scanlon, "Rights, Goals and Fairness" [1977], reprinted in *The Difficulty of Tolerance: Essays in Political Philosophy* (Cambridge: Cambridge University Press, 2003), pp. 26–41.

political philosophy but also, perhaps even more importantly, in recasting the public argument about international responsibility for human rights.[24] This is his analysis of the structure of the duties associated with basic rights.

To grasp the significance of this analysis, we should recall that, when *Basic Rights* was published, most philosophers were inclined to believe that "liberty" rights differ from "welfare" rights in the nature of the duties associated with them. "Liberty" rights were thought to be connected with "negative" duties, and "welfare" rights with "positive" ones. The inference typically drawn was that "liberty" rights are relatively inexpensive to enforce, since all they require of other people is their forbearance, whereas "welfare" rights, which impose real and possibly substantial costs on others, are expensive. Indeed, it has sometimes been argued that the costs of satisfying "welfare" rights are so great that there is no feasible way they could be met. This leads to the conclusion that universal human rights to such things as adequate nutrition, housing, and medical care (all of which are recognized in the 1948 Universal Declaration) should be regarded as statements of aspirations or ideals, rather than as grounds upon which people could justifiably make claims against another or their state.[25]

Shue holds this deflationary position to be myopic. It is a mistake, he argues, to believe that rights divide in any simple way between those imposing negative and positive duties. When we reflect about particular rights, we see that this is not what we actually believe. Moreover, when we reflect about the reasons why rights should matter to us, we see that this is not what we ought to believe. Consider again the right to the security of one's body—a right that many advocating the deflationary position accepted as a paradigm case of a genuine human right. If we limit ourselves to the simple two-person case, it might seem plausible that the only duty entailed by A's right to bodily security is B's duty to forbear from any form of physical interference with A's body. But in a world of more than two people, we are likely to think that in at least some cases A's right entails other duties as well: C, for example, may have a duty to defend or protect A against B's efforts to interfere. Certainly this is the traditional view.[26] And if we

---

[24] For an example, see International Commission on Intervention and State Sovereignty (ICISS), *The Responsibility to Protect* (Ottawa: International Development Research Centre, 2001), whose central chapters (3 through 5) track closely Shue's tripartite Correlative Duties discussed below.

[25] Possibly the most influential statement of this position can be found in Maurice Cranston, *What Are Human Rights?* (London: Bodley Head, 1973), pp. 65–71. Significantly, Cranston held that there was no difficulty in showing that there is a *bona fide* human right to security.

[26] It dates at least to Cicero: "[T]he man who does not defend someone, or obstruct the injustice when he can, is at fault just as if he had abandoned his parents or his friends or his country." *On Duties*, trans. M. T. Griffin (Cambridge: Cambridge University Press, 1991), 1.23.

imagine a world containing not just a handful of casually interacting individuals but also social institutions, we may also think that people have obligations to use their institutions to protect people's security and to help them protect themselves. This shows that the duties associated with security rights are more complicated than the simple picture recognizes.

Shue argues that, as a general matter, rights can ground duties that take three basic forms. He describes these as duties "to avoid depriving," "to protect from deprivation," and "to aid the deprived" (p. 52). Of these, only the first can be classified as "negative" in the usual sense. Taken together, these duties may impose far more significant costs on their bearers than the simple picture suggests. Forbearing from interfering with somebody's physical security may seem cheap, involving at most opportunity costs. But as Shue points out, establishing and maintaining effective institutions to protect people's security is seldom cheap—think of the cost of an effective police force, to say nothing of effective national defense.[27]

This analysis of duties makes an important polemical point, which is that the conventional complaint about welfare rights (that they impose significant costs on others and therefore can't be counted as genuine rights) can equally well be made about security rights. These types of rights are symmetrical when looked at in terms of the duties they impose on others: both types impose both "negative" and "positive" duties, and the satisfaction of both types of rights has the potential to be costly to at least some duty-bearers. So one can't have it both ways. Either there are no genuine rights to physical security, or the line between genuine and "aspirational" rights can't be drawn neatly between rights to security and to subsistence. The distinction between these types of rights simply does not have the significance that was attributed to it by adherents of the deflationary view.

Looked at as a philosophical position, the Correlative Duties Argument is open to two challenges—coming, as it were, from opposite directions. Without trying to resolve them here, we point them out as important aspects of the philosophical agenda set by *Basic Rights*. First, someone who is generally sympathetic to the tripartite analysis of duties might nevertheless believe that it casts the net too narrowly. One way to put that idea is to say that rights, or anyway basic rights, give rise to an array of reasons for action for agents who are in a position to act in ways that might secure the satisfaction of the right. From this perspective, the conventional view can seem arbitrary in paying attention only to those agents

---

[27] For an elaboration, see Stephen Holmes and Cass Sunstein, *The Costs of Rights* (New York: Norton, 1999).

whose actions could directly obstruct a person's enjoyment of a right. If it is within the power of other agents to prevent the obstruction or to remediate its effects, why should we not think that the right gives rise to reasons for action for these agents as well?

But once we start down this path, the objector might ask, why stop with Shue's three types of duties? Surely there might be other kinds of actions or omissions, in addition to forbearance, protection, and aid, that would reduce the chances of a right's being violated or increase the chances of a violation being remediated. Consider, for example, investment in economic infrastructure aimed at improving a society's productive capacity: under some circumstances this might be the most effective way to reduce severe poverty in the society, yet it does not fit easily into any of the three categories of duty. (One might consider such investment "aid," but this would only be true in an extended sense of that idea; the investment might not, by itself, satisfy the subsistence needs of any severely impoverished person, nor remove any obstacle that obstructs the provision of an existing resource to such a person.)

The nature of the most effective actions and omissions, of course, will depend on the details of the case, but the general point is clear enough. When there are other kinds of actions open to an agent, why should we not say that this agent might have duties to perform them? What this question suggests is that Shue's own analysis is in its own way myopic. Perhaps, as Jeremy Waldron has suggested, we should say that rights are associated with "waves of duties" that might in principle extend indefinitely far from the actual or potential rights violation.[28]

This is a friendly objection in the sense that it seeks to extend the reach of Shue's own insight about the structure of duties. Indeed, in later writings, Shue himself accepts a version of it.[29] The difficulty, however, is that it strengthens the second objection we have mentioned to the Correlative Duties Argument. This objection, which has been set forth with particular clarity by Onora O'Neill, holds that there is a significant difference between rights for which a complete assignment of duties can be given and those for which the assignment of duties is necessarily incomplete, and that this distinction supervenes on the distinction between security and subsistence rights.[30] Put crudely, the argument is that security rights in particular, and liberty rights more generally, do not face an "allocation problem": everybody

---

[28] Waldron, *Liberal Rights*, p. 25.

[29] For example, in the 1996 Afterword to *Basic Rights*, pp. 157–61.

[30] See, for example, Onora O'Neill, "The Dark Side of Human Rights," *International Affairs*, 81 (2005), 427–39. This is one of several related objections pressed in O'Neill's article.

has correlative duties to respect them. By contrast, subsistence rights, and welfare rights more generally, leave the allocation of duties underdetermined. These rights are claims to performances rather than to forbearances, and the mere assertion of a claim is not enough to identify the agents which have duties to satisfy it. That question is simply left open.

The significance of this point, for those who find the objection persuasive, is just this. The distinctive point of rights, according to this view, is to enable us to make claims and demands against one another, and to identify particular agents of whom we would be justified in saying that they would be wrong not to act as the right requires. In the case of security rights, there is no difficulty in saying who has committed a wrong when A's physical security has been violated: it is the agent whose action constituted the violation. But in typical cases of violations of subsistence rights (for example, in circumstances of widespread poverty), it is not at all clear who has committed the wrong. There may be many agents whose actions and omissions, taken together, explain why people's subsistence needs are unmet, but there is typically no one agent or set of agents of whom we can say that they acted wrongly.[31] Accordingly, the objection concludes, in cases like this it is not possible for claims of right to serve the purpose we expect of them.

Earlier we said that the intuitive idea underlying Shue's tripartite analysis of duties is that a rights violation might give rise to a variety of reasons for action pertaining to a range of differently situated agents. The present objection might be framed as a dissent from this idea: it holds that the idea fails to distinguish, as we do in ordinary moral reflection, between reasons for action and duties to act. In this respect, the second challenge is hardly a friendly objection: it goes to the heart of Shue's position.

2. The Significance of Institutions

It is a complicated question whether the Correlative Duties Argument can be defended against the objection just sketched.[32] We would draw particular attention to one line of response found in *Basic Rights* and developed in some of Shue's subsequent writings. This line of response is especially

---

[31] Not even the set of all agents: unless we think in terms of rights implying a second-order duty upon the set as a whole to organize themselves so that rights are satisfied (more of which shortly).

[32] This question is examined in illuminating detail in Elizabeth Ashford's contribution to this volume.

pertinent for the purposes of this volume because it connects the abstract analysis of duties to matters of policy.

The objection treats subsistence rights as problematic because there is usually no particular agent or group of agents to whom responsibility for deprivations can be attributed. It is not that nobody has any reason to care about severe poverty. We all have such reasons. There is philosophical controversy about their nature and extent. But, at a minimum, everybody has reasons of beneficence for concern about other people's unmet urgent material needs. The question is whether we have *duties* corresponding to these reasons. The conventional view is that if these reasons ground any duties at all, the duties are "imperfect" in the sense of being incompletely specified. We may have duties to do something for someone, but we do not know to whom, in particular, we owe the duties or what, in particular, the duties require us to do.

Why is this? One reply is that we lack institutions with the capacity to undertake policies that would result in reducing or eliminating the deprivations and to assign responsibilities to specific agents to carry them out. Following Shue, we might say that institutions play a *mediating* role: they organize social action in such a way that individuals are enabled to carry out what, in the absence of institutions, would be "imperfect"—that is, incompletely specified—duties to protect and to aid those threatened with deprivation.[33]

Mediating institutions transform "imperfect" duties into "perfect" ones. Pre-institutionally, people have imperfect duties toward others. The rich, for example, have an imperfect duty to assist the poor; but since it is an imperfect duty, no poor person has any claim-right against any given rich person. A mediating institution—a formal collective entity, archetypically a state, embracing rich and poor—serves in effect as a "consolidator" of those imperfect duties. All of the rich have a perfect duty to pay taxes to the state. The state in turn has a perfect duty to provide assistance to all its citizens who are in need. This phenomenon is familiar enough domestically, in contemporary welfare states. We might think about the duties associated with global subsistence rights in the same general way. They could be "perfected" through the establishment of appropriate institutions capable of assigning the duties whose performance would prevent deprivations and give aid to those deprived. It is important to add the caveat that "appropriate institutions" at the global level need not resemble too closely

---

[33] "Mediating Duties," *Ethics*, 98 (1988), 687–704. See also the discussion in the 1996 "Afterword" to *Basic Rights*, pp. 166–73. These topics are further discussed in the chapters by Christian Reus-Smit and Neta Crawford in this volume.

those of the welfare state in domestic-level societies. One need not argue—and Shue does not do so—for anything as ambitious as a world state.[34]

So far, so good; but how far does this take us? The mere perception that institutions can define and allocate duties to act does not offer any guidance about the basis on which institutions should do so. If, for example, a global poverty regime were to require me to contribute to poverty reduction, I can always ask, "Why me?" To deflect O'Neill's challenge, we need to know how such a question should be answered.[35]

Shue's reply might best be described as pragmatic. For any right, the reasons on the basis of which corresponding duties might be assigned are likely to be diverse. Some reasons, in his terms, are "closely tied" to the justification of the right: right-bearers may, for example, have a "special history" with potential duty-bearers that explains why these agents have responsibilities to these right-bearers. The most straightforward example would be a case in which some agents inflict a harm on others: the harm-inflicters plainly have duties to remediate the harm.[36] But most cases will not be like this. The potential duty-bearers are more likely to be blameless. In these (more common) cases, the reasons have two components: the first is a recognition of the urgency, for the right-bearer, of the form of protection that the right confers; the second is some set of pragmatic judgments about the resources and capacities of potential duty-bearers ("ability to pay," for example). If provision of the protection is sufficiently urgent, if there is a set of potential duty-bearers with the resources and capacities to provide it, and if the costs of doing so can be allocated (by some institutional arrangement) among members of the set in such a way that no individual is forced to bear an unreasonable cost, then, Shue argues, we have arrived at an allocation of duties that is both "perfect" and reasonable. His conclusion is worth quoting in full: "correlated with a particular right like the right to food are actually several kinds of duties, some ... general and some ... special—and some will be, strictly speaking, neither general nor special but the fruit of new relationships created by new institutions designed expressly to allocate previously unallocated duties."[37]

Readers will have to decide for themselves if this response to O'Neill's challenge is persuasive. Our own view is that it points in the right direction but that more might usefully be said. The key insight is that when basic

---

[34] We return to the idea of mediating institutions below, in connection with the question whether protection against environmental degradation should count as a basic right, and if so how the appropriate "social guarantee" might be imagined.

[35] The chapters by Neta Crawford and Judith Lichtenberg in this volume address this challenge in very different ways.

[36] "Mediating Duties," p. 700.   [37] Ibid., p. 703.

rights are embodied in institutions capable of allocating the costs of satisfying them, we need not provide a single reason, applicable to all potential contributors, to explain why they have duties to contribute. One of the ways that institutions mediate is by aggregating the various reasons that pertain to different relationships governed by the institutions into a single coherent set of policies. This important insight is often overlooked by proponents of the "no rights without duties" view.

The point about which we believe more might be said concerns the array of reasons that can properly underlie the allocation of such duties. Shue focuses on "special histories" consisting of relationships that directly affect the well-being of right-bearers by posing a threat of harm. But of course "special histories" might be defined by other features as well. Consider, for example, cases analogous to "negligence," in which an agent fails to perform an action open to him at reasonable cost whose performance would have prevented or alleviated a harm; cases of "external harm" in which an agent engages in a relationship with another agent that produces a harm for third parties not involved in that relationship; and cases of "historical injustice." In all of these cases, and doubtless in others as well, there may be a morally salient feature of the relationship that explains why those who benefit from participating in it (or whose participation imposes real or opportunity costs on other participants or third parties) may have reasons to contribute to satisfying the basic rights of others. And of course we might also allocate responsibility in a purely forward-looking way, on the basis of capacity to help rather on the basis of any history of harm or neglect.[38] We leave it as an open question how a more variegated theory of special responsibilities might be developed.[39] We observe only that, while Shue's analysis points the way, there is more to be said.

3. Basic Environmental Rights

Shue does not claim that security and subsistence are the only basic rights. He observes that there may be others (p. 67, e.g.). But the only other candidate considered in any detail in the book is the right to political participation.[40] Here, we raise the question whether a case might be made

---

[38] Robert E. Goodin, *Protecting the Vulnerable* (Chicago: University of Chicago Press, 1985), pp. 117–35.

[39] Richard Miller's contribution to this volume might be interpreted as an attempt to develop such a theory, although within a framework that prescinds from talk of "basic rights."

[40] This is the subject of part of chapter 3 of *Basic Rights*, whose argument anticipates the case made subsequently by Amartya Sen for the "universal value" of democracy: Sen, *Development as Freedom* (New York: Knopf, 1999), chs. 6 and 10.

out for basic environmental rights. We offer some speculations on this question, which Simon Caney takes up in detail in his contribution to this volume.

Shue has written influentially on many important topics other than basic rights, not least among them climate change.[41] Despite having said many wise things on that subject, he himself has not done much to forge any strong connections between his work on climate change (or environmental issues more generally) and basic rights.[42] It seems to us that this is a large and fertile area where the moral architecture of *Basic Rights* might profitably be extended.

Environmentalists frequently make common cause with other moral crusades to augment their case. The eco-feminism movement is one clear example.[43] The "environmental justice" movement is another.[44] The question we want to explore here is whether "basic environmental rights"—understood in Shue-like terms of "claims to a livable environment, socially guaranteed against standard threats"—might be a useful rubric under which to pursue environmental concerns, both philosophically and politically.[45]

Of course, two good arguments for the same conclusion are always better than one. It is therefore wholly understandable, and highly commendable, that when arguing that the rich of the world should do their fair share in

---

[41] For an overview see Shue's chapter on "Climate" in *Companion to Environmental Ethics*, ed. Dale Jamieson (Oxford: Blackwell, 2001), pp. 449–59.

[42] In "Exporting Hazards," *Ethics*, 91 (1981), 579–606, Shue argues against the export of hazardous wastes or production products abroad as a violation of our *duty* "not to harm," almost never speaking of anyone's right not to be harmed. Indeed, he remarks in one telling footnote that he wants to "avoid resting anything essential here on positions adopted in *Basic Rights*" (p. 603, fn. 30).

[43] Among them Val Plumwood, *Feminism and the Mastery of Nature* (New York: Routledge, 1993).

[44] Andrew Dobson, *Justice and the Environment* (Oxford: Oxford University Press, 1999); David Schlosberg, *Defining Environmental Justice* (Oxford: Oxford University Press, 2007).

[45] We are hardly the first to moot the notion of "environmental rights." Principle 1 of the 1972 "Declaration of the United Nations Conference on the Human Environment," reaffirmed twenty years later in the "Rio Declaration on Environment and Development," reads in part: "Man has the fundamental right to freedom, equality and adequate conditions of life, in an environment of a quality that permits a life of dignity and well-being, and he bears a solemn responsibility to protect and improve the environment for present and future generations." Similar verbiage finds its way into some national constitutions, such as when Article 21 was added to the section of the Dutch constitution dealing with human rights in 1983. Similarly, under the Arhus Convention, which came into force in 2001, "every person has the right to live in an environment adequate to his or her health and well-being" in all the European nations ratifying that Convention. And there is a set of "UN draft principles on human rights and the environment," tabled at the forty-sixth session of the UN Commission on Human Rights in 1994. See Maria Adebowale et al., "Environment and human rights: a new approach to sustainable development" (London: International Institute for Environment & Development, 2001), available at <http://www.ring-alliance.org/ring_pdf/bp_envrights.pdf>.

helping to avert rather than exacerbate global environmental problems, Shue tries (as he puts it) "to construct an argument that is logically independent of other arguments I have given elsewhere," in *Basic Rights* among others places.[46] In his work on climate, Shue typically argues from considerations of fairness and justice, and notions of a "guaranteed minimum" deriving from those considerations.[47] That is a good argument too. We dissent neither from that argument nor from Shue's larger convergence strategy in offering it. Our observation is merely that, in his anxiousness to get that argument onto the table, he neglects how his arguments about basic rights lead to broadly similar conclusions.

One easy way to subsume a claim to a livable environment within the framework of Shue's *Basic Rights* would be to treat it as a subspecies of his "security rights."[48] There has recently been a "securitization" of all and sundry. Issues that were traditionally analyzed in other terms altogether are now often redescribed as matters of "security."[49] Environmental integrity is no exception. Environmental disasters pose two sorts of threats to one's physical security: not only do they threaten it directly; they also threaten it indirectly, as refugees from environmental disasters elsewhere crowd into adjoining territories, undermining social order. Both of these security-style arguments for environmental protection have been trumpeted for fully two decades or more.[50]

Those two security-style arguments for environmental protection are very different, of course. The first points to the right of people not to be poisoned, parched, or flooded. The second points to the right of people not to have their homeland invaded by refugees from being poisoned, parched, or flooded where they presently live. The rhetorical trope of "security"

[46] "Exporting Hazards," p. 603, fn. 30.

[47] "Subsistence Emissions and Luxury Emissions," *Law & Policy*, 15 (1993), 39–59; "Avoidable Necessity: Global Warming, International Fairness, and Alternative Energy," *Theory & Practice: Nomos XXXVII*, ed. Judith Wagner DeCew and Ian Shapiro (New York: New York University Press, 1995), pp. 239–64; "Global Environment and International Inequality," *International Affairs*, 75 (1999), 531–45.

[48] This is precisely Shue's own approach in the rare occasion on which he does speak of rights in an environmental context. Speaking of harming others by exporting to their country hazardous production processes, Shue writes, "My attempt in this article to describe one kind of prohibited physical harm is intended to be an elucidation of what in *Basic Rights* is called a 'standard threat' to rights to security and thus an elucidation of part of what security rights are rights to guarantee against"; "Exporting Hazards," p. 603, fn. 30. See similarly his "Bequeathing Hazards: Security Rights and Property Rights of Future Humans," in *Global Environmental Economics: Equity and the Limits to Markets*, ed. Mohammed Dore and Timothy Mount (Malden, Mass.: Blackwell, 1999), pp. 38–53.

[49] Barry Buzan, Ole Waever, and Jaap de Wilde, *Security: A New Framework for Analysis* (Boulder, Colo.: Lynne Rienner, 1998); ICISS, *The Responsibility to Protect*, ch. 2.

[50] Richard A. Falk, *This Endangered Planet* (New York: Random House, 1971). Jessica Tuchman Mathews, "Redefining Security," *Foreign Affairs*, 68 (1989), 162–77.

derives its political power precisely from eliding the two. Philosophically, however, they are very different. It is relatively easy to see how a case might be constructed for treating the first as a Shue-style basic right, as we shall elaborate below. It is far less easy to see how the second—the right to keep others out of whatever territory you happen to be squatting upon at present—could generally be construed as a basic right, in those terms.

Indeed, many people would think that morally speaking there is something akin to Bernard Williams' "one thought too many" going on in that second argument.[51] There is something outrageously egocentric, from a moral point of view, in saying that we should protect the environment, not because other people will die if we do not, but rather because those people who are rightly fearful for their lives will invade our turf if we do not. In the moral scales, it is their imminent death rather than our prospective inconvenience that should matter vastly more.

The strategy of subsuming environmental protection under the basic "security right" of those who would be directly poisoned, parched, starved, or flooded remains open. But it seems to us better—to better represent what is truly fundamental—instead to regard environmental rights *themselves* as basic, rather than a mere aspect of something else (security) that is what is truly basic.[52]

Basic rights are "basic" because the conditions they protect are necessary for the enjoyment of any other rights. A right to a livable environment, socially guaranteed against standard threats, seems plainly to be one such precondition. The argument is strictly parallel to that for the other basic rights. To put the point a little differently than Shue himself prefers to put it: agency presupposes existence; you have to be alive to exercise any rights.[53] And literally not having a livable environment extinguishes your life as surely as does being shot or starved (the threats against which basic rights of security and subsistence protect you).

We are inclined to agree with Thomas Pogge, in his chapter in this volume: that sort of argument (which we shall henceforth call the "right-to-life

---

[51] To adapt for other purposes a phrase from Bernard Williams, "Persons, Character and Morality," in *Moral Luck* (Cambridge: Cambridge University Press, 1981), p. 18.

[52] A project pursued in Simon Caney's chapter in this volume.

[53] Shue, *Basic Rights*, p. 186, n. 3, canvasses the possibility of arguing "that both security and subsistence are needed for survival" and therefore "both are included in a right to survival, or right to life." He pronounces himself "by no means hostile to this approach," but offers three reasons for weakly preferring his own "admittedly somewhat more circuitous path of argument." The first two do no more than show that this approach has identical drawbacks to his, while the third is merely that this approach might more easily be misunderstood as being restricted to negative rights alone. The mildness of those objections tempts us to assimilate the "right to life" approach to the same larger family of arguments for basic rights as Shue's own.

argument") buys us less than we would ideally like. Ideally, we want an argument for giving people strong protection against being merely shot-but-not-killed, against being starved-but-not-to-death. But all that the sort of argument sketched above gives us is a case for strong protection against conditions that are life-ending, or anyway that seriously threaten to be.

Likewise with the argument sketched above for "basic environmental rights to a livable environment." The only right that is deemed "basic" and accordingly entitled to strong protection is a right against environmental conditions that are literally unlivable, that would literally lead to one's death. We can extend the scope of that a little by adding some reasonable qualifications, such as "seriously threaten to lead to one's death" and "substantially sooner than one would otherwise have died." The basic structure of the argument does not require that the threat will necessarily kill you absolutely immediately or with absolute certainty. Nonetheless, there will still be lots of severely degraded environments in which life, of a sort, is nonetheless possible. Just as Shue would like his argument for security and subsistence rights to extend to the non-fatal situations just mentioned, so too would we have liked our argument for environmental rights to extend to cover foul but not fatal environmental degradation. But while the right-to-life version of the argument does not extend to them, Shue's may still: insofar as they seriously compromise people's agency, serious but non-lethal threats might still be things against which people should be thought to have "basic rights."

Basic environmental rights are subject to the same important challenge we discussed earlier in connection with basic subsistence rights: "who has the duties?" To say someone has a right is to say that someone else has a correlative duty. If we cannot identify anyone as holding a correlative duty, it might seem that we cannot ascribe any right.

The problem of identifying an agent responsible for securing rights arises particularly where some coordinated collective action is required and where no organization yet exists to perform that function. In this respect, the environmental case is even more difficult than the case of severe poverty. In cases like these, to say (a) that someone has a right that some set of people is morally responsible for securing, and (b) that that right cannot be secured without them organizing themselves in order to do so, is to say (c) that morally they are duty-bound to so organize themselves.[54]

Consider this analogy. The right to habeas corpus protects people against arbitrary detention by requiring public officials to bring a prisoner before

---

[54] Goodin, *Protecting the Vulnerable*, p. 139.

the court issuing the writ. The right to habeas corpus thus clearly presupposes the existence of a court to issue the writ and before which the prisoner can be brought. But suppose some dictator has suspended all courts in his country. Legally, the dictator would then be completely at liberty to detain anyone for as long as he liked: there is no longer any court to issue a writ against him. But morally, shouldn't the same reasons for thinking that the right of habeas corpus is morally important in a jurisdiction with courts also provide us with a morally important reason for (re)establishing a system of courts in which it can be claimed, in a jurisdiction currently without courts?

As we observed earlier, when people organize themselves for coordinated collective action, they create what Shue calls "mediating institutions." Among other things, mediating institutions are needed to solve "many hands" problems. The structure of those problems is that any of many could provide the needed assistance, or the needed forbearance. If others do so, you do not need to. And it being costly, there is a temptation to let someone else do it. But if everyone waits for someone else to do it, then no one does it.

In the case of subsistence rights, mediating institutions are required as consolidators of positive duties to protect and assist. In the case of "environmental rights," they are needed to coordinate negative duties "not to harm." The damage done by any increment of pollution—greenhouse gas or whatever—is a non-linear function. The environment has a certain absorptive capacity. Low levels of pollution (greenhouse gases or whatever) do little damage. Modest increases of pollution, above that, do little more damage. But above a certain level, increasing levels do disproportionate damage; and above some further threshold, the damage proves truly catastrophic.

Looking at the situation from the point of view of any given person, firm, or country, one's own marginal contribution is slight. But summing across everyone's marginal contributions, the consequences are large, tending toward catastrophic.[55] The function of mediating institutions in those circumstances is to allocate the "duty to desist" fairly across all those whose desistance is morally required, just as the function of mediating institutions in the case of subsistence rights is to allocate the "duty to contribute" fairly across all those whose contribution is morally required.

When talking of "mediating institutions," we typically think of state-like institutions. In connection with "security rights" we think of state-like

---

[55] It is a notorious fallacy to treat *every* case as the marginal one. See e.g. G. A. Cohen, "The Structure of Proletarian Unfreedom," *Philosophy & Public Affairs*, 12 (1983), 3–33.

institutions with police powers. In connection with "subsistence rights" we think of state-like institutions with taxing powers, and powers to transfer the proceeds of those taxes (in cash or in kind) to people in need. In connection with "environmental rights" we might think most naturally of state-like institutions with regulatory powers.

Here, again, we must recall that "mediating institutions" need not be of that heavily institutionalized sort. Treaty regimes can serve as "mediating institutions," too, and Kyoto or its successors qualify in those terms. To serve effectively as "mediating institutions," those treaty regimes might need better enforcement mechanisms and heavier penalty clauses than they presently contain. But treaty regimes containing serious penalties of a reciprocal sort in case of violation might serve a mediating role just as well as more familiar institutional forms.

4. Too Many Rights?

There is recurring complaint about what seems like a proliferation of human rights.[56] Many of those complaints come from human-rights skeptics. But often enough they come from friends of human rights, anxious that the strength of the claim associated with really important rights not be watered down by the addition of too many new and in many ways less important rights claims. The more rights there are, the greater the danger that we will face "rights–rights trade-offs," being forced to sacrifice some rights in order to fulfill others. The possibility of basic environmental rights, and perhaps yet other basic rights, might suggest a similar complaint.

If all of these rights are truly basic, and there is no way of satisfying all of them simultaneously, then trade them off for one another is just what we must do.[57] But before doing that, we ought to be very sure that they really are all on a par with one another. Doubts about precisely this are what underlie much resistance to constitutionalizing social rights, like a right to a paid vacation. That is simply not on a par with the right not to be tortured, which should not be traded off (at anything like parity, anyway, and arguably not at all) for it. Such concerns have come to plague "second-" and

---

[56] Maurice Cranston, *What Are Human Rights?* and "Human Rights, Real and Supposed," in *Political Theory & the Rights of Man*, ed. D. D. Raphael (London: Macmillan, 1967), pp. 43–54; Carl Wellman, *The Proliferation of Rights: Moral Progress or Empty Rhetoric?* (Boulder, Colo.: Westview, 1999).

[57] Jeremy Waldron, "Rights in Conflict," *Liberal Rights*, ch. 9; Cass Sunstein, "Health-health Tradeoffs," *University of Chicago Law Review*, 63 (1996), 1533–72.

"third-generation rights," quite generally. With some of the rights in those categories, such concerns may well be justified. But insofar as some "second-generation rights" like the right to subsistence and some "third-generation rights" like the right to a livable environment can be shown to be "basic" in the strong sense that Shue proposes, they should be fully on a par with any "first-generation right" like the right to security that is basic in the same way.

On the strong right-to-life version of the argument, all those rights are deemed basic because they protect against threats to life itself, and to the pursuit of any other rights all of which can only be exercised by a living agent. There are many ways agency might be extinguished: among them, by being beaten to death, starved, or poisoned. Or on Shue's version of the argument, there are many ways effective agency can be seriously undermined: by being badly beaten, starved, or poisoned, without being killed. It is equally important to protect against all of them, if a person's agency and capacity to enjoy her other rights is to be preserved. And that is the animating thought behind the whole *Basic Rights* agenda.

Whether we should think of any of these rights, however basic, as absolute and lexically prior to all other rights or objects of value is, perhaps, another matter. At places in *Basic Rights* Shue suggests they should be. The seemingly incontrovertible premise that rights to physical security should be regarded as absolute is the bedrock upon which Shue's *Basic Rights* argument was built. But when what Waldron in his chapter below calls the "9/11 argument" translates that into a quest for absolute security against any and all conceivable terrorist threats, the proposition seems less incontrovertible.[58] Indeed, as Waldron goes on to show, it is illogical that basic rights, understood (as Shue does) as prerequisites for the enjoyment of all other rights, should take precedence over absolutely all other rights whose enjoyment justifies us in thinking they are basic and important. Thus there is scope for rights–rights trade-offs, not only among basic rights themselves, but also between basic and non-basic rights. Even if we back away from the bright-line of "no trade-offs," however, the point remains that the terms of trade should be weighted very heavily indeed in favor of rights that are truly basic.

---

[58] See similarly Robert E. Goodin and Frank Jackson, "Freedom from Fear," *Philosophy & Public Affairs*, 35 (2007), 249–65.

2

On Rights and Institutions

Christian Reus-Smit

Buried within Henry Shue's writings on human rights lie two tantalizing ideas. The first is found in his oft-quoted article, "Mediating Duties." His central concern there is how universal human rights can be secured in a world in which the capacities of individuals with correlative duties are limited. If all human beings have a right to food, and all other human beings have a correlative duty to satisfy that right, does that mean that I, as an individual, have a responsibility to provide food aid to all starving children? Shue's answer is no, we should look to national and international institutions to "mediate" our duties, to meet the rights of the world's starving because our own individual capacities are limited.[1] The second idea is found in his classic work, *Basic Rights*. There he voices the idea of what I shall call "rights as power mediators," the idea that rights are normative media that are intended to structure power relations between rights-holders and duty-bearers, to give the former protection or support that their material capacities could never give them. In Shue's words:

People who cannot provide for their own security or subsistence and who lack social guarantees for both are very weak, and possibly helpless, against any individual or institution in a position to deprive them of anything else they value by means of threatening their security or subsistence. A fundamental purpose of acknowledging any basic rights at all is to prevent, or to eliminate, insofar as possible the degree of vulnerability that leaves people at the mercy of others.[2]

---

[1] Henry Shue, "Mediating Duties," *Ethics*, 98 (1988), 687–704.
[2] Henry Shue, *Basic Rights: Subsistence, Affluence, and U.S. Foreign Policy,* 2nd edn. (Princeton, N.J.: Princeton University Press, 1996), pp. 29–30.

This chapter takes these ideas and turns them to new purposes. For Shue, the first idea is a philosophical one—we *ought* to look to institutions to satisfy universal human rights where our capacities to do so as individuals are limited. My goal, in contrast, is to recast the mediating role of institutions as an empirical-theoretic proposition, not a philosophical one. I want to suggest that rights are necessarily "institutionally referential," that (among other things) the most basic individual rights require an institution that is charged with satisfying and protecting them. For this reason, struggles for individual rights have always championed an institutional solution, a particular institutional arrangement that can meet the needs of rights claimants. Since the sixteenth century, the preferred institutional solution has been the sovereign state. With regard to the second idea—the idea of rights as power mediators—my goal is not to recast Shue's formulation but to elaborate it. Shue's purpose, like that of most philosophers of human rights, is to explain the nature of rights as distinctive moral claims and to justify why they should condition our political practices. Explaining their nature and function as power mediators is not his objective, nor is it that of most rights theorists. My goal is to flesh out what it means to think of rights in this way, to explore their role in structuring social power relations.

Seeing rights as institutionally referential, and elaborating their function as power mediators, exposes a paradox in the relationship between rights and the sovereign state. Because rights demand an institutional referent, and because recurrent rights struggles have embraced the sovereign state as their favored institutional solution, the politics of individual rights has historically been one of the major engines driving the globalization of the system of sovereign states, serving to simultaneously delegitimate successive empires and license states as their institutional replacements. But it is also the case that as the system has evolved, the power relationship that rights have been most frequently invoked to mediate has been that of the individual and the sovereign state. To paraphrase Shue, individuals have come to invoke their basic rights most frequently "to prevent, or to eliminate, insofar as possible the degree of vulnerability that leaves people at the mercy of" their states. This paradoxical relationship between rights and the sovereign state—which sees rights as both an engine and civilizer of the system of sovereign states, and the state as both institutional solution and problem—is occluded by most accounts of human rights and world politics. The international system is seen as having its own generative dynamics, with international human rights emerging as exogenous normative principles to address its pathologies.

1. Rights as Distinctive Moral Claims

Moral claims take many different forms, and rights claims are but one distinctive kind. To accuse someone of blasphemy against one's god is a moral claim, as is the proposition that religious and secular authorities should be constitutionally separated. My concern here, however, is with a particular category of moral claims, which I term "entitlement claims." These are the claims that individuals or groups make against other individuals, groups, or institutions for the protection or provision of certain goods. These claims can take a variety of forms.[3] One could appeal to the charitable responsibilities of others to secure such goods, invoking the idea that the well off in society are obliged to assist the destitute or profoundly disadvantaged. One could also appeal to the social utility that would result from the provision of such goods, to the benefits all of society would gain from meeting all of its members' basic needs.

These types of entitlement claims feature in the complex mix of moral argument we witness every day. In the modern era, however, one kind of entitlement claim eclipses all others—the rights claim. The discourse of contemporary world politics is replete with rights claims from, and on behalf of, citizens deprived of their civil liberties, refugees deprived of the membership that might guarantee such liberties, indigenous peoples for self-determination, ethnic groups for protection against genocide, women and children for protection from domestic violence, famine victims for the sustenance needed to stave off starvation, religious communities for freedom of worship, and the list goes on. So central are rights claims to the moral discourse of contemporary world politics that we are often blind to the fact that moral argument can take different forms, that rights cultures, in which rights constitute the principal form of entitlement claim, are but one kind of moral culture, and in the history of human civilization they may well be in the minority.

Shue contends that a "right provides the rational basis for a justified demand."[4] In other words, if A has a right to B then she has a powerful justification for demanding that another person, with correlative duties,

[3] It should be noted here that some philosophers contend that the idea of "claims" is only appropriately associated with that of rights. Joel Feinberg argues, for example, that it is only in the context of rights that claiming truly makes sense. My own preference, however, is to understand claims more broadly. While rights claims may have a special force in particular social milieus, it seems unduly restrictive to assert that other kinds of moral appeals do not constitute claims, or that in non-rights cultures there was no such thing as moral claims. See Joel Feinberg, *Rights, Justice, and the Bounds of Liberty* (Princeton, N.J.: Princeton University Press, 1980), pp. 143–58.

[4] Shue, *Basic Rights*, p. 13.

provide or secure B. One may be invested with a right by national or international law, one can gain rights by entering into a contract, or, more controversially, one can have rights by virtue of being human. The thing about rights is that they are special entitlements, ones that license demand-like claims. A "rights claim ('I *have* a *right* to that') is more than a reminder or an appeal; it also involves a powerful *demand* for action. And this demand brings into play an array of special social practices that rest on the privileged position of the right-holders."[5] Because of this, rights claims asserted in trivial contexts sound jarring. Insisting that someone give me back my pencil because I have a property right to it is not necessarily wrong, it's just an overreaction. In appropriate political, cultural, and historical settings, legal, contractual, or moral rights are normative trump cards. Or as Joel Feinberg once put it, rights "are especially strong objects to 'stand upon,' a most useful sort of moral furniture."[6]

Why do rights entitle right-holders to demand the object of the right from those with correlative duties? Why are rights normative trump cards or such sturdy "moral furniture"? The answer is easiest when it comes to legal rights. If I have a right under law—whether it derive from a national bill of rights or a formal contract—I can (a) identify an authoritative source to demonstrate the existence of that right, and (b) appeal to the legal and policing apparatuses of the state to have that right upheld. These qualities of legal rights have encouraged legal positivists to see them as the only genuine rights, as they are said to be free of the metaphysical justifications that often accompany other kinds of rights. The answer is more difficult when it comes to universal moral rights.[7] If I claim a right to life or liberty, that right is essentially moral in nature. Its normative veracity derives from something other than the prevailing framework of law, even if I am fortunate enough to live in a state in which that right is legally codified and enforced. In fact, my need to claim my right to life or liberty will be most intense in situations where it is not legally guaranteed.

Traditionally, moral rights have been justified through appeal to natural law. Nowhere is this more apparent than in John Locke's contention that the "*State of Nature* has a Law of Nature to govern it, which obliges every

---

[5] Jack Donnelly, *Universal Human Rights in Theory and Practice* (Ithaca, N.Y.: Cornell University Press, 1989), p. 10.

[6] Feinberg, *Rights, Justice, and the Bounds of Liberty*, p. 151.

[7] Of course not all moral rights are universal. Moral rights are those to which one has a just, as opposed to a legal, title. Some moral rights apply to one person only, like the moral right to know what is going on within one's own house. Other moral rights apply to anyone in a particular situation, like those of a parent. Universal moral rights, in contrast, are held by all humans equally. See Maurice Cranston, *What Are Human Rights?* (London: Bodley Head, 1973), p. 21.

one: And Reason, which is that Law, teaches all Mankind, who will but consult it, that being all equal and independent, no one ought to harm another in his Life, Health, Liberty, or Possessions."[8] Through the exercise of reason, therefore, humans can deduce the laws of nature, set down by God, which impose duties upon us not to violate the fundamental rights of others and, in turn, give us rights against their predations. As Western societies secularized, and the international system became more culturally diverse, the persuasiveness of these arguments declined. The most prominent alternative has been to justify the fundamental moral rights of humans by casting them as essential to human dignity. Feinberg writes that

Having rights enables us "to look others in the eye," and to feel in some fundamental way the equal of anyone. To think of oneself as the holder of rights is not to be unduly but properly proud, to that minimal self-respect that is necessary to be worthy of the love and esteem of others. Indeed, respect for persons (and this is an intriguing idea) may simply be respect for their rights, so that there cannot be the one without the other; what is called "human dignity" may simply be the recognizable capacity to assert [rights] claims.[9]

2. Rights as Institutionally Referential

Rights are institutionally referential in three senses. First, they are *institutionally ambitious*. In social orders where individual rights and rights claims are culturally novel, where there is, as yet, no established framework of social norms that give such rights social meaning and purchase, arguments for the recognition and protection of individual rights are institutionally constitutive in ambition. That is, when individuals seek support or protection by invoking their rights they are, among other things, seeking to construct a set of intersubjective understandings that acknowledge the normative force of such rights. Second, rights are *institutionally presumptive*. In social orders where rights and rights claims are culturally acknowledged (if not protected), existing institutional rules, norms, or principles give rights meaning and rights claims veracity. Rights gain political force when they are socially recognized, and it is within the intersubjective framework of institutional norms that social recognition is embedded. Invoking a legal right appeals to a legal institution that gives that right meaning and force; invoking a social right appeals to norms and

---

[8] John Locke, *Two Treatises of Government* (Cambridge: Cambridge University Press, 1988), p. 271.
[9] Feinberg, *Rights, Justice, and the Bounds of Liberty*, p. 151.

understandings that make that right intelligible and persuasive; and invoking one's international human rights today appeals to the international human rights regime for institutional legitimacy and political purchase. Finally, rights are *institutionally dependent*. The protection and satisfaction of rights requires an enabling or executing institutional context. I explain this in greater detail below, but it is sufficient to propose here that rights without protective or enabling institutions may well exist—metaphysically, at the level of social understandings, or within laws cast aside by tyranny—but they will be inherently weak. Even so-called negative rights, which supposedly require other actors to do nothing more than refrain from obstructing or harming rights-holders, in reality require institutions for their protection.

It is worth noting that these different senses in which rights are institutionally referential involve different ideas of "institutions." In general, institutions can be defined as "stable sets of norms, rules, and principles that served two functions in shaping social relations: they constitute actors as knowledgeable social agents, and they regulate behavior."[10] Institutions can be formal or informal: the latter being codified (like criminal law), the former existing solely in the realm of intersubjective understandings between social actors (like table manners). Institutions can also exist without any formal organizational structure, or they can have more or less elaborate bureaucratic and administrative architectures. The evolution of the General Agreement on Tariffs and Trade (GATT) into the World Trade Organization (WTO) involved a shift from the former to the latter. The first and second senses in which rights are institutionally referential sees institutions as formal or informal sets of norms, rules, and principles, but does not require institutions to be organizationally developed. When individuals make rights claims they are either (in the second sense) declaring that they have entitlements that derive from a formal or informal set of institutional norms that grant individuals like them such rights or (in the first sense) seeking, in part, to constitute such norms. In contrast, the third sense in which rights are institutionally referential depends, in most cases, on institutions being organizationally developed. It is generally assumed that for rights to be adequately protected or satisfied there needs to be an enabling institution that has sufficient organizational capacity to be able to "act" in their defense. This is not always the case, though. We know now that under the right circumstances international institutional norms can provide transnational advocacy

[10] Christian Reus-Smit, *The Moral Purpose of the State* (Princeton, N.J.: Princeton University Press, 1999), p. 13.

networks with normative resources in their legitimacy struggles with authoritarian states.[11]

We are concerned here with the third sense in which rights are institutionally referential, the notion that they require enabling or executing institutions. Shue explains the importance of institutions to rights in the following way. He is concerned, first and foremost, with universal rights that are not "costless," that can only be protected or satisfied through the expenditure of effort or resources. The right to food is his example. He takes it as given that such a right is universal, that it is an entitlement all humans can rightly claim. He argues, however, that universal rights that are demanding—that require positive actions to fulfill—do not (and cannot) translate into universal duties. While it may be true that every human has a right to food, it cannot be true that every other human has an equal duty to satisfy that right. Most people simply do not have the time or resources needed to alleviate the suffering of all of the world's starving. In Shue's words, "I could not give a penny to each hungry child, even if it were a good idea—I do not even have the time to give one minute's thought to each hungry child. In addition, if rights are universal, I am naturally entitled to consume some of my resources myself."[12] This does not mean, however, that nobody is responsible for the protection or satisfaction of demanding universal rights, especially since all rights have correlative duties. The key, Shue argues, is establishing an appropriate division of labor among duty-bearers: "All negative duties fall upon everyone [because they are costless to observe], but the positive duties need to be divided up and assigned in some reasonable way."[13]

The standard way of thinking about this is in terms of "concentric circles," with our strongest obligations being to right-holders who are socially close to us—our intimates, fellow community members, and compatriots. Shue accepts the priority of intimates, but rejects "the progressive character of the decline in priority as one reaches farther from the center." There is "insufficient reason to believe," he argues, "that one's duties to people in the next county, who are in fact strangers, are any greater than one's positive duties to people on the next continent."[14] Having demonstrated the failings of the concentric circles approach, Shue proposes an institutional solution. It is true that the universal right to food is

---

[11] Margaret Keck and Kathryn Sikkink, *Activists Beyond Borders: Advocacy Networks in International Politics* (Ithaca: Cornell University Press, 1998); and Thomas Risse, Stephen Ropp, and Kathryn Sikkink, eds., *The Power of Human Rights: International Norms and Domestic Change* (Cambridge: Cambridge University Press, 1999).

[12] Shue, "Mediating Duties," p. 690.   [13] Ibid.   [14] Ibid., p. 692.

demanding, and that no individual has the capacity to meet this unrealized right of the world's starving. But it is also true that "the aggregate of individually small investments by large numbers of persons could reach a significant sum, especially if cooperation and coordination occurred among those acting in fulfillment of duty."[15] It is institutions, Shue argues, that can provide such cooperation and coordination. They can not only protect and satisfy rights more efficiently than uncoordinated individual actions, but they have the additional benefit of "respite," of providing a "psychological barrier" between the suffering of the world's poor and duty-bearers with tragically limited individual resources. It is thus "highly worthwhile," he concludes, "for the major international actors—governments, industries, bureaucracies, and regimes—that now control many aspects of our lives to be assigned, and brought into compliance with, a reasonable set of tasks for implementing the positive duties of individual persons."[16]

As noted in the introduction, Shue's argument about rights and institutions is a philosophical one: his goal is to give us good reasons why institutions *ought* to mediate our positive duties to protect or satisfy costly universal human rights. My goal is to transform this philosophical proposition into an empirical-theoretic one, to suggest that rights are necessarily institutionally referential, not just desirably so. More than this, I want to argue that historically rights struggles have been institutionally focused, and that since the sixteenth century the sovereign state has been the predominant institutional referent.

Before proceeding, it is important to dispense with one frequent misconception, the idea that we can, and should, distinguish between "negative" and "positive" rights, the former requiring duty-bearers to simply abstain from rights-violating conduct, the latter demanding additional effort and resources for their satisfaction. If this distinction were to hold, one could rightly argue that only positive rights are institutionally referential in our third sense, that only they require supporting or executing institutions. Ultimately, however, the distinction is unsustainable. As Shue demonstrates, quintessential negative rights, like the individual's right to physical security, cannot be protected without substantial effort and resources. "Ordinarily it is ... a matter of some people refraining from violations and of third parties being prevented from violations by the positive steps taken by the first and second parties."[17] Similarly, fulfilling

---

[15] Shue, "Mediating Duties," p. 695.   [16] Ibid. p. 698.

[17] Shue, *Basic Rights*, p. 39. For a similar argument, see Jack Donnelly, *Universal Human Rights in Theory and Practice*, 2nd edn. (Ithaca, N.Y.: Cornell University Press, 2003), pp. 30–1.

archetypical positive rights, such as the right to food, can involve powerful economic actors refraining from exploitive practices, like discriminatory terms of trade, as much as positive initiatives. "A demand for the fulfillment of rights to subsistence may involve not a demand to be provided with grants of commodities but merely a demand to be provided some opportunity for supporting oneself."[18]

The case for rights being inherently institutionally referential is best made with reference to the right to physical security, or what Thomas Hobbes called "the right to self-preservation." Is it possible to conceive of such a right as *not* institutionally referential? For social-contract theorists, like Hobbes and John Locke, this was a natural right, an entitlement individuals had prior to the establishment of civil or political society, an entitlement readily apparent to all humans imbued with "right reason." This would appear to be a situation in which the right to physical security is institutionally referential in neither of our second or third senses (though it may still be in our first): it exists without reference to social norms (as reasoning through the content of natural law is not the same as reasoning with reference to intersubjective social meanings); and it exists without enabling institutions. It is clear, though, that Hobbes, Locke, and others believed that a natural right to physical security was radically insufficient, that rights which existed outside the realm of a social compact—outside the realm of formal or informal intersubjective understandings—and without supporting and executing institutions were rights that would be forever assailed. This led Hobbes to his oft-quoted conclusion that "the natural state of men, before they entered into society, was a mere war, and that not simply, but a war of all men against all men."[19] Locke's conclusion was similar: while individuals possess rights in the state of nature, they are impossible to enjoy as they are "constantly exposed to the invasion of others."[20] Individuals escape this condition of vulnerability by contracting to establish political society and a sovereign authority, in doing so converting their natural rights into civil rights. The key thing, though, is that the social contract gives rights institutional referents in both the second and third senses: as commonly observed, it establishes an executing institution in the form of the sovereign, but it also establishes a set of intersubjective understandings, or social norms,

[18] Shue, *Basic Rights*, p. 40.
[19] Thomas Hobbes, *De Cive or The Citizen* (New York: Appleton-Century-Crofts, 1949), pt. 1, ch. 1, p. 29.
[20] John Locke, "The Second Treatise of Government: An Essay Concerning the True, Original, Extent and End of Civil Government," in *Two Treatises of Government* (Cambridge: Cambridge University Press, 1988), p. 350.

among right-holders. It is the constitution of such understandings to which Hobbes refers when he imagines what individuals pledge at the moment of contract: "I Authorize and give up my Right of Governing my selfe, to this Man, or to this Assembly of men, on this condition, that thou give up thy Right to him, and Authorize all his Actions in like manner."[21] Locke also highlights the social contract's role in constituting intersubjective understandings: *"the beginning of Politick Society* depends upon the consent of the Individuals, to joyn into and make one Society; who, when they are thus incorporated, might set up what form of Government they thought fit."[22]

The institutionally referential nature of rights is more starkly apparent as we move away from the notion of natural rights. As noted above, it is possible to conceive of natural rights as presocial, as existing independently of any framework of intersubjective understandings that give them meaning, as existing in a state of nature where there are no enabling or supporting institutions: I have a natural right by virtue of the laws of nature, laws that exist without human convention; I understand this right through the exercise of reason, an entirely atomistic interpretive process. But if we see all rights—including universal rights—as human artifacts then they are social by definition.[23] There are, of course, human artifacts that are not social, even ideational ones. If I stand up and claim that the international system was really the creation of aliens but nobody agrees with me the idea is a human artifact—my own little creation—but it is not, in any meaningful sense of the word, social: it is neither the product of human dialogue, nor does it reside in the intersubjective space between human actors; it is entirely subjective. But once we move away from the idea of rights as metaphysical principles, they appear as human artifacts that are deeply social. As Jean-Marie Coicaud observes, "The very idea of a right presupposes the existence of a community. In a world in which but a single person lived, right would have no room to exist."[24]

This is partly because the political veracity of rights depends on social recognition: to claim a right in a social universe in which there is no

[21] Thomas Hobbes, *Leviathan* (Cambridge: Cambridge University Press, 1991), ch. 17, p. 120.

[22] Locke, "Second Treatise," p. 337.

[23] Jack Donnelly's "Universal Declaration model" sees human rights as precisely such artifacts: "human rights have become a hegemonic political discourse, or what Mervyn Frost calls 'settled norms' of contemporary international society, principles that are widely accepted as authoritative within the society of states": Donnelly, *Universal Human Rights*, 2nd edn., p. 38.

[24] Jean-Marie Coicaud, *Legitimacy and Politics: A Contribution to the Study of Political Right and Political Responsibility* (Cambridge: Cambridge University Press, 2002), p. 11.

recognition of that right is to claim a right that is without social purchase. To claim a right is either (in the sense of rights as institutionally ambitious) to seek to construct a new set of intersubjective understandings about individual entitlements, or (in the sense of rights as institutionally presumptive) to appeal to a set of pre-existing understandings about the entitlements individuals enjoy in that social universe. Moving beyond the notion of natural rights makes our starting point, therefore, not the state of nature imagined by Hobbes, Locke, and others, but the realm of the social contract, the realm of understandings about the mutual recognition of social rights. And once we have reached this point, there is no reason to believe that Hobbes' and Locke's argument that the protection or satisfaction of rights requires the existence of enabling institutions no longer holds. In Hobbes' words, the "society proceeding from mutual help only, yields not that security which they seek for ... but that somewhat else must be done, that those who have once consented for the common good, to peace and mutual help, may by fear be restrained, lest afterwards they again dissent, when their private interest shall appear discrepant from the common good."[25]

For classical social contract theorists it was axiomatic that the referent institution for the protection of individuals' rights was the sovereign state: a power created, in Hobbes' view, "to conforme the wills of them all, to Peace at home, and mutuall ayd against enemies abroad."[26] Or as Locke put it, "The great and chief end therefore, of mens uniting into commonwealths, and putting themselves under Government, *is the preservation of their property*," understood as their "Lives, Liberties, and Estates."[27]

This idea that rights require referent, protective institutions, and that sovereign states are the most appropriate referents, has received a number of modern defenses, of which Hannah Arendt's is particularly noteworthy. Arendt's primary concern was the Versailles settlement's consecration of the nation-state as the legitimate form of political organization in Europe, a consecration which held that ethnically defined nations were entitled to their own sovereign states, a consecration that in practice granted self-determination to some "nations" while constituting the remaining peoples as "minorities" or "displaced persons."[28] It was the plight of these latter peoples that exposed for Arendt the tragic limitations of the "inalienable rights of man." The Versailles settlement established "the

---

[25] Hobbes, *De Cive*, pt. 2, ch. 5, p. 65. [26] Hobbes, *Leviathan*, pt. 2, ch. 17, pp. 120–1.
[27] Locke, "Second Treatise," p. 350.
[28] Hannah Arendt, *Imperialism: Part Two of the Origins of Totalitarianism* (New York: Harcourt Brace Jovanovich, 1968), ch. 5.

supremacy of the will of the nation over all legal and abstract institutions," and the accompanying "Minorities treaties" failed to protect unenfranchised ethnic groups while constituting them as permanent anomalies, peoples whose rights were protected not by their states but by woefully underdeveloped international law. Refugees were in an even worse situation. The homogenizing logic of national self-determination produced new waves of refugees, but the replacement of the historical concept of "stateless" people with "displaced persons" left them with no protection, even international. "The postwar term 'displaced persons' was invented during the war for the express purpose of liquidating statelessness once and for all by ignoring its existence. Nonrecognition of statelessness always means repatriation, *i.e.*, deportation to country of origin, which either refuses to recognize the prospective repatriate as a citizen, or, on the contrary, urgently wants him back for punishment."[29] What the Versailles settlement highlighted for Arendt was the poverty of rights without political membership, of rights without the protections that sovereign states accord their citizens: "The Rights of Man, after all, had been defined as 'inalienable' because they were supposed to be independent of all governments; but it turned out that the moment human beings lacked their own government and had to fall back upon their minimum rights, no authority was left to protect them and no institution was willing to guarantee them."[30]

Discussions of the relationship between individual rights and world politics focus almost exclusively on the potential for international human rights to civilize the domestic political practices of extant sovereign states. The international system is assumed to be the product of a distinct set of political dynamics—of which war-fighting and economic competition are considered especially important—and the human rights regime is seen as an exogenous normative structure which may, or may not, have the capacity to constrain the exercise of state power. The discussion so far suggests, however, that the politics of individual rights may have had a deeper, more constitutive effect on the system of sovereign states. Rights, we have seen, are inherently and necessarily institutionally referential, and classical theorists of rights consistently saw the sovereign state as the preferred institutional solution. I want to suggest, though, that this is more than a theoretical nicety, more than a philosophical predilection to be noted. The history of the international system since the sixteenth century has been punctuated by recurrent rights

---

[29] Arendt, *Imperialism*, p. 159.   [30] Ibid., pp. 171–2.

struggles, struggles that have taken the common form of peoples challenging the legitimacy of imperial political structures and championing the sovereign state as a liberating, protective institution. These struggles have been a critical factor in the dissolution of empires and the attendant proliferation of recognized sovereign states. Individual rights, from this perspective, have been a force for systemic change, altering over time the international system's structure of political agency, contributing to the transformation of a world of empires into a globalized system of states.

The evolution of the international system from a small core of nascent sovereign states in sixteenth- and seventeenth-century Europe to the current global system occurred through five waves of expansion: those associated with the Westphalian settlement (1648), the independence of the Americas (1810–1821), the Versailles settlement (1918), post-1945 decolonization (1945–1970), and the post-Cold War break-up of the Soviet Union and Yugoslavia. Elsewhere I have explained how after 1945 the struggle for civil and political rights and the construction of the international human rights regime served to delegitimate European colonialism and license the proliferation of post-colonial states.[31] But a connection between the politics of individual rights and the constitution of states out of empire was apparent as early as Westphalia. It was a century of conflicts over individual liberty of conscience that led to the Thirty Years War, and the Treaties of Westphalia resolved these conflicts (in a way that the Peace of Augsburg a century earlier had failed to do) by combining a new order of emergent sovereign states (which mapped onto the pluralistic confessional landscape) with constraints on the sovereign's right to enforce religious belief and practice.[32] Similar stories can be told about at least two of the three remaining waves of expansion: the independence of the Americas and the post-Cold War break-up of the Soviet Union and Yugoslavia. In the former case, enlightenment ideas about the individual's right to political representation were crucial, and in the latter "Helsinki" human rights norms played a crucial role in opening political space for the "Velvet Revolutions."[33]

---

[31] Christian Reus-Smit, "Human Rights and the Social Construction of Sovereignty," *Review of International Studies*, 27 (2001), 519–38.

[32] Christian Reus-Smit, *Individual Rights and the Making of the International System* (Cambridge: Cambridge University Press, forthcoming).

[33] See Brian Loveman, *The Constitution of Tyranny: Regimes of Exception in Spanish America* (Pittsburgh: University of Pittsburgh Press, 1994); and Daniel Thomas, *The Helsinki Effect: International Norms, Human Rights, and the Demise of Communism* (Princeton, N.J.: Princeton University Press, 2001).

3. Rights as Power-mediators

In addition to rights being institutionally referential, they have a second, less remarked upon, dimension—their status and function as power mediators. Rights are not just normative principles that inspire particularly strong entitlement claims: they are principles intended to structure power relationships between individuals, individuals and groups, and individuals and political institutions, especially where those relationships are characterized by unequal distributions of material resources. If I seek to defend my home against a neighbor by claiming that I have a property right, I am seeking to structure the power relationship between us by invoking a normative principle with both legal and moral standing, hopefully achieving an outcome that my sheer material capacities could never guarantee. A political prisoner who invokes his or her right not to be tortured is seeking to do a similar thing, but in far more dire circumstances.

Before we can fully comprehend this dimension of rights we need to consider the nature of power.[34] I shall follow Max Weber in defining power as "the probability that one actor within a social relationship will be in a position to carry out his will despite resistance, regardless of the basis on which this probability exists."[35] The key aspect of this definition is Weber's stress on the inherently relational nature of power, on the fact that power is necessarily an attribute of social relationships, not a possession of an atomistic actor. The lone individual, living outside society but controlling abundant material resources, cannot be said to have power in any politically meaningful sense. It is only when an actor seeks to have a transformative effect in relation to other actors that they can be said to have, or not to have, power. And it is only in this relational context that the resources they conscript, material or otherwise, will have political or social meaning and salience. Power "can develop only through *exchange* among actors involved in a given relation. To the extent that every relation between two parties presupposes exchange and reciprocal adaptation between them, power is indissolubly linked to negotiation: *it is a relation of exchange, therefore of negotiation*, in which at least two persons are involved."[36]

---

[34] The ideas on power advanced here are elaborated in Christian Reus-Smit, "International Crises of Legitimacy," *International Politics*, 44 (Nos. 2/3: March/May 2007), 157–74, and *American Power and World Order* (Cambridge: Polity Press, 2004), ch. 2.

[35] Max Weber, *The Theory of Social and Economic Organization* (New York: Free Press, 1957), p. 152.

[36] Michel Crozier and Erhard Friedberg, *Actors and Systems: The Politics of Collective Action* (Chicago: University of Chicago Press, 1980), pp. 30–1.

It is possible, if uncommon, for power relations to be based simply on unequal distributions of material resources, which is the way that many scholars understand power in international relations. In this situation, those actors with the most guns or money can impose their will through coercion or bribery. These kinds of power relations are, however, socially pathological. If power relations were always structured in this way, then society would be impossible, and so would all of the goods that society facilitates. This would indeed be a world akin to Hobbes' state of nature, "where an Invader hath no more to feare, than another mans single power; if one plant, sow, build, or possess a convenient Seat, others may probably be expected to come prepared with forces united, to dispossesse, and deprive him, not only of the fruit of his labor, but also of his life, or liberty, And the Invader again is in the like danger of another."[37]

Because of the socially pathological nature of unadulterated material power relations, all societies (including international societies, I would contend) develop normative media for structuring power relations in less socially destructive ways. The purpose of such media is not to eradicate power relations, as if this were possible, but to transform them—to qualify and compromise material relations with notions of legitimate social agency and action. The nature of these media varies greatly from one cultural and historical context to another. In some cultures, patronage norms structure power relations, in others caste norms perform the structuring role, and as modernity has globalized, rights norms have become ever more central. These normative media structure power relations in different ways—patronage, caste, and rights cultures generate different kinds of power formations. Material factors are clearly important—different kinds of economic system distribute material power resources in different ways, for example. But the purpose of a society's normative media is to channel power in different ways than the distribution of material power resources would dictate, and the nature of that society's normative media, and the way that it restructures power, is determined largely by prevailing cultural understandings. A simple counterfactual reinforces this point: If we were to strip all known caste, patronage, and rights societies of their normative media, would their distinctive power relations remain unchanged? The answer is almost certainly no.

Why do those who command disproportionate material resources, and who might benefit from the naked exercise of material power, allow normative media to evolve in ways that restructure power relations? Since

---

[37] Hobbes, *Leviathan*, ch. 13, p. 87.

most elites are born into a social order in which the operative normative media are well established, the question is more appropriately posed as: Why do those with bountiful material resources allow a society's normative media to persist? The answer is legitimacy. If an actor's power, practices, or values are considered legitimate by other social actors, he or she can reap the premium of voluntary compliance and cooperation. But legitimacy is a social phenomenon—one's power, practices, or values are only legitimate to the extent that others in society deem them to be. Furthermore, assessments of one's legitimacy are always made with reference to existing or emergent norms of rightful agency, conduct, or belief. This means that elites have an interest in the maintenance, even construction, of normative media that may tame their power but simultaneously legitimate it. A side benefit of this legitimating role is that normative media also stabilize and regularize power relations. Caste norms, patronage norms, and rights norms embed different configurations of power, situating individual power relations, between particular actors at particular times, within socially sanctioned frameworks of hierarchy, exchange, and recognition.

As noted earlier, most theoretical writings on rights are concerned with their nature as distinctive moral entitlements. However, authors have frequently alluded to rights as power mediators, even if they have not explored this fully. This is strongest in the writings of classical critics of absolutism. Locke's description of our natural right to freedom as a "fence against tyranny" is emblematic. He writes that "To be free from such force is the only security of my Preservation: and reason bids me look on him, as an Enemy to my Preservation, who will take away that *Freedom*, which is the Fence to it."[38] Contemporary theorists of rights also note the status of rights as power mediators, even if they grant this less attention than their classic predecessors. We already noted Shue's claim that the "fundamental purpose of acknowledging any basic rights at all is to prevent, or to eliminate, insofar as possible the degree of vulnerability that leaves people at the mercy of others."[39] John Vincent made a similar claim when he wrote that "rights are invoked against the situation in which some people are at the mercy of others, not out of pity, but from concern for the same values that underpin our dignity as individuals. Rights are thus a weapon of the weak against the strong."[40]

Before proceeding, a point of clarification is needed. To describe rights as power mediators is not to suggest that they work simply as intervening

---

[38] Locke, *Two Treatises*, p. 279.   [39] Shue, *Basic Rights*, pp. 29–30.
[40] John Vincent, *Human Rights and International Relations* (Cambridge: Cambridge University Press, 1986), p. 17.

variables between real, material sources of power and political outcomes. We might imagine here thick and thin conceptions of mediation. An old-style capacitor in an electronic circuit works as a thin mediator, altering the current that passes through it, while the original power source remains distinct and unchanged. This is the mediation of intervening variables. Normative media exhibit a thicker form of mediation than this. When I invoke my human rights to prevent a materially preponderant actor from harming me, I am appealing to intersubjective meanings that grant me, as a human being, such rights. These meanings are sources of power, different in form from the material resources my oppressor brings to bear, but sources nonetheless. They are resources in struggles over the terms of legitimate agency and action, both of which are important ingredients of power. Rights claims, and the norms they appeal to and help reproduce, don't just alter power through transmission, therefore, they help constitute it.

Societies in which rights constitute the prevailing normative media can be described as "rights cultures," just as Renaissance Italian society can be described as a patronage culture or traditional Indian society as a caste culture. Rights cultures exhibit a number of distinctive features which condition endogenous power relations in distinctive ways. First, rights cultures tend to be individualistic, which is not to say that they lack communal bonds or that their members display little if any social conscience; only that such cultures depend on the intersubjective belief that society is comprised of individuals who are integral moral agents and who are invested with moral and legal rights to protect their capacity for such agency. Second, rights cultures are formally equalitarian. This does not mean that they are without social hierarchies or disparities of power—they generally have both in abundance. It simply means that the individuals who navigate these hierarchies and disparities possess, equally, socially sanctioned rights of a moral or legal character. With certain caveats, patronage and caste cultures sanctify and cement social hierarchy. The norms of rights cultures, in contrast, constitute power relations by overlaying hierarchies constituted by birth, wealth, and position with a framework of equalitarian principles designed to provide common protections and entitlements. Third, the norms that constitute rights cultures are non-particularistic, in the sense that the relationship between right-holders and duty-bearers is not meant to be qualified or augmented by particularistic ties. The fact that one has positive social relationships with duty-bearers should be no more relevant to the respect of one's rights than if one had negative relationships with them. Finally, rights cultures tend toward codification. Claiming a right always raises the question of the authoritative source of that right, and codification is the social process of constructing such sources. At historical junctures where ideas of natural right have prevailed, this process has taken the form of exegesis, the distilling of such rights from authoritative texts that supposedly encapsulate the law of nature or God's law. In more recent, secular contexts the tendency, domestically and internationally, has been toward the codification of rights in contract, statute, or treaty.[41]

Rights take different forms and these differences shape rights cultures, and the power relations they engender, in distinctive ways. This is usually thought of in substantive terms—that there are civil and political rights, social and economic rights, etc. While these differences are important, differences in scope have been equally, if not more, important historically. The scope of rights varies across two dimensions: territorial reach, and societal depth. Some rights are territorially bounded, like citizenship rights, while others have no such bounds, like universal human rights. Some rights are held only by particular categories of persons, like minority rights, and others are thought to belong to all humans. Citizenship rights are territorially bounded *and* categorically restricted. With this understanding of the scope of rights in mind, we can identify a number of particularly important forms of rights: statist rights, which pertain only to members of a particular, territorially defined polity; non-universal systemic rights, such as the minority rights enshrined in the Versailles settlement, that apply to particular groups in particular contexts, but form part of the normative and legal structure of the international system; and universal systemic rights, or international human rights, which, as we have said, have come to apply to all humans without territorial restriction.

The power relationship that rights are most commonly invoked to mediate is that between the individual and the sovereign state. That this should be so is not surprising. The sovereign state is, by definition, a political institution that concentrates and demarcates political power: it centralizes it in the hands of national governments, and it fences it in territorially. This gives the agents of the state—governments and their bureaucratic supports—extraordinary capacities for good, but also for more or less extreme forms of violence and oppression. It is the all too frequent exercise of these latter capacities that led Barry Buzan to observe that it is the sovereign state—protector of national security—that

---

[41] On this tendency internationally, see the special issue "Legalization and World Politics," *International Organization*, 54 (No. 3: 2000).

has been, historically, one of the principal sources of individual insecurity.[42] It is against these exploitive and oppressive practices of sovereign states that rights are commonly invoked, and this is true of each of the categories of rights identified above. Citizens invoke their constitutional rights to contain the exercise of state power, among other things; indigenous peoples invoke their constitutional and international human rights for the same reason; and minorities invoke their constitutional, non-universal systemic rights, and international human rights, all for the purpose of constraining and reshaping their power relationship with the agents of the state. Torture victims do the same, refugees do likewise, and even gays seeking the right to marry are invoking their international human rights to condition state power. At times appeals to rights are designed to circumscribe the exercise of state control, to fence off certain actions as beyond the scope of legitimate state authority. At other times, rights are invoked to extend the exercise of state control, to establish it as right and proper that the state should use its authority in areas normally considered beyond its ambit. When women invoke their international human rights to force their states to protect them against domestic violence they are seeking just such an extension of state power, an extension into what traditionalists have historically considered the private sphere.

4. The Generative Paradox of Rights and States

The literature on individual rights and world politics takes a distinctive form. It begins by imagining a preformed international system, one characterized by particular understandings and practices of sovereignty, one generated by a distinctive set of constitutive social forces, principally war and economic competition. Against this is cast the international human rights regime, a set of norms constructed to reduce the pathological human consequences of a world organized into autonomous, territorial states. As I have argued elsewhere, this is a tale of two separate regimes, the latter an exogenous construction intended to civilize the former.

This perspective is especially apparent in conventional discussions of sovereignty and human rights. Sovereignty is seen as an extant regime

---

[42] "For perhaps a majority of the world's people threats from the state are among the major sources of insecurity in their lives": Barry Buzan, *People, States and Fear: The National Security Problem in International Relations* (Brighton: Wheatsheaf Books, 1983), p. 26.

confronted by a historically new human rights regime. Richard Claude and Burns Weston offer a quintessential statement of this view:

Consider ... the classical international law doctrine of state sovereignty and its corollary of nonintervention, the central props of our inherited state-centric system of world order. These values associated with this doctrine (a legal license to "do your own thing") and corollary (an injunction to "mind your own business") rest in uneasy balance with human rights concerns (which seem to tell us that "you are your brothers' and sisters' keeper").[43]

So pervasive is this approach that it is shared by skeptics and optimists alike. Stanley Hoffmann argues that international human rights norms have "questioned two sacred elements of sovereignty: the right to wage war, and the right to do what you like to your citizens."[44] Similarly, Kathryn Sikkink claims that the "doctrine of internationally protected human rights offers one of the most powerful critiques of sovereignty as currently constituted, and the practices of human rights law and human rights foreign policies provide concrete examples of shifting understandings of the scope of sovereignty."[45]

The two ideas that lie buried within Shue's writings on human rights, and which have been elaborated in previous sections, suggest a markedly different perspective on individual rights and world politics. They point to what I shall call the "generative paradox of rights and states." From conventional perspectives there is nothing paradoxical about this relationship—the system of sovereign states exists and the human rights regime has evolved to round off its nastier edges. Scholars disagree about whether the regime is having the desired effect, but nobody considers the relationship paradoxical—tragic, vexed, unclear, etc., but not paradoxical. But this is because conventional perspectives see only one dimension of rights, their nature and function as power mediators. They focus on the power relationship between the individual and the sovereign state and then ask whether international human rights can mediate this relationship. But once we introduce our other dimension of rights—their institutionally referential nature—we have a very different picture, one genuinely paradoxical. Theoretically, we have seen that rights require an

---

[43] Richard Pierre Claude and Burns H. Weston, "Human Rights as a Challenge to State Sovereignty," in *Human Rights in the World Community: Issues and Action*, ed. Richard Pierre Claude and Burns H. Weston (Philadelphia: University of Pennsylvania Press, 1989), p. 3.

[44] Stanley Hoffmann, "Reaching for the Most Difficult: Human Rights as a Foreign Policy Goal," *Daedalus*, 112 (No. 4: Fall 1983), 19–49 at p. 22.

[45] Kathryn Sikkink, "Human Rights, Principled Issue-Networks, and Sovereignty in Latin America," *International Organization*, 47 (1993), 411–41 at p. 411.

institutional referent, and that in practice rights struggles since the sixteenth century have defined the sovereign state as that referent. Our two dimensions of rights thus have contradictory impulses: the institutionally referential dimension encouraging the constitution of sovereign states, the power-mediating dimension encouraging the compromising of sovereignty.

This paradoxical relationship between rights and states has played an important generative role in the development of the global political order. As we have already seen, since the sixteenth century recurrent political struggles have appealed to the moral grammar of individual rights to simultaneously delegitimize empire and license the creation of new sovereign states. Of the five waves of expansion that have produced our present global system of states, the politics of individual rights was centrally implicated in at least four: Westphalia, independence of the Americas, post-1945 decolonization, and the break-up of the Soviet Union and Yugoslavia. In each of these cases rights served both as mobilizers of political action—constituting actors' identities and interests in distinctive ways—and as rhetorical resources, normatively powerful principles that could be invoked to delegitimize imperial political structures, justify resistance politics, and license the creation of new political units. My claim here is not that individual rights, and the politics they engendered, were sole or sufficient causes of international systemic expansion. Rather, it is that they were necessary conditions: without these ideas and the struggles they inspired and licensed, the break-up of Europe's empires would have had different impetuses, taken different forms, produced different outcomes, and occurred with different timing.

In arguing that the politics of individual rights helped produce the present system of sovereign states I am not suggesting that the states so generated were necessarily more observant of their subjects' or citizens' rights than the imperial institutions they replaced—tragically, all too frequently they were not. This should not be surprising, however. If it is not easier to destroy something than create it, as the old truism goes, it is certainly different. The political conditions of late empires—their structures, institutions, processes, material capacities, and ideational supports—constituted a distinctive terrain for rights-based political resistance. But the disintegration of empire saw new political conditions emerge, and the project of political resistance had to give way to that of political construction. But the challenge of constructing new rights-protecting sovereign states (democratic or otherwise) has always proven formidable. New political elites have frequently confronted economic collapse, the continued opposition of recidivist groups, and the persistent institutional legacies of empire. Added to all of this, the political coalitions that formed to confront empire often fragment once the project turns from resistance to political construction.

This brings us to the second generative impact that the paradoxical relation between rights and states has had on the global political order. The often tragic underperformance of sovereign states in the field of basic rights has encouraged the development of institutional referents beyond the state. It is useful here to conscript, with modification, John Ruggie's concept of the "unbundling of territoriality." For Ruggie, the development of a system of territorially demarcated sovereign states, each claiming exclusive authority within their borders and denying any higher authority beyond, produced a dilemma: how could states deal with challenges "that could not be reduced to territorial solution?"[46] The need to deal with this problem has encouraged states to unbundle aspects of their territoriality onto various kinds of international institutions. This "institutional *negation* of exclusive territoriality serves as the means of situating and dealing with those dimensions of collective existence that territorial rulers recognize to be irreducibly transnational in character."[47] We have seen precisely this kind of unbundling of territoriality in the field of international human rights protection. States have invested uneven degrees of political authority on a variety of international human rights institutions—from the Covenants on Civil and Political and Social and Economic Rights to the International Criminal Court—because of the pathological limitations of unbridled and absolute sovereignty, or what Ruggie calls "absolute individuation." Human rights differ, however, from Ruggie's standard model of territorial unbundling. He assumes that it is states unbundling territoriality in functional areas that are uniquely transnational in character. But in the field of human rights the unbundling has often been driven by non-state actors, human rights protection is not functional in the same way that managing free trade or limiting climate change is, and human rights are only a transnational issue because of states failing in their responsibilities.

The fact that rights struggles have historically championed the sovereign state as the institutional alternative to empire has, however, cast a shadow over the development of institutional referents beyond the state.

---

[46] John Gerard Ruggie, "Territoriality and Beyond: Problematizing Modernity in International Relations," *International Organization* 47 (1993), 139–74 at p. 164.

[47] Ibid., p. 165.

Empires were transnational political authorities, and the sovereign state was conceived as a form of institutional liberation. Despite the profound limitations of many states as human rights protectors, the specter of past empire, and the tight clutch in which new sovereignty is held by post-colonial states, has constrained the development of more effective international human rights institutions. Nowhere is this more starkly apparent than with post-1945 decolonization. First-wave post-colonial states, like India, Pakistan, Brazil, the Philippines, Chile, and Columbia, were vigorous supporters of the development of an international bill of rights, and subsequently used these rights to delegitimize colonialism and license decolonization.[48] Once the great European empires were dissolved, however, and the first truly global system of sovereign states constructed, post-colonial states, including those listed above, became equally vigorous defenders of highly categorical notions of sovereignty.

5. Conclusion

There are many myths of history that international relations scholars tell themselves. Among these is the myth that rights came to influence world politics only in the twentieth century, that they only become important with the post-1945 development of the international human rights regime. In Kathryn Sikkink's words, "Before the Second World War, human rights were not considered an appropriate topic for international scrutiny and rule formation."[49] This widespread misconception is only possible because scholars focus almost exclusively on the second dimension of rights, their nature and function as power-mediators, and specifically on the role of rights in mediating the power relationship between individuals and the sovereign state. After all, universal human rights have been codified internationally precisely for the purpose of mediating this power relationship. Acknowledging the first dimension of rights—their institutionally referential nature—encourages a very different view of the history of rights and world politics. Combining these two dimensions reveals the generative paradox of rights and states, a paradox that has,

[48] See Reus-Smit, "Human Rights and the Social Construction of Sovereignty," pp. 531–6.

[49] Kathryn Sikkink, *Mixed Signals: U.S. Human Rights Policy in Latin America* (Ithaca, N.Y.: Cornell University Press, 2004), p. 26. If we are speaking about universal human rights, then this statement is not untrue—the international politics of such rights is largely a late-twentieth-century phenomenon. But the general assumption is that it is only with the advent of such politics that individual rights of any sort became important in world politics.

for the last five centuries, been deeply implicated in the constitution of the global political order, contributing not only to the expansion of the system of sovereign states itself but also the unbundling of territoriality onto international human rights instruments. Buried within Shue's philosophical writings on human rights lie, therefore, conceptual signposts toward a more comprehensive historical sociology of rights.

3

Another Turn of the Wheel?

Basic Rights in International Society

Andrew Hurrell

One of the oldest ways of thinking about international relations is to view the international realm in terms of a logic of reproduction and recurrence. Yes, there will be relatively good times when ideas about governance, order, even justice flourish. But these will inevitably give way to a harsher world in which clashes over power and deep divergences over values will threaten institutionalized cooperation once more and relegate consideration of rights and justice to the margins of global politics. This familiar way of thinking is embedded in many classical realist writings; it is embodied in the academic narratives of how the idealism of the 1920s gave way to the realism of the 1930s and 1940s; and it can be seen again in the move from the 1970s (characterized by much liberal discussion of transnationalism, interdependence, the declining utility of military force, and the growing role of moral issues) to the 1980s (characterized by the revival of Cold War tensions, by the spread of conflict in the Third World, and by the end of the North–South dialogue).

One way of considering the present conjuncture is to pose this question anew. Are we not witnessing another turn of the wheel as the neo-Grotian or liberal solidarist moment of the 1990s gives way to a more unstable and conflict-prone world? Are not the structures and dynamics of contemporary international politics best understood in terms of a return to Westphalia? If this is indeed the case, then should not the idea of basic rights be consigned to the dreamland of the political theorist? This chapter addresses these questions and uses them as a framework, first to contextualize Shue's writings on basic rights; and second to raise some questions about the position of the idea of basic rights within international society.

It is one of the characteristics of Shue's work that it speaks both to the philosophical literature and to more empirically minded students of global politics. His work has reflected many of the most important changes that have taken place in the normative character of international society; it has contributed directly to some of those changes and to the surrounding debates (for example in relation to basic rights, to the conditionality of sovereignty, to *jus in bello*, and to torture); and it has provided a consistently valuable critical framework by which these changes might be assessed and evaluated.

The empirical also plays a distinctive part in Shue's work as a political philosopher, in at least three ways. In the first place, Shue seeks to build his arguments up from what he takes to be relatively uncontroversial and minimalist understandings about how the world works and what motivates groups and individuals. In terms of political arrangements, for example, he discounts the likelihood of any radical international institutional reform, taking the state as the core actor and concentrating on finding ways of allocating the default duties that arise when states are unable to meet the basic rights of their citizens. He accepts that this is a "practical judgement, and an especially shaky one" but goes on: "if the state cannot be eliminated, as one certainly might wish, the question becomes whether it can be civilized."[1]

A second way in which the empirical matters has to do with the importance of strategic argument and action in Shue's understanding of basic rights or, perhaps more accurately, his understanding of the relationship between basic rights and the mechanisms necessary for their actual enjoyment. "This form of analysis means treating the securing of rights as ends and arriving at adequate arrangements through means/end, or strategic, reasoning."[2] This cannot of course be based on an unconstrained instrumental or consequentialist logic, but it does bring assessments of the empirical firmly into the picture.

Knowing how to protect the right against violation, or to restore the right after violation, depends on historical and empirical understanding of the relevant social, historical, political, legal, and psychological factors. As long as theorists remain

---

[1] Henry Shue, "Afterword," in *Basic Rights: Subsistence, Affluence and U.S. Foreign Policy*, 2nd edn. (Princeton, N.J.: Princeton University Press, 1996), p. 174.
[2] Ibid., p. 160.

narrow specialists, adequate analysis of how to institutionalize a right requires interdisciplinary collaboration. It is certainly nothing that ethical theory alone can settle.[3]

Thirdly, Shue suggests that our judgments about the development of better institutions must reflect empirical understanding both of how and why institutions develop and of their potential and limits.

With the securing of at least the basic rights of everyone as the goal sought, a full treatment would investigate alternative institutional structures, not behind a veil of ignorance but with as much information relevant to the comparative feasibility of the various structures as can be pulled together, and in light of considered but defeasible judgements about fairness in the assignment of duties grounded in basic rights.[4]

This chapter is divided into three sections. It begins by situating Shue's analysis of basic rights within the broader development of a liberal solidarist conception of international society, especially as this was understood in the period immediately following the Cold War. The second section then sketches some of the principal arguments in favor of the view that we are witnessing a return to Westphalia and draws out the implications of these arguments for basic rights. In the concluding section I suggest why such a view is at least incomplete and why the idea of basic rights continues to show a perhaps surprising degree of resilience.

1. Basic Rights and Liberal Solidarism

The second half of the twentieth century witnessed a transformation in ideas about the nature and possibilities of international order. At the level of practice, there were important changes in patterns of institutionalization; a dramatic increase in the scope, density, and intrusiveness of international rules; far-reaching developments in both the making of international law and the basis on which legal, moral, and political norms were to be justified; and increasing efforts to move towards the more effective implementation of international norms.[5] At the level of normative ambition the changes were still more far-reaching and led

---

[3] Ibid., p. 161.

[4] Henry Shue, "Limiting Sovereignty," in *Humanitarian Intervention and International Relations*, ed. Jennifer Welsh (Oxford: Oxford University Press, 2006), pp. 11–28 at p. 22.

[5] For one view of these changes see Andrew Hurrell, *On Global Order: Power, Values and the Constitution of International Society* (Oxford: Oxford University Press, 2007).

inexorably to the belief—at least within Western liberal societies—that international order had to be reconceived and reconceptualized. A minimally acceptable order came increasingly to be seen as involving both limits on the freedom of states to resort to war and the creation of international rules that affected the domestic structures and organization of states, invested individuals and groups within states with rights and duties, and sought to embody some notion of a general common good. The scope of legitimate expectations increased exponentially. Indeed it is easy to lose sight of just how profound and radical these changes have been.

The hugely increased normative ambition of international society is nowhere more visible than in the field of human rights and democracy: in the idea that the relationship between ruler and ruled, state and citizen, should be a subject of legitimate international concern; that the ill treatment of citizens should trigger international action; and that the external legitimacy of states and their position within international society should depend in some way on their domestic political arrangements. Such ideas are central to liberal solidarist conceptions of international society. Whether seen from the perspective of law, morality, or politics a key conceptual change is the move from the idea of the state as sovereign to the idea of the state as agent—an agent acting both in the interests of its own citizens and on behalf of an international community that is increasingly supposed to embody and reflect shared interests and shared values.

At one level Shue's work on basic rights can be related to a specific set of debates in the 1970s about the role of human rights in U.S. foreign policy. But it also reflects a broader set of developments that were taking place in the institutional architecture of human rights. This is most immediately discernible in arguments concerning the interdependence and indivisibility of different sets of human rights. At the political level, such arguments were central to the bargains being negotiated amongst different groups of states. No bargain would have been possible between East and West and North and South that did not accept international recognition of civil and political rights on the one hand and economic and social rights on the other.

Shue's work explained how this interdependence worked at a deeper level—both conceptually and substantively. He challenged the view that security rights are prior to, or more important than, subsistence rights. He suggested that, on closer analysis, distinctions between civil and political and economic and social rights, or between rights that demand merely abstention and forbearance rather than positive action and the provision of significant resources, break down and become untenable. Security and subsistence rights both matter; both have a similar structure; and neither can be understood in terms of any simple distinction between positive and negative. As he put it: "it is simply not the case that all, or most, civil and political rights can be fulfilled entirely or mostly by negative duties, while all, or most, economic and social rights must be fulfilled entirely or mostly by positive duties."[6] For example, civil and political rights certainly demand that states and their agents do not engage directly in harm-causing activities, but they also require the provision of an effective police service and judicial system.

If Shue's analysis of basic rights gave much sharper focus to notions of the indivisibility and interconnectedness of rights, it also offered a potential way of dealing with what many saw as the excessive expansion of the rights agenda and the consequent dilution of their potential political impact.[7] Shue's core claim is, after all, that we can identify *basic* rights—basic in the sense that their fulfillment is essential to the fulfillment of all other rights. One dimension of this debate is philosophical and is well represented in other chapters of this book. But another dimension is more political. To what extent does Shue's notion of basic rights succeed in narrowing down a set of what he calls "strategically critical rights" that can play a potentially constructive role in the messy and contested politics of human rights?[8] There are some grounds for doubt. It is true that Shue's core notion of subsistence rights is minimalist, involving some opportunity to support oneself. But what precisely is entailed in the idea of subsistence remains somewhat unclear and legal efforts by the UN Committee on Economic, Social, and Cultural Rights to develop consensus on both the content of a minimum core of such rights and on the obligations imposed by socio-economic rights on states has proved elusive.[9] Moreover, the potential for expansion is greatly increased if we add in Shue's discussion of liberty rights.[10] Again, Shue is anxious to keep the focus minimal, concentrating on a loosely defined right to political participation that is not tied to any particular kind of political system. Yet, even in the "Afterword" to *Basic Rights*, the notion of a right to vote creeps in.[11] This

---

[6] Shue, "Afterword," p. 155.

[7] For a discussion and critique of the expansion of rights, see Philip Alston, "Conjuring Up New Human Rights: A Proposal for Quality Control," *American Journal of International Law*, 78 (1984), 607–21.

[8] Shue, "Afterword," p. 157.

[9] On the influence of Shue's work in this area and on the difficulties involved see David Bilchitz, *Poverty and Fundamental Rights: The Justification and Enforcement of Socio-Economic Rights* (Oxford: Oxford University Press, 2007), especially pp. 90–1 and 183–7.

[10] Shue, *Basic Rights*, ch. 3.   [11] Shue, "Afterword," p. 163.

then opens up the sorts of arguments about a right to democratic governance that became such an important feature of Western discussions about the post-Cold War international order.[12]

Even if the internal logic is compelling, it is not clear that the idea of basic rights has actually helped to secure consensus on a shared notion of which rights are to be given greatest priority and political support. Rather, we have continued to see a high degree of politicization and contestation. On one side, whatever the legal status of the international covenants, many Western governments (and the international economic institutions which they dominate) have continued to downplay economic and social rights. On the other, the political appeal of a developmentalism that stresses the imperatives of state-building and national development above human rights and democracy has certainly not disappeared in many parts of the developing world and in many emerging economies. Moreover, for many governments, the alleged international right to democratic governance has widely been used for narrow national and partisan purposes and the very uneven and uncertain process of democratization in many countries has increased contestation as to the nature of democracy.

But the most important aspect of Shue's work concerns the duties that need to be performed if rights are to be made secure: duties to refrain from harm-causing; duties to protect those whose basic rights are violated; and duties to aid and assist. As he put it: "My primary contention has been that taking rights seriously means taking duties seriously."[13] I would like to draw out three points here. The first concerns the complexity of the question of where and on whom duties fall; the second relates to the role of institutions and institutional reform; and the third focuses on the idea of conditional sovereignty.

1.1. The Complexity of Duties

As the Introduction to this volume has suggested, there is much room for debate as to what exactly is involved in the idea of "social guarantees against standard threats," "secure access to rights," or "genuinely effective means to fulfill." Equally, there are complex questions involved in the allocation of duties and in attempts to specify (and limit) what is actually required in order to protect basic rights. This is especially the case given that the most critical duties might not be those that are temporarily or

---

[12] Within the international legal community see especially Thomas Franck, "The Emerging Right to Democratic Governance," *American Journal of International Law*, 86 (1992), 46–91.

[13] Shue, "Afterword," p. 167.

geographically nearest to the rights violation. Whilst the philosophical and conceptual issues remain important, I would like to suggest that Shue's core intuition is right and that the messiness of the situations within which human rights abuses take place and the changing character of human rights abuses have served to reinforce the importance of these intuitions.

When *Basic Rights* was written, it was plausible to lay primary emphasis on human rights abuses that were directly attributable to the actions of authoritarian states and the agents of those states. Even in such cases, Shue wanted to argue that duties were complex in terms of the mixture of positive and negative actions that were required to make rights meaningful. But the conventional picture seemed reasonably clear and coherent. We could legitimately think of an international human rights system as one that concentrates on the protection of individuals against the nefarious actions of their state; that is built around legal notions of state responsibility; and that assumes that pressure can be exerted on states which, in turn, possess the levers necessary to improve the situation. In other words that states which are part of the problem can also be potentially part of the solution. In extreme cases, where the state cannot be encouraged or pressured to alter its ways, then the system needs to find ways of specifying what outsiders are entitled or obligated to do in order to assist those whose rights are being violated.

If we continue to press Shue's two core questions—what does it actually take to enable people to be secure against a range of predictable threats and what duties are required to implement these basic rights?—then the changing character of the threats have worked to increase the complexity and to expand the range of actions that are required and the number of agents on which the duties to act will fall.

In many parts of the world "traditional" human rights violations perpetrated by state agents as part of a deliberate state policy no longer exhaust or even dominate the catalogue of violations. In Latin America, for example, although much of the regional human rights agenda is still taken up by the legacies of authoritarianism and issues of transitional justice (amnesty laws, proper compensation, the right to know about details of past violations), these forms of human rights abuses have tended to decline with the end of military governments in the region. Increasing attention has therefore been given to violations that involve challenges to the rule of law (access to justice, due process) and to the rights of vulnerable groups (especially the rights of indigenous peoples in relation to land ownership and access to healthcare, the rights of women, and the rights of children). The focus of attention has shifted to structural violence by police against marginal communities, collapsed prison systems, and deeply problematic judiciaries. The causes do not lie in the exercise of excessive or arbitrary state power but are rather the consequences of state weakness. Sustained and "structural" human rights violations occur on a large scale. But in many cases the direct role of state authorities may be difficult to demonstrate, or may indeed be entirely absent. The capacity of weak and inefficient state institutions to address such violations may be extremely limited.

If we broaden the picture and look across many parts of the developing world, it is important to note that this problem is by no means confined to cases of societal collapse, civil war, and the total breakdown of central authority. Indeed, working with a single and rigid category of "failed states" is an extremely unhelpful way of approaching this phenomenon. It is more helpful to consider the multiple forms of violence, the blurred character of relations between public and private power, and the way in which really existing states have always diverged from neat Weberian models. The historical legacies of processes of state formation in different parts of the world have therefore continued to shape both the character of human rights violations and the capacity of states to address them.

The crucial point is that our understanding of the duties required by basic rights cannot easily escape from this messiness—from the difficulty of assigning individual moral responsibility in a world of impossible choices, mixed motives, and human frailty; from the complexity of the causal chains that might plausibly explain the nature of the threats and of the links between structural factors on the one hand and group and individual action on the other; and the geographical expansiveness of the chains of causality that link rights violations in one part of the world to the lives of distant strangers. In such a world, seeking to identify clear perpetrators as the sole basis on which to assign responsibility can only be one part of the story, although obviously still an important part. Even security rights face serious and complex allocation problems in terms of assigning responsibilities.

1.2. Duties and Institutions

A second aspect of the focus on duties is visible in *Basic Rights* but becomes a far more central part of Shue's subsequent work: namely the duty to create institutions to protect those whose basic rights are under threat; to provide the positive forms of assistance necessary for the social guarantee of basic rights across international society; and to ensure that the often risky or costly duties are allocated fairly. In the 1970s, the focus was on U.S. foreign policy and the politics of aid in the context of the Cold War. The object was explicitly anti-interventionist—to stop the United States from offering material aid and support to brutal regimes in the interests of Cold War geopolitics. In the "Afterword" to the second edition of *Basic Rights* Shue points out that the focus on aid reflected the particular concerns of the time and the need to cut off or condition U.S. foreign assistance: "this obscured the importance of the second general kind of duty, the duty to protect, and most specifically what I labelled … the duty to protect people from violation of their rights by the design of better institutions."[14] Or, as he explains, in "Mediating Duties":

> If institutions are players of as much importance as I have maintained throughout and can implement positive duties effectively, among the most important duties of individual persons will be indirect duties for the design and creation of positive-duty performing institutions that do not yet exist and for the modification or transformation of existing institutions that now ignore rights and the positive duties that rights involve.[15]

Note that the changes required involve both the reform of existing global social institutions and structures that are harm-causing (as argued by theorists such as Pogge) and the creation of new institutions.[16] Note too that there are a number of reasons why institutions matter, some clearly specified in Shue's work, others only hinted at and deserving of further elaboration. Perhaps clearest is the argument that institutions are needed in order to allocate duties fairly and to avoid an over-demanding set of duties that would strain individual motivation and would itself be unfair: "Expecting individuals endlessly to be willing to step into the breaches left by the failures of others to do their prior duties is wildly unfair. These lives would simply be consumed by (default) duties—this is precisely to ignore that for duty-bearers too, as much as for victims of rights violations, this is the only life they will live."[17] But there is also a suggestion that fairness in allocating duties is important in order to secure political support for costly action to protect the basic rights of distant strangers (as in Shue's discussion of the case of Somalia).

Beyond fairness in allocating duties, institutions might matter morally in two further ways—first, as a means by which imperfect duties can be turned

---

[14] Shue, "Afterword," p. 159.

[15] Shue, "Mediating Duties," *Ethics* 98 (1988), 687–704 at p. 703.

[16] See, for example, Thomas Pogge, *World Poverty and Human Rights* (Cambridge: Polity Press, 2002).

[17] Shue, "Afterword," p. 172.

into perfect duties that can strictly bind agents and should be fulfilled in all circumstances; and second, in order to create conditions in which victims and potential victims can be empowered. "The best arrangement is often one that allows victims of rights violations to become the agents of their own salvation, but this depends upon institutions that support empowerment."[18]

By contrast, there is rather little debate in Shue's work on what sorts of institutions might be most effective in delivering rights-protecting action, particularly in the most serious cases that demand coercive intervention. Clearly "institutional" action of some kind is needed because of the limits of what individuals can do on their own to help protect basic rights on a global level. But what kind of institutional action? On one side, there are good arguments that coercive intervention may be best undertaken through formal organizations such as the United Nations or regional bodies—both because of their legitimating role and their capacity to provide a standard range of efficiency-enhancing benefits to states. On the other side, many believe that effectiveness will continue to depend on the willingness of major states to act. Indeed the focus of Shue's commentary on both Northern Iraq and Rwanda is on the actions and, in the latter case, reprehensible omissions of the United States.[19] There is, then, a tension between the moral importance of institutions and beliefs as to what might actually constitute the most effective forms of institutional action, perhaps pointing to the broader need to bring moral cosmopolitanism and legal or political cosmopolitanism into closer alignment.

1.3. Conditional Sovereignty

If we ask what principles might shape these institutions, already in 1996 Shue is developing the notion of conditional sovereignty. "It seems to me, however, that one plausible step would be building a general, global consensus that state sovereignty is conditional upon the protection of at least basic rights."[20] As he turns to consider this in more detail, he begins by recasting the idea of state sovereignty and by taking and developing one of the classic arguments of international society theorists, namely that even hard, traditional "Westphalian" sovereignty has been misconstrued.

Thus, it cannot be that initially states have some effective right to (external) sovereignty, like a right to wage war, that mysteriously "inheres in each state individually," and only later do they gain an effective right to non-intervention when a transition occurs from system of states to society of states and collective

---

[18] Shue, "Afterword", p. 167.   [19] Ibid., pp. 175–6.   [20] Ibid., p. 174.

understandings emerge. Until shared rules emerge, no rights hold ... Thus, if sovereignty is a right, sovereignty is limited. Sovereignty is limited because the duties that are constitutive of the right, and without which there can be no right, constrain the activity of every sovereign belonging to international society.[21]

Shue's writing here is both reflecting and directly contributing to one of the most important aspects of the liberal solidarism of the 1990s, namely the view that sovereignty is conditional and that states are only fully legitimate to the extent that they act on behalf of their citizens and do not abuse their rights. One important area of debate (and contestation) has focused on humanitarian intervention. Although the issue is a very old one, the post-Cold War period saw a clear increase in the willingness of states to use force for humanitarian purposes.[22] In addition, humanitarian motivations and goals played an important role in the way in which understandings of what might constitute a threat to international peace and security have been broadened. For many liberal commentators, a clear normative shift was taking place towards an acceptance of a norm of humanitarian intervention.[23]

Similarly, increased attention was being given within international society to recasting sovereignty in terms of sovereignty as responsibility, and to the need to develop an internationally recognized responsibility to protect. As the International Commission on Intervention and State Sovereignty put it in 2001: "It is acknowledged that sovereignty implies a dual responsibility: externally, to respect the sovereignty of other states, and internally, to respect the dignity and basic rights of all the people within the state."[24] The adoption by the General Assembly of the idea of a responsibility to protect at the UN World Summit in September 2005 has been viewed as evidence of normative change that has, at least to some degree, been reflected in international legal practice. Such moves clearly expand the normative ambition of international society—by permitting coercive intervention without the consent of the affected state, and by shifting the burden of responsibility from those seeking to intervene to the state said to be in breach of its responsibility to protect.

[21] Shue, "Limiting Sovereignty," p. 15. See Reus-Smit (Chapter 2 of this volume) on the role of the sovereign state (section 2) and the idea of rights as power mediators (section 3).

[22] See J. L. Holzgrefe and Robert Keohane, eds., *Humanitarian Intervention: Ethical, Legal and Political Dilemmas* (Cambridge: Cambridge University Press, 2004); Jennifer Welsh, ed., *Humanitarian Intervention and International Relations* (Oxford: Oxford University Press, 2006).

[23] For example, Nicholas Wheeler, *Saving Strangers: Humanitarian Intervention in International Society* (Oxford: Oxford University Press, 2000).

[24] ICISS, *The Responsibility to Protect: Report of the International Commission on Intervention and State Sovereignty* (Ottawa: International Development Research Centre, 2001), p. 8.

On the other side, however, there are important grounds for questioning how far these changes have developed. Many doubt that anything approaching a clear legal norm of humanitarian intervention has crystallized, stressing the limited number of cases of classically defined humanitarian intervention (Iraq, Somalia, Haiti, and Kosovo) and arguing that interventions without explicit UN authorization (most notably Kosovo) cannot be considered as legal.[25] Moreover, there remains very little consensus on interventions that are not authorized by the UN Security Council. The Report of the UN High Level Panel on Threats, Challenges and Change, issued in December 2004, identified five "basic criteria for legitimacy" before the use of force should be authorized: seriousness of the threat, proper purpose, last resort, proportionate means, and the balance of consequences. Yet, as the international debates surrounding the responsibility to protect made clear, many states were resistant to any set of guidelines that could open the door to unilateral military intervention. As Bellamy points out, by 2005 a significant dilution had taken place in the idea of a "responsibility to protect":

R2P no longer proposed criteria to guide decision-making about when to intervene; there is no code of conduct for the use of the veto; and there is no opening for coercive measures not authorized by the Security Council. The threshold on when R2P is transferred from the host state to the international community was raised from the point at which the host state proved itself "unable and unwilling" to protect its own citizens to that at which the state was "manifestly failing" in its responsibility to do so.[26]

At best, then, even if international society has moved very gingerly towards the notion of a responsibility to protect, progress has been contested and limited. Even in cases of potential genocide, political action is in a very important sense optional. The core institutional structure for authorizing and legitimizing international action is inherently built around selective security rather than collective security.[27] The gap between the shallowness of these changes and Shue's view of what justice requires is abundantly clear:

Thus, in my view, it would be preposterous to suggest that there is a universal negative duty not to commit genocide but that there is no positive duty to protect

[25] See, for example, Michael Byers and Simon Chesterman, "Changing the Rules about Rules? Unilateral Humanitarian Intervention and the Future of International Law," in Holzgrefe and Keohane, *Humanitarian Intervention*, pp. 177–203. See also Adam Roberts, "The So-called 'Right' of Humanitarian Intervention," *Yearbook of International Humanitarian Law*, 3 (2000), 3–51.

[26] Alex J. Bellamy, "The Responsibility to Protect and the Problem of Military Intervention," *International Affairs*, 84 (2008), 615–39 at p. 623.

[27] Adam Roberts and Domink Zaum, *Selective Security. War and the United Nations Security Council Since 1945*. Adelphi Paper 395 (London: IISS, 2008).

intended victims. The twentieth century made it clear that significant numbers of people are perfectly willing to violate their negative duty not to commit genocide, and to do so with unyielding determination. We consequently have as great a need here for a workable allocation of default duties as is imaginable.[28]

How far might we push the idea of conditional sovereignty? An increasing number of commentators have argued that non-democratic states should lose their previously sovereign right to particular weapons systems, particularly weapons of mass destruction. Others have suggested that such states could become legitimate targets for coercive regime change. Others again believe that only democratic states should participate in the core institutions of a reformed international society, sometimes proposing that a league of democratic states should have a privileged political, legal, and moral position in the upholding of international order.

As against such positions, Shue has stressed the limits and dangers of intervention and the difficulty of ensuring that the proposed cure to violations of rights does not involve more dangers than the disease. As he puts it: "external military intervention is always the last resort because of its inherent tendencies to be self-defeating."[29] Even if the limits to intervention are not immutable, they are undoubtedly extremely deep-rooted. Equally, Shue has been insistent that the rules of international society cannot be solely a matter for democratic states to decide upon amongst themselves. In particular, he criticized Rawls for focusing his Law of Peoples too narrowly around the foreign policy of a particular kind of state, and neglecting the rules that might shape relations with non-aggressive repressive states, especially those that do not accept Western liberal notions of reasonable pluralism.[30]

If the "public" at the international level consists of the states that are not at war with each other, it may be better for the "public" to be as nearly global as possible . . . Irrespective of whether it would count as Rawlsian international public reason, we need to find or make a basis for a normative consensus about international conduct amongst more of those who disagree about the principles of domestic conduct.[31]

What I am endorsing is attempting to reason about, and to develop reciprocally acceptable rules for foreign policy while including in the conversations states with objectionable domestic institutions that, for example, even violate human rights.

---

[28] Shue, "Limiting Sovereignty," p. 18.   [29] Shue, "Afterword," p. 177.

[30] Henry Shue, "Rawls and the Outlaws," *Politics, Philosophy and Economics*, 1 (2002), 307–22.

[31] Ibid., p. 318.

There is no contradiction in a position like mine that says, in effect, do not encourage states in their oppressive domestic institutions and policies, but do try to reason with them about foreign policies and international institutions and to arrive at mutually acceptable, non-aggressive norms of foreign policy.[32]

Shue, of course, recognizes the tension inherent in such a position and argues both for a range of non-coercive actions to protect rights and for the development of specific guidelines to help decide when coercive intervention is justified. "The price of peace can be too high, just as the threshold for war can be too low."[33]

2. Back to Westphalia

In the previous section I have considered some of the ways in which Shue's writing on basic rights meshed with trends taking place in the post-Cold War period. Yet, even in relation to the 1990s, it is important to underscore the limits and the constraints. As we have seen, there were indeed some signs of a growing consensus that sovereignty should be made conditional on the ability and willingness of a state to protect the rights and welfare of its citizens. The difficulty was that this responsibility was not devolved to a politically and normatively coherent set of institutions but rather to an "international community" whose actions continued to depend on the power, interests, and preferences of its most powerful members. The end of the Cold War, it was argued, had allowed for a broader definition of "national interests" and greater room for the promotion of genuinely liberal goals. But the problems of selectivity and of cross-cutting political pressures did not disappear.

Moreover, a great deal depends on how we understand the way in which the post-Cold War international system was developing. For much of the 1990s the dominant theoretical stories were liberal. One version sees the origins of human rights regimes in terms of norm mobilization by norm entrepreneurs within global civil society; their evolution in terms of processes of transnational socialization and the creation of a norm cascade; and their dominant mode of action not in terms of a logic of domination and adaptation as realists would suggest, nor in terms of the logic of consequences and interests as institutionalists argue, but rather in terms of a logic of appropriateness in which argument and persuasion play crucial

---

[32] Shue, "Rawls", p. 320.   [33] Ibid., p. 319.

roles.[34] A second version is what one might label a systemic or Kantian liberalism in which the attractive power of a dynamic and successful core of liberal states would lead to a gradually expanding process of socialization in which previously recalcitrant or rejectionist states were being pulled into the liberal fold and in which liberal values were being internalized. Thus states such as India or Brazil that had previously exemplified the Third World suspicion of human rights found themselves drawn more and more into an increasingly dense set of practices in which concern for human rights was a natural and unavoidable part of international relations, and, especially, of the operation of major international institutions. In contrast, others have viewed the spread of liberal values in the 1990s as reflective of the consolidation of the power of the Western industrialized world and interpreted the spread of human rights in terms of processes of hegemonic imposition or coercive socialization. Equally, a growing group of so-called "human rights realists" have pointed to the gaps that exist between the expansive architecture of the international human rights system and the actual safeguarding of those rights. They argue that where human rights institutions work at all, this has far more to do with material incentives than with the diffusion of norms and the internalization of values.[35]

As we move out of the 1990s and consider the early years of this century, it is not difficult to draw up a list of factors that point towards a far harsher view of international relations and a far more constrained, unstable, and threatening position of human rights—the return of Westphalia. Let me sketch some of the most important of these trends, albeit in very brief outline.

The first, and most obvious, concerns the renewed salience of security. As with previous critiques of liberal claims concerning change and transformation, this lies at the heart of the realist view that international politics is naturally dominated by logics of power and insecurity and by the centrality of military force. Hence, at the national level, we have witnessed the reassertion of claims about the centrality of national security and the apparent obviousness of Schmittian arguments that it is "our" security that matters most; that leaders have a duty to protect national security

---

[34] See, in particular, Margaret Keck and Kathryn Sikkink, *Activists Beyond Borders* (Ithaca, N.Y.: Cornell University Press, 1998). For an interest-based account see Andrew Moravcsik, "The Origins of Human Rights Regimes: Democratic Delegation in Postwar Europe," *International Organization*, 54 (2000), 217–52. For a power-based account see Stephen D. Krasner, "Sovereignty, Regimes and Human Rights," in *Regime Theory and International Relations*, ed. Volker Rittberger (Oxford: Clarendon Press, 1993), pp. 139–67.

[35] See, for example, Emilie Hafner-Burton, "Trading Human Rights: How Preferential Trade Agreements Influence Government Repression," *International Organization*, 59 (2005), 593–629.

even at the cost of liberty and the protection of human rights; and that state control should be reasserted over borders, over citizens and, of course, over aliens. Hence, at the international level, there is a parallel set of Schmittian arguments, namely that, in seeking to constitutionalize international politics, liberal solidarists had detached law from effective power. Again, on this view, security is a prior value and all international political orders depend ultimately on a strong state or group of states willing and able to provide a minimal degree of security which will necessarily involve the threat and use of coercive force. Finally, and related, there is the renewed centrality of war in its classic and Clausewitzian sense—as a reciprocal, dynamic, and unpredictable form of conflict in which there is a constant tension between the internal logic of violence and the political objectives that this violence is supposed to help achieve. As Waldron's chapter in this volume discusses, these developments have sharpened in quite problematic ways the problems that arise from Shue's inclusion of security as a basic right.[36]

Many of the traditional problems associated with the protection of human rights have been intensified by the changed security environment created by the attacks on the United States of 9/11 and by the unfolding of the so-called long war on global terrorism. The repercussions on human rights have been clear, and clearly negative—in terms of the human rights violations committed by the United States and its major allies and in terms of the incentives and political space for other groups in many regions to emulate Washington's rhetoric and behavior. The war on terrorism has been viewed by the United States as a struggle in which, to quote George Bush, "there are no rules" and where it is deemed justifiable to "deny protection to people who do not deserve protection."[37] The existence of legal black holes and sites of so-called secret rendition, the creeping practice of extra-judicial killings of terrorist suspects, the curtailing of civil liberties within many Western democracies, and the return of arguments justifying torture have had a deep and negative impact on the international human rights landscape.

However, it is important to note that the renewed salience of security forms only one part of a broader picture. Three further factors should be noted.

First, there is the continued or renewed power of nationalism, no longer potentially containable politically or analytically in a box marked "ethnic

---

[36] See the chapter by Jeremy Waldron below.

[37] Bush Press Conference, September 17, 2001; available at <http://archives.cnn.com/2001/US/09/17/gen.bush.transcript/>.

conflict" but manifest in the identity politics and foreign policy actions of the major states in the system. On this view, nationalism as a force and as a powerfully felt community of fate shows little sign of declining in many of the largest states of the world (and has been powerfully reasserted in Russia, in China, and in the United States); and demands for national self-determination, the exploitation of such claims by outside states, and newer forms of resistance to alien rule continue to underlie a very great number of violent conflicts in the world, including many associated with the growth of terrorism.

Second, there are the various ways in which economic globalization has fed back into the structures and dynamics of a Westphalian state system rather than pointing towards its transcendence. Hence, as in previous rounds of debate, analysts have noted the resilience of the state as an economic actor in seeking to control economic flows and to police borders; and in seeking to exploit and develop state-based and mercantilist modes of managing economic problems, especially in relation to resource competition and financial instability. Most important is the insistence that the most important effect of liberal economic globalization has been on the distribution of inter-state political power. If the debate over power shifts in the 1990s concentrated on the shift of power from states to firms and non-state actors, the "power shift"[38] of the past decade has focused on rising and emerging powers, on state-directed economic activity, and on the mismatch between existing global economic governance arrangements and the distribution of power amongst those with the actual power of effective economic decision.

And third, there is the renewed centrality of the balance of power as both a motivation for state policy and as a core element of international political order. The relevance and utility of balance-of-power theory is not limited to those cases where unbalanced power poses a "direct security challenge to other states," and needs to include "soft" as well as "hard" balancing strategies.[39] It is for this reason that balance-of-power thinking continues to play such a central role in the foreign policy of second-tier states such as China, India, Russia, or Brazil, and helps shape U.S. policy towards important regions of the world—Asia most notably. Equally, it is difficult to make analytical sense of security in many parts of the world except with reference to the balance of power. And balance-of-power

---

[38] Jessica T. Matthew, "Power Shift," *Foreign Affairs*, 76, 1 (1997), 50–66.

[39] See Andrew Hurrell, "Hegemony, liberalism and global order," *International Affairs*, 82 (2006), 1–19 at pp. 12–16; Stephen G. Brooks and William C. Wohlforth, "Hard Times for Soft Balancing," *International Security*, 30 (2005), 72–108 at p. 103.

politics often play a decisive role in the operation of multilateral institutions, especially in terms of the informal understandings and trade-offs amongst the major states, without which effective multilateralism is unlikely to prove effective. The link, then, between the old pluralist world of power politics and the solidarist world of institutions is close and persistent.

Taken together, these factors lend credence to the argument that we are witnessing a return to Westphalia and to a world in which the range of challenges to basic rights has increased and in which the obstacles to the institutionalized protection of those rights have grown more pronounced. Not all of the trends, of course, involve direct threats to basic rights. But the cumulative impact is important. For example, patterns of economic development, particularly in relation to Asia, suggest that the relationship between successful economic development and political democracy/ human rights turns out to be more complex and ambiguous than the Western triumphalism of the 1990s would pretend. Equally, if one of the core reasons for the growth and pervasiveness of international human rights was the dominance of the Western industrialized countries and the hegemonic position of the United States, then a shift to a more balanced distribution of power is likely to have very important conse-quences. On the one hand, it brings to the fore states with different views on the content of human rights and the role that they should, or should not, play in international politics. On the other, the constraints of balance-of-power politics complicate the promotion and protection of human rights, for example by undermining attempts to impose human rights conditionalities on flows of trade, aid, and investment, or by the accept-ance of spheres of influence as a necessary part of the management of the balance of power.

3. Conclusion: Another Turn of the Wheel?

The trends sketched out above undercut Shue's hopes that the state might not remain the central actor in world politics, that state behavior might be civilized, at least to some degree, and that more effective institutions might emerge to promote and protect basic rights. They also reinforce the sense that liberal solidarist ambition has become divorced and disconnected from power-political forces.

There are, however, two sets of reasons for resisting the argument that we are simply witnessing another turn of the wheel and for believing that notions of basic rights will continue to have a significant role within international society. The first set of reasons has to do with the material and structural changes associated with globalization and the impact that these changes are having both on the foreign policy goals of individual states and on potentially shared goals of global governance. Thus it may be true that security has reappeared as a major international issue. But contemporary security issues cannot be understood in terms of old-style Westphalian power politics, but are intimately bound up with new forms of interconnectivity that relate the many different forms of contemporary violence (religious, political, entrepreneurial, criminal) with global communications, with networks of migration and diaspora politics, and with patterns of economic and social inequality. Equally, the management of globalization inevitably involves the creation of deeply intrusive rules and institutions and debate on how different societies are to be organized domestically. This is a structural change. If states are to develop effective policies on economic development, environmental protection, the resolution of refugee crises, the fight against drugs, or the struggle against terrorism, then they need to engage with a wide range of international and transnational actors and to interact not just with central governments but with a much wider range of domestic political, economic, and social players.

There is no reason for believing that material and structural changes of this kind will mesh easily with the promotion of basic rights. Indeed it is not difficult to envisage a situation in which states are pressed to tackle the problems associated with globalization in ways that work directly to the detriment of the basic rights of the weakest and most marginal. Think, for example, of a global climate change regime negotiated by a new concert of the major powers, each recognizing some shared interests but driven also by considerations of relative power and by intense competition for natural resources and for the ecological space for continued growth and development. On the other hand, climate change also provides a good example of what Shue has called "the unavoidability of justice"—whether in terms of how we are to value the welfare of future generations, or to judge the allocation of the burdens of adaptation and mitigation, or to decide upon the kinds of societal change that will be involved in tackling climate change.[40] Within this unavoidable debate about justice, basic rights could assume an important role, precisely in helping to protect the interests of those most adversely affected by climate change and least able to participate politically in the decisions that affect their fate.

---

[40] Henry Shue, "The Unavoidability of Justice," in *The International Politics of the Environment*, ed. Andrew Hurrell and Benedict Kingsbury (Oxford: Oxford University Press, 1992), pp. 373–97.

A second set of factors connects more directly with the language of rights, but again not necessarily in an easy or straightforward manner. Structural and material changes have affected the nature of foreign policy goals and global governance challenges. They have also affected the politics of legitimacy. All political orders face the fundamental problem of legitimating power and there are good reasons for believing that this challenge has become harder within the contemporary global order: because of the inevitability of deep intrusion and intervention in securing both national foreign policy goals and shared governance objectives; because of the manifest failures of attempts at hegemonic or imperial ordering; and because of the weakness of other forms of legitimation at the international level (for example, the disillusionment with claims to specialist economic or scientific knowledge and the weakness of institutional mechanisms capable of providing satisfactory levels of procedural legitimacy).

The trends outlined in the previous section should make us question the easy assumption that the language of rights has become a universal moral currency. And yet human rights remain a pervasive feature of debates on global governance and of what constitutes a legitimate modern state. There is now a denser and more integrated network of shared institutions, discourses, and practices within which social expectations of rights have become more securely established. Nor is it clear that power-based or incentive-based models of human rights politics fully capture the contemporary politics or impact of human rights—think, for example, of the power of legitimating ideas; the links between international human rights and patterns of internal social and political change; and the extent to which even very resistant states, such as China, have found it difficult to avoid enmeshment in the discourse of rights and in the legal and institutional operation of the human rights system.

The transnational dimension is especially important. Indeed one limitation of Shue's rather statist focus in his analysis of basic rights and conditional sovereignty is that it underplays the increasingly transnational character of human rights politics: in terms of the transnational political spaces that have been created; and in terms of the increased dialogue and interaction between national legal orders and international and regional constitutionalism. Thinking of human rights in transnational terms focuses attention on the interaction between international human rights developments and national-level political and legal debates and processes of domestic constitutionalization. Whether we are thinking of food security in India, or housing in South Africa, or the calling to account of those responsible for human rights violations in Argentina, the transnationalization of human rights has provided domestic actors and domestic courts with new political and legal opportunities to pursue their interests.[41]

The relationship between rights-threatening practices and the evolution of rights-protecting discourses, institutions, and policies is far from straightforward.[42] During the Cold War, the confrontation between East and West led directly on both sides to involvement in, or complicity with, appalling violations of basic rights. And yet rights became powerful emblems of success in the ideological battlefield. However much they were resisted both by Western foreign policy practitioners and by authoritarian regimes, and however much they were violated in practice, contestation over rights became a part of the fabric of high politics and the very gap between legitimating claims and the widespread violation of rights became a central element in the growth of human rights institutions and in processes of political change, most notably in the former Soviet Union. In the more recent period, whilst the threats and challenges to human rights have undoubtedly grown more serious, the resilience of rights-protecting practices has also been evident.[43]

Although much of Shue's work stresses the need for philosophical work on basic rights to stay close to changing political realities, there is a consistent theme that points the other way—to the role of considerations of justice in the constitution of a better international society. In both the Afterword to *Basic Rights* and in later work, Shue rejects the claims of ethical particularists such as David Miller or Michael Walzer in relation to the unchangeable limits of human motivation or the absence of any meaningful notion of society above the level of the nation-state.[44] It would be wrong, argues Shue, to think that we can only discuss global institutions after the emergence of a global community whose shared values could then be reflected within those institutions.

[41] See, for example, Ellen Lutz and Kathryn Sikkink, "The Justice Cascade: The Evolution and Impact of Foreign Human Rights Trials in Latin America," *Chicago Journal of International Law*, 2 (2001), 1–33.

[42] On the difficulties for the human rights movement posed by the harsher international environment, see Stephen Hopgood, *Keepers of the Flame: Understanding Amnesty International* (Ithaca, N.Y.: Cornell University Press, 2006), especially ch. 8; and David Kennedy, *The Dark Sides of Virtue: Reassessing International Humanitarianism* (Princeton, N.J.: Princeton University Press, 2004).

[43] See, for example, Rosemary Foot, "Human Rights and Counterterrorism in Global Governance: Reputation and Resistance," *Global Governance*, 11 (2005), 291–310.

[44] David Miller, "Justice and Global Inequality," in *Inequality, Globalization and World Politics*, ed. Andrew Hurrell and Ngaire Woods (Oxford: Oxford University Press, 1999), pp. 187–210, esp. pp. 190–1; Michael Walzer, *Spheres of Justice: A Defense of Pluralism and Equality* (New York: Basic Books, 1983), esp. pp. 29–30.

Rather than waiting for a society somehow to emerge on its own before asking its members to think about what would make it a just society, one can attempt to build a society through agreement in theory or practice on just arrangements. And nothing prevents attempts to seek agreement among those who initially disagree, not that the attempts to reach agreement are guaranteed to succeed.[45]

Or, making a similar point a decade later:

This is exactly wrong, it seems to me. Understandings of justice *do* constitute—or determine—societies. It is profoundly inaccurate to suggest that only after a society has formed can "it" begin to shape shared understandings of justice (and other normative matters). On the contrary, the coming together around shared convictions—often convictions about what the main issues are, not agreement about the answers, is a major element in the formation of a society at any level.[46]

In the Preface to the second edition of *Basic Rights*, Shue regrets that, in cutting out the original final chapter dealing with U.S. foreign policy, he also omitted the quotation from Camus' *The Plague* with which that chapter ended. In that quotation Rieux stresses the importance of speaking out, of bearing witness on behalf of the victim, and of taking the victim's side: "That is why I decided to take, in every predicament, the victim's side, so as to reduce the damage done." Given the negative trends highlighted in this chapter that certainly work to increase the damage being done to basic rights, one might end with a further quotation from Camus, this time highlighting the absence of any possibility of a stable or definitive victory and the on-going nature of the challenge.

However, he knew that his chronicle could not be the story of definitive victory. It could only be the record of what had to be done and what, no doubt, would have to be done again, against this terror and its indefatigable weapon, despite their own personal hardships, by all men who, while not being saints but refusing to give way to the pestilence, do their best to be doctors ... Indeed, as he listened to the cries of joy that rose above the town, Rieux recalled that this joy was always under threat.[47]

---

[45] Shue, "Afterword," p. 179.   [46] Shue, "Limiting Sovereignty," p. 25.
[47] Albert Camus, *The Plague*, trans. Robin Buss (Harmondsworth, Mddx.: Penguin, 2001), p. 237.

4

Are There Any Basic Rights?*

Judith Lichtenberg

The year 1980, when *Basic Rights* first appeared, seems in some ways a relic of a bygone world. Global population has since increased by 50 percent, to more than 6.6 billion. Information technology not available in 1980 to the richest people in rich countries is used today by hundreds of millions in developing countries. In 1980 AIDS was about to make its first public appearance. The 1979 takeover of the American embassy in Tehran now seems more an omen than something terrible in itself. Today the term "globalization"—suggesting a single humanity—is on everybody's lips. Environmental problems such as global warming, which fail to respect national boundaries, confirm our interconnectedness. Yet the moral issues Henry Shue addressed have not changed except to become more pressing, and *Basic Rights* remains a major contribution to political philosophy and the theory of human rights.

The central aim of the book is well known. Shue argues that subsistence rights—rights to a minimum level of well-being, sometimes called welfare rights or economic rights—are on a par with rights to physical security, rights "not to be subjected to murder, torture, mayhem, rape, or assault" (p. 20), whose reality is not in question.[1] Shue challenges the standard view that security rights are prior to or more important than subsistence rights—or even that the arguments establishing their priority imply that subsistence rights do not exist. He argues that this view rests on the claims that

---

* I received helpful comments on an earlier draft from the editors of this volume, an anonymous reviewer, and participants in the spring 2008 Georgetown Law and Philosophy seminar.

[1] *Basic Rights: Subsistence, Affluence, and U.S. Foreign Policy* (Princeton, N.J.: Princeton University Press, 1980); 2nd edn., with a new "Afterword," 1996. Page numbers—which are the same for both editions, except for the "Afterword" to the second edition (which replaces the last chapter of the first)—will be given in parentheses in the text.

(a) security rights are negative in the sense that they involve only "refrainings"; (b) subsistence rights are positive—requiring positive actions and the allocation of resources; and (c) for these reasons, negative rights take priority over positive rights.[2] Shue attacks each of these claims.

Shue's arguments persuaded me when I first heard them in the 1980s. But I now worry that he succeeded too well. Yes, he makes a compelling case that security rights are not "negative" rights and subsistence rights "positive": each kind of right has central negative as well as positive features. Yet his account of rights is sufficiently demanding to raise the question of whether there are *any* rights of the sort he is discussing. Parity arguments are dangerously double-edged: if it is shown that A and B are relevantly alike, we can conclude either that if we accept A we must accept B, or that if we reject B we must reject A. One person's modus ponens, as they say, is another's modus tollens.

In this chapter I examine the charge that basic rights are unacceptably demanding to see whether it stands up.

1. Basic Rights

Shue's subject is *basic* rights, which concern "the morality of the depths … the line beneath which no one is to be allowed to sink" (p. 18). Rights are basic "only if enjoyment of them is essential to the enjoyment of all other rights" (p. 19). Basic rights may differ somewhat from human rights or from what others, such as H. L. A. Hart, have called natural rights.[3] But basic, human, and natural rights are sufficiently similar that I will not distinguish them sharply, as I believe others have also not done. All concern fundamental moral rights that have a claim to be politicized or institutionalized in some way.

According to Shue, "A moral right provides (1) the rational basis for a justified demand (2) that the actual enjoyment of a substance be (3) socially guaranteed against standard threats" (p. 13). The heart of a right is the duties that correlate with it, because "to have a right is to be in a position to make demands of others" (p. 13). We know little of value about a right unless we know which duties it entails and on whom they fall; without these, rights amount to no more than aspirations.

---

[2] Or, more precisely, the negativity of negative rights makes them prior to would-be positive rights, whose positivity renders them inferior as rights or not rights at all.
[3] H. L. A. Hart, "Are There Any Natural Rights?" *Philosophical Review*, 64 (1955), 175–91.

One of Shue's distinctive contributions is that he makes explicit that rights must provide *social guarantees* against standard threats. Rights do not simply entail moral duties on the part of others: the performance of these duties must be assured so rights-holders can rely on having the substance of their rights.

The claim of social guarantees points to a persistent ambiguity in the notion of a right. Abstractly, a person can have a *right* to another's action or forbearance without a *guarantee* of action or forbearance: philosophers, at least, often talk about rights in this way. In this sense a right entails a duty or duties, which a person is morally obligated to fulfill. But of course duties are sometimes ignored. Nevertheless, guarantees or enforcement is often implicit in discussions of rights, from John Stuart Mill to Robert Nozick.[4] Despite the conditions he sets out for rights, Shue probably does not intend to make social guarantees essential to *all* moral rights; for one reason or another, some rights cannot or should not be guaranteed. For example, people have a moral right not to be lied to, implying a corresponding duty of others not to lie. Yet few would argue that in general the right not to be lied to should be enforceable or socially guaranteed. How do we decide which rights should be enforceable or carry social guarantees? Perhaps this is the default position. After all, if rights are so important—the sorts of claims that by definition can be *demanded*—then they ought to carry guarantees unless there are good reasons why not. The invasions of privacy necessary to enforce truth-telling in all situations constitute one such reason.

But the moral rights Shue is concerned with—basic rights, human rights—must, to have teeth, include social guarantees. A full account of such rights will describe the duties correlative to them, who bears the duties, and how they relate to the guarantees.

2. The Tripartite Analysis of Duties

This brings us to Shue's tripartite analysis of the duties corresponding to basic rights, which is where serious concerns about the demandingness of

---

[4] Shue quotes Mill: "To have a right, then, is, I conceive, to have something which society ought to defend me in the possession of"; *Utilitarianism* (Indianapolis: Bobbs-Merrill, 1957), p. 66. The most obvious way to assure social guarantees is through law. But institutions depending on custom or tradition rather than law can also assure the performance of duties corresponding to basic rights.

his account arise. According to Shue, to every basic right three kinds of duties correspond:

I. Duties to *avoid* depriving.
II. Duties to *protect* from deprivation.
III. Duties to *aid* the deprived. (p. 52)

What I am calling the traditional or standard view, according to which security rights are negative and (would-be) subsistence rights are positive, assumes that the duties corresponding to rights are exhausted by the first category. Thus, your right not to be killed or maimed is met as long as others do not kill or maim you. The duties corresponding to such negative rights fall on everyone (although exceptions may be granted for self-defense and the like); all people must do to fulfill their duties is to refrain from killing or maiming—not an unreasonable demand, it seems. The question immediately arises for subsistence rights: on whom do the duties fall? The skeptic suggests that the answer would also have to be "everyone," as it is for negative security rights, or at least everyone who is able to act effectively. And then we immediately encounter two kinds of problems. Most obvious is what may be called Singer-type problems of overdemandingness.[5] As Shue admits in "Mediating Duties," a perennial rationale for not acknowledging duties to distant strangers "is the fear that so many unfulfilled rights of so many people threaten to overwhelm those who take on the corresponding duties."[6] How much does each person have to do? Does it depend partly on what others do—in particular, whether they are doing their duty? If not, a conscientious person might have to do so much that her life would be swallowed up; in any case she will have to do much more than most people actually do.

The second, related problem concerns the specification of duties. If people have duties, it is imperative that they know what these duties are. But exactly what the "duties to avoid depriving" are that correspond to subsistence rights, and (at least as important) to whom they belong, is not obvious as it is for security rights, where all a person has to know, it seems, is "Don't!"[7]

---

[5] These problems have been much discussed since the publication of Peter Singer's article "Famine, Affluence, and Morality," *Philosophy & Public Affairs*, 1 (1972), 229–43. Surprisingly, I find no mention of Singer's essay in *Basic Rights*. As a maximizing consequentialist, Singer faces a more severe problem than Shue, who is not. Nevertheless, given the magnitude of deprivation in the world, the demands imposed by Shue's view could still be very great.

[6] *Ethics*, 98 (1988), 687–704 at p. 695.

[7] Onora O'Neill casts doubt on the universality of subsistence or welfare rights on these grounds—that, unlike negative rights, they do not clearly imply what duties follow, and that the corresponding duties must belong "to specified others rather than to all others"; Onora O'Neill, "The Dark Side of Human Rights," *International Affairs*, 81 (2005), 427–39 at p. 428. For a critique of O'Neill's view see Elizabeth Ashford's contribution to this volume.

Shue offers two insights that address these problems. First, because basic rights involve social guarantees, duties to avoid depriving do not exhaust the duties entailed by such rights. The second category of duties, duties to protect from deprivation, will require positive actions and investment of resources—such as police, courts, and a legal system—even for the supposedly negative security rights. Such duties are in fact so central that without them talk of basic or human rights makes no sense. To assert the existence of human rights is to insist not simply that it is wrong for people to violate fundamental human interests but that such interests must be *protected*.

Second, when appropriate protections are in place, subsistence rights need not be especially demanding; in particular, they need not involve some people transferring their own resources to others. As Shue puts it, "A demand for the fulfillment of rights to subsistence may involve not a demand to be provided with grants or commodities but merely a demand to be provided some opportunity for supporting oneself" (p. 40). He expands on this point in the Afterword to the second edition: the right to have x may entail

a duty to stay out of people's way while they take x for themselves, or a duty to teach them to read so they can figure out how to make or grow x, or a duty to let them form a political party so that they can effectively demand that the government stop exporting x (instead of having the CIA arm their police so that they can suppress all dissent). (p. 164)

Thus, even the first kind of duty entailed by a basic right to subsistence, the duty to avoid depriving, may not be "positive" when the second kind, the duty to protect from deprivation, is in place.

Of course, duties to protect from deprivation also often go unfulfilled. These duties would seem to fall primarily on governments, or at least collective bodies, not individuals—who, qua individuals, are rarely able to act effectively as protectors of rights. But many governments fail, whether through malice, negligence, or inability, leaving hundreds of millions of people with their basic rights unprotected and unfulfilled. Such failures trigger Shue's third category of duty: duties to aid the deprived.

On whom do these duties fall? Presumably on all those able to aid the deprived—after all, the governments of those in need have already failed as protectors of rights, leaving individuals, other governments, and non-governmental institutions to provide remedies. But this conclusion seems to land us back with the problem of overdemandingness. Shue admits that "while it would be unhelpful to say merely that no right can be safely enjoyed unless numberless people perform innumerable duties, this is in fact the case" (p. 157). But surely this must concern Shue, both because his argument for softening the line between security and subsistence rights seeks in part to allay the worry about overdemandingness, and because, more generally, he cares too much about improving people's well-being to produce a theory that leaves everything as it is. "Institutional design," he tells us, "must combine judgments about what it is fair to expect people to do, what it is efficient to ask people to do, and what it is possible to motivate people to do" (p. 170). Expecting some to do more because others have done less is unfair, and it would create perverse incentives. Moreover, "prevention is always better than cure" (p. 173), so it is preferable to avoid getting to the stage where protecting people's rights can be achieved only by fulfilling duties to "aid the deprived."

Shue's tripartite analysis of the duties corresponding to basic rights is in most respects convincing. If basic rights matter so much—if they represent those moral claims that a person may *demand*—then simply postulating moral duties corresponding to them seems insufficient. Such duties establish what people and institutions morally ought to do or not do, how they must act to act permissibly. But many individuals and many institutions fail to do what they ought; and if rights are so important it seems there need to be compensations for such failures. We need *guarantees*. So we posit duties to protect people's rights. But those entrusted with such duties may also fail, so it seems we need further duties as back-ups. We need *guarantees*. So we posit duties to aid.

Now we have a glut of duties, perhaps even a regress of duties. And that raises concerns about whether Shue's account demands too much—more of too many people than is realistic or satisfiable.

3. Who Bears the Duties and What Do They Require?

In attempting to wrestle with the problem of overdemandingness, we must ask what sorts of entities, and who in particular, bear the duties corresponding to basic or human rights. It may seem natural to assume that individuals are among their main addressees, and this explains much of the skepticism about welfare or subsistence rights, which seem to demand a great deal of mere mortals. But a common view holds that individuals do not bear the primary duties corresponding to human rights. For example, James Nickel writes that "Human rights are political norms dealing mainly with how people should be treated by their governments and institutions.

They are not ordinary moral norms applying mainly to interpersonal conduct (such as prohibitions of lying and violence)."[8] Similarly, Thomas Pogge argues that "human-rights violations, to count as such, must be in some sense official ... human rights thus protect persons only against violations from certain sources."[9]

Pogge describes his view as an "institutional" understanding of human rights, which he contrasts with an "interactional" understanding according to which "each such right entails certain directly corresponding duties"—a view that, he suggests, emphasizes individual duties. According to Pogge, Shue subscribes to an interactional account of human rights.[10] Shue disagrees. I shall argue that he is right that Pogge mischaracterizes his view.

How well does the distinction between the duties of institutions, including government, and the duties of individuals, hold up? There are at least two reasons to believe it is exaggerated. The first is conceptual: the duties of institutions ultimately fall to individuals, because institutions are ultimately constituted by individuals, and it is they who render institutions actors. Government neglect or abuse of human rights means the neglect or abuse by *human agents* within the government. Of course, the acts of institutions often depend on the aggregate or joint acts of individuals, not of individuals acting alone. And they are acts of individuals in their capacity as agents of government, not as private persons. So to say that human rights make demands of institutions and not individuals is to say that they make demands of individuals-in-their-roles-within-institutions, not individuals in their private capacity.

More important than this conceptual point is a moral argument. If human rights held solely against governments and other political institutions, then individuals outside government or in their non-governmental capacities might be beyond the reach of criticism for failing to prevent, protest, or compensate for government violations of human rights. That seems implausible in itself, but it would in addition create perverse incentives, encouraging delinquent governments to continue in their ways in the expectation that they could get away with it. For human rights to be

---

[8] James Nickel, "Human Rights," *Stanford Encyclopedia of Philosophy*, at <http://plato.stanford.edu/entries/rights-human/>, emphasis in original; see also James Nickel, *Making Sense of Human Rights*, 2nd edn. (Oxford: Blackwell, 2007), p. 10.

[9] Thomas Pogge, "How Should Human Rights Be Conceived?" *Jahrbuch für Recht und Ethik*, 3 (1995), 103–20; reprinted in *The Philosophy of Human Rights*, ed. Patrick Hayden (St. Paul: Paragon House, 2001), 187–211. A somewhat different version appears as chapter 3 of Pogge's *World Poverty and Human Rights* (Cambridge: Polity Press, 2002). The passage quoted here is from p. 192 of *The Philosophy of Human Rights*.

[10] Ibid., pp. 199–200.

effective, then, they must impose burdens on individuals as well as institutions. And despite his institutional understanding of human rights, Pogge himself makes the very strong individualistic claim that "since citizens are collectively responsible for their society's organization and its resulting human-rights record, human rights ultimately make demands upon (especially the more privileged) citizens."[11]

It is not clear, then, how Pogge's institutional view differs from Shue's. Shue certainly recognizes that the duties basic rights entail are mostly and in the first instance duties of governments and other institutions. Shue and Pogge also agree that the duties entailed by basic or human rights also place strong demands on individuals.

Even if we assume, then, that the duties corresponding to human rights fall primarily on the governments of those whose human rights they are, Nickel's assertion that "Human rights are political norms dealing mainly with how people should be treated by their governments and institutions" is open to a variety of interpretations, narrow and broad. The breadth of interpretations is reflected in the deep ambiguity of the phrase "how people should be treated by their governments." For example, does it imply only government action, or can it encompass omissions as well? What constitutes "treatment"?

The U.S. Supreme Court asserted a narrow interpretation in *Deshaney v. Winnebago County Social Services Department.* It held that a state's failure to protect a boy who became profoundly retarded after he had been violently abused by his father over a long period did not violate the Due Process Clause of the Fourteenth Amendment of the U.S. Constitution.[12] Such conduct would presumably be covered by Articles 3 (asserting a right to the security of the person) and 5 (prohibiting torture and "cruel, inhuman or degrading treatment or punishment") of the *Universal Declaration of Human Rights.* The question is whether the government is implicated when the acts have been committed by private persons. The Supreme Court said no.

By contrast, consider Pogge's account of the ways governments can disrespect human rights:

1. Governments can create or maintain "(unjust) laws that permit or require human-rights violations."
2. They may do so " 'under the color of law,' i.e. by perversely construing existing legislation as licensing human-rights-violating policies."

---

[11] "How Should Human Rights Be Conceived?" p. 200.   [12] 489 U.S. 189 (1989).

3. A government may refrain from human rights violations but "reserve for itself the legal power to order or authorize" them.

4. It may pass human rights legislation but not enforce it.[13]

5. It may organize or encourage private groups to violate human rights.

6. Even if it does not organize or encourage them, a government may "stand idly by" when private groups violate human rights. (Similarly, Pogge says that "Unofficial violations of a right that is on the list of human rights do not constitute human-rights violations; but official indifference toward such private violations does constitute official disrespect."[14])

7. Citizens may fear "violent interference or punitive measures" so much that they refrain from conduct protected by human rights standards or legislation. In such cases, lack of government interference in protected conduct does not signify respect for human rights.[15]

Pogge divides government misconduct regarding human rights into two categories: official government violations, and manifestations of "official disrespect."[16] The line between these is not always clear: Pogge includes the first two categories as violations, whereas the others manifest official disrespect, presumably a less serious but nonetheless unacceptable offense. Others might draw the line in a different place. By including manifestations of official disrespect as impermissible, Pogge elides the distinction some would make between violating a person's rights and allowing them to be violated.

Cases like *Deshaney* fit under the sixth category: the government "standing idly by" while a private person violates a person's human right not to be subjected to cruel and inhuman treatment.[17] "Standing idly by" suggests that the government is aware of the mistreatment. In the *Deshaney* case this was so: the Winnebago County Department of Social Services had

---

[13] Although Pogge mentions passing human rights legislation but not enforcing it as one way to violate people's human rights, it seems clear that such legislation being "on the books" is not necessary, according to Pogge, to violate human rights. Human rights are pre-existing, whether or not they are legally in force.

[14] "How Should Human Rights Be Conceived?" p. 197.

[15] Ibid., pp. 193–7.   [16] Ibid., p. 192.

[17] If human rights are in the first instance rights against a person's government, how can we talk about "a right not to be subjected to cruel and inhuman treatment" full stop? Is it part of the very meaning of the right that the correlative duty is a duty of government? I take it the answer is no, otherwise a violation by a private party would not be a violation of a human right. But it appears that even those who believe human rights are rights against governments talk as if private violations are violations.

taken various steps to protect the child, so it was clearly aware of the abuse; the problem was that the agency did not remove the child from his father's custody. But perhaps a stronger condition is appropriate: the government shows official disrespect in those cases when it *ought* to be aware of (private) mistreatment, whether it is in fact or not. Pogge suggests as much when he says that "Avoidable insecurity of access (beyond certain reasonably attainable thresholds) [to the object of human rights] constitutes official disrespect."[18]

This complex spectrum of types of problematic government conduct and attitudes toward mistreatment of individuals leaves several questions unanswered. If we distinguish between direct violations of human rights by governments and manifestations of official disrespect ("standing idly by" and the like), do governments have strict duties to avoid both? When we consider civil, political, and security rights, duties to refrain from direct violations look much easier to meet than duties to refrain from all possible manifestations of official disrespect; and committing direct violations may seem to demonstrate greater *mens rea* and be particularly reprehensible. Are the duties to be distinguished in terms of strength, and, if so, how? Shall we say that all these duties are strict, but some are stricter than others?

With subsistence or economic rights, the distinction between direct violations and manifestations of official disrespect becomes hard to draw. Pogge's list and the accompanying descriptions conjure up violations of civil, political, or security rights. Suppose one endorses Shue's basic right to subsistence, or (a possible instantiation of it) Article 25 of the *Universal Declaration*, according to which "Everyone has the right to a standard of living adequate for the health and well-being of himself and his family," and suppose this is a right in the first instance against one's government. When people lack an adequate standard of living, it will rarely be easy to tell whether governments have engaged in direct violations or are manifesting official disrespect—or what the difference amounts to.[19]

Even if human rights impose duties in the first instance against one's government, then, there is enormous variation in how we interpret these duties and in deciding when and to what extent governments have failed to live up to them, by explicit violations or by something less, yet still blameworthy. On the broad interpretation that appears to follow from both

---

[18] "How Should Human Rights Be Conceived?" p. 200. In a note to this passage, Pogge argues that "What is new about my understanding is that it links rights fulfillment with insecurity rather than violation" (note 19, p. 209). This claim does not adequately credit Shue, whose concept of social guarantees performs the same function.

[19] The discussion in section 5 may help explain why.

Shue's and Pogge's accounts, governments themselves have onerous duties, both negative and positive. But individuals are not off the hook. They have duties when governments fail, as they so often do. But in addition they have ongoing indirect duties "to create, maintain, and enhance institutions that directly fulfill rights."[20] That these duties are indirect does not mean, Shue admits, "that they are any less onerous in the magnitude of time, money, energy, and so forth that they require to be invested. In principle, indirect duties could be more demanding than direct duties."[21] The thought that although I am not required to contribute a large portion of my income to relieve suffering I have a duty to invest a great deal of time attempting to influence the political process or reform social institutions will not comfort those concerned about the demandingness of Shue's version of human rights.

4. The Strategy of Emphasizing Negative Duties

Shue demonstrates that the standard view of basic rights biases the case against subsistence or economic rights, which appear disproportionately demanding. When we recognize that security rights necessarily require positive action and that subsistence rights can sometimes be satisfied by forbearance, the differences between the two kinds of rights diminish. If we accept the existence of security rights—which, it is implicit in the argument, everyone does—then we should also accept the existence of subsistence rights.

Pogge too aims to "narrow the gap" between civil and political rights on the one hand and social and economic rights on the other. But whereas Shue insists that both security and subsistence rights contain negative as well as positive elements, Pogge argues that "The most remarkable feature of ... [Pogge's institutional understanding of human rights] is that it goes beyond minimalist libertarianism without denying its central tenet: that human rights entail only negative duties."[22] Pogge accuses Shue of a "maximalist" approach that leans heavily on positive duties.

Pogge's strategy is attractive. Positive rights, usually identified with duties to render aid, are controversial, in great part because they seem to demand so much, while everyone accepts negative rights, associated with duties not

---

[20] "Mediating Duties," p. 696. And Pogge agrees, as we saw earlier; "How Should Human Rights Be Conceived?" p. 200.
[21] "Mediating Duties," p. 697.
[22] "How Should Human Rights Be Conceived?" p. 202.

to kill or harm.[23] Pogge acknowledges that he confines his conception of human rights to negative rights to keep them "widely acceptable."[24] So as long as you keep your hands to yourself, the theory goes, you can succeed in fulfilling the negative duties thought to correlate with negative rights.

But Pogge's strategy can be criticized on at least four grounds. Shue covers the first, showing that this picture is misleading at best—because even so-called negative rights require a complex and costly infrastructure, including positive duties; and because when this infrastructure is in place, the rights typically thought positive may not be.[25] Second, one might insist that it is deeply inhumane to think that those in desperate need have a right to our assistance only if we are somehow causally responsible for their plight. (Shue, of course, is not committed to this view; and I shall not discuss it further here.) Third, one can question Pogge's suggestion (not necessarily explicit) that negative duties are significantly less demanding than positive duties.[26] Finally, one may doubt that negative and positive duties can be sharply distinguished. I consider the third point in the remainder of this section and the fourth in the next.

Pogge argues that on his institutional view (in contrast to the "maximalist interactional view" he attributes to Shue), a human right to "the necessities of subsistence ... involves no duty on everyone to help supply such necessities to those who would otherwise be without them." It would be more accurate to say that the necessities of subsistence involve no duty on everyone *as such* to help meet those needs. But in fact citizens today have powerful duties, he believes, which flow from their participation in activities and institutions that cause harm to poor people in developing countries. These are not pure positive duties of aid but rather duties to compensate for the ways the behavior of the rich affects the prospects of the poor. Citizens have duties "to ensure that the social order they collectively and coercively impose upon each of themselves is one under which each has secure access to these necessities, insofar as this is feasible."[27] Key

---

[23] There is another difference between negative and positive rights and duties underlying resistance to the latter. It involves a kind of existential claim: you may be held responsible for making the world worse than it would have been had you never been born, but you may not be held responsible (or not to the same extent or in the same way) for not making it better. I take up this issue in the next section.

[24] Thomas Pogge, "Recognized and Violated by International Law: The Human Rights of the Global Poor," *Leiden Journal of International Law*, 18 (2005), 717–45 at p. 720. For the "narrowing the gap" idea, see *World Poverty and Human Rights*, p. 70.

[25] For more on the costs of infrastructure, see Stephen Holmes and Cass Sunstein, *The Costs of Rights* (New York: Norton, 1999).

[26] I develop this argument in "Negative Duties, Positive Duties and the 'New Harms'," *Ethics*, 120 (2010), 557–78.

[27] Pogge, "How Should Human Rights Be Conceived?" p. 203.

is the assumption that the more affluent of the world "collectively and coercively" impose a set of institutions on the global poor; if they did not, they would not, on Pogge's view, lie under a duty.

Pogge draws our attention to central changes in the causes and consequences of the way we live that have occurred over the last few decades. (He is not alone, of course, in emphasizing these changes.) With economic, environmental, and electronic globalization rapidly increasing, as well as near-consensus about the threat of severe climate change, we can no longer escape knowing that our everyday habits and conduct contribute to harming other people near and far, now and in the future. Our clothing may have been produced in sweatshops, our rugs and other artifacts made by young children. Western consumers may "buy stolen goods when they buy gasoline and magazines, clothing and cosmetics, cell phones and laptops, perfume and jewelry,"[28] because the current international system of commerce allows corrupt dictators in resource-rich countries to profit hugely at the expense of their impoverished citizens. Turning on the air-conditioning, driving our cars, flying to distant locations for conferences or vacations, using plastic or paper bags, drinking bottled water, and innumerable other activities we take for granted contribute to climate change, whose effects will be felt most harshly by the world's poorest people.

Fulfilling negative duties, then, may require that we refrain from many practices integral to our daily lives. Not the least of these duties will be learning which of our routine activities are unacceptable—where our clothes and other possessions come from, under what conditions they were made, and so on. These tasks alone will be costly and time-consuming. With Pogge, as with Shue, it is not always clear how such duties are to be discharged—whether indirectly, by lobbying, organizing, or educating others, or directly, by refraining from those activities that, when combined with the similar activities of many others, undermine poor people's access to necessities. Pogge often suggests that the duties are mainly indirect, to be met by collective, institutional change rather than personal virtue, and in so doing he downplays their demandingness. But if we have duties to ensure that the social order we live under provides secure access to everyone's human rights, we will be busy indeed—especially because "all human beings are now participants in a single, global institutional order" so that "all unfulfilled human rights have come to be, at least potentially,

---

[28] Leif Wenar, "Property Rights and the Resource Curse," *Philosophy & Public Affairs*, 36 (2008), 2–32 at p. 2.

everyone's responsibility."[29] If these are merely negative duties, then much of the attraction of the merely negative has disappeared.

5. The Fuzzy Distinction Between Negative and Positive Duties

Pogge would probably reply that he focuses on negative duties not because they are easy to satisfy but because in fact the rich have harmed the world's poor. He agrees with the libertarians that "the distinction between causing poverty and merely failing to reduce it is morally significant."[30] But the distinction is harder to draw than Pogge and others, including Shue, suggest.

The reason has to do with what may be called the baseline problem. When a driver's car strikes a pedestrian, we know that the driver harms the pedestrian, because if the driver had not acted as he did the pedestrian would not have suffered serious injuries. We know that that the 9/11 attackers caused the deaths of 3,000 people, because those people would not have died had the attackers not crashed their planes into the World Trade Center, the Pentagon, and a Pennsylvania field. But when harm involves complex causal chains involving many intervening actions and events over a long period, it is impossible to establish the counterfactual: to know how things would have been had the allegedly harmful events not occurred.

Consider Shue's hypothetical example, which also invokes the harm principle. A peasant landowner grows a quarter of the black beans sold in a village and employs six men who hold the only paying jobs there. "A man from the capital" offers him a contract to grow flowers for export instead; he accepts. Black bean prices soar, creating hardship for many; in particular the laborers, whose own land could not support their livelihoods, lose their jobs. The motives of the landowner need not have been morally questionable. And the bad consequences for the workers do not result from a single act or a single agent. Nevertheless, the malnutrition resulting from the economic change is not simply bad luck, the result of a natural disaster. It is, Shue argues, "a social disaster. The malnutrition is the product of specific human decisions permitted by the presence of specific social institutions and the absence of others": by "the requirement in the contract for a switch away from food, by the legality of the contract, and by the

---

[29] Thomas Pogge, "Cosmopolitanism and Sovereignty," *Ethics* 103 (1992), reprinted in *World Poverty and Human Rights*, at p. 171.

[30] Pogge, *World Poverty and Human Rights*, p. 13.

performance of the required switch in crops" (p. 44). Shue articulates the underlying principle:

In general, when persons take an action that is sufficient in some given natural and social circumstances to bring about an undesirable effect, especially one that there is no particular reason to think would otherwise have occurred, it is perfectly normal to consider their action to be one active cause of the harm. (p. 44)

We may think the laborers have a legitimate grievance because the actions of the landowner and his colleagues made the workers significantly worse off than they had been. But why is the state of affairs immediately prior to the flower contract the baseline against which to judge the decline in their well-being? Suppose the landowner had employed the workers for five or seven years, but previously they had been unemployed and lived below subsistence. Would they still have had cause for complaint? How long does it take for the employed state to become the norm? Why privilege the immediate past?

Pogge contrasts his own harm-based view with the theory that "What matters for the moral assessment of an economic order under which many are starving is whether there is a feasible institutional alternative under which such starvation would not occur."[31] He rejects this way of construing the issue, but it is not clear what, on Pogge's view, the baseline is according to which the starving have been harmed. The moral standard should not be every possible alternative—that is too broad—but we must appeal to some such alternatives.[32] To what shall we compare the current global institutional order? What would have happened in its absence?[33] Although

---

[31] *World Poverty and Human Rights*, p. 13. He associates this approach with consequentialist as well as "veil-of-ignorance reasoning à la Rawls."

[32] For this kind of argument directed at Robert Nozick's defense of private property and his Lockean proviso, see Will Kymlicka, *Contemporary Political Philosophy: An Introduction* (Oxford: Clarendon Press, 1990), pp. 112–17; and G. A. Cohen, "Self-Ownership, World-Ownership, and Equality," in *Left-Libertarianism and Its Critics: The Contemporary Debate*, ed. Peter Vallentyne and Hillel Steiner (Houndmills, UK: Palgrave, 2000; a revised version of this essay, which was originally published in 1986, constitutes chapter 3 of Cohen, *Self-Ownership, Freedom, and Equality*, Cambridge: Cambridge University Press, 1995). As Cohen argues, the question is "why should institutionally primitive common ownership be the only alternative to capitalism which is allowed to count"? (p. 262). A "defensibly strong Lockean proviso" will say that "no one should be worse off in the given economic system than he would have been under some unignorable alternative" (p. 263).

[33] I leave aside the non-identity problem: if certain seemingly harmful large-scale events had not occurred, different people would have lived; since those now living would not have been born, they cannot have been harmed by the events in question. See Derek Parfit, *Reasons and Persons* (Oxford: Oxford University Press, 1986). Even if we assume the same persons existed as would have in the absence of these events, knowing what would have happened to them if ... is difficult at best. My parents met as a result of Hitler's rise to power and their emigration from Germany during the 1930s. Suppose Hitler had not come to power and they had still somehow met and begat me. What would my life have been like? Not at all like it is; but more than that it is impossible to say.

intuitively we may think that certain large-scale economic institutions and events have harmed people, the baseline problem makes it impossible to establish such claims except by comparison with other possible ways of organizing economic and social life.

This theory is confirmed by the natural understanding of why exploitation is objectionable.[34] In exploiting Worker, Boss does not necessarily make him worse off than Worker would have been had Boss not been in the picture; on the contrary, Worker might have been even worse off, having no means of employment whatever. We object to exploitation not because Boss necessarily makes Worker worse off but because we believe that people are owed certain minimum conditions of treatment—conditions that can be met under "feasible institutional alternatives."

In many contexts—discrete harms to individuals of the sort treated in tort law—the appropriate baseline is the situation immediately prior to the change. Such accidents are like acts of God that disrupt causal chains whose paths are otherwise clear: in these cases we speak unproblematically of negative duties not to cause harm. But in the realm of social and economic life, considered over anything but the shortest time periods, it is impossible to establish the default or baseline. The economic acts, policies, and conditions now in place do not disrupt causal chains whose paths are otherwise predictable.

Without a baseline, the distinction between negative and positive duties blurs. In contracting to grow flowers rather than black beans, did the landowner and his colleagues, or the system within which they operated, violate a negative duty not to harm the workers? A duty not to deprive them of a livelihood? How does this differ from a duty to ensure the workers a livelihood? The terms we use, and the fact that they contain grammatical negatives (like "not" and "deprive") may suggest the presence of negative duties. But grammar can mislead. Much depends on where we take up the story: for example, with the landowner employing the workers to harvest the black beans, or earlier. Where we begin will affect our view of the appropriate baseline—of how to answer the question "How would things have been had a given chunk of behavior not occurred?"

These issues elude simple analyses. Here again tort law is instructive. In *Newton v. Ellis*, the defendant had dug a hole in the highway; a passerby fell in the hole and was injured. Ellis was held liable for failing to put up a light

---

[34] Natural perhaps but not universal. Libertarians like Robert Nozick limit impermissible behavior—or at least behavior that may be prohibited by the state—to conduct that makes a person worse off than she would be in the absence of that behavior. See *Anarchy, State, and Utopia* (New York: Basic Books, 1974), pp. 178–81.

illuminating the hole. Although the failure to light the hole might be described as an omission, when properly viewed it forms part of the act of digging the hole—thus, in legal terms, a case of "misfeasance" rather than "nonfeasance."[35] The test of what "would have happened had the agent not been on the scene in the first place" explains the result. Ellis violated a negative duty not to harm, not a positive duty to render aid.

Newton v. Ellis might appear to support the view that today's rich and powerful violate negative duties by *causing* harm to the world's poor rather than simply failing to prevent harm to them. On this view, the failure to pay workers decent wages (for example) is part of the larger act that begins when corporations or landowners hire those workers—thus misfeasance rather than nonfeasance, a negative rather than a positive duty. There is something right about this way of looking at the matter but also something mistaken. What is mistaken is that, as I have argued, we do not know what condition the workers would be in if the corporations were not on the scene at all—the baseline problem. What is plausible, on the other hand, is the idea that *engagement* with others triggers duties that might not otherwise exist. Perhaps the world's rich and powerful would owe nothing to the poor had they never interacted with them. In a world of Robinson Crusoes, to use Robert Nozick's metaphor, duties between the rich and poor might not exist.[36] But engagement creates new duties. On Pogge's view, that people everywhere in the world now inhabit a single institutional order constitutes engagement in the relevant sense and creates duties. But it does not follow that the duties are negative or arise simply from the harm principle. In such cases, I have argued, the very distinction between negative and positive duties begins to fade.

The conclusion is not that workers and others in such cases have no rights to better treatment than they get. It is rather that these are not most plausibly construed as negative rights not to be harmed. Shue's fundamental intuition that people have basic rights to minimal economic security—to "unpolluted air, unpolluted water, adequate food, adequate clothing, adequate shelter, and minimal preventive public health care"—expresses the moral truth at issue more clearly. Such rights will sometimes require that others act, and sometimes that they refrain from acting. But it is the

---

[35] *Newton v. Ellis*, 119 Eng. Rep. 424 (K.B. 1855), p. 428.

[36] Nozick, *Anarchy, State, and Utopia*, p. 185. Such situations may be characterized by ignorance, isolation, and inability. Each may affect the existence or degree of duties to aid. We may think today's rich owe something to the poor at least partly because of economic and social engagement or interdependence in the Poggean sense. But in addition, some will argue that *awareness* of distant deprivation and the *ability* to act effectively also create responsibilities to act, irrespective of causal responsibility for harm.

right to be in a certain condition (to "subsist," or better), rather than the right not to be harmed, that is the primary notion.[37]

Analysis of the baseline problem puts another nail in the coffin of the distinction between negative and positive duties. When we think beyond simple and short-term cases, the problem of determining the appropriate baseline confounds our efforts to draw the line between them.

6. Making Duties Less Onerous

Shue's basic rights impose strenuous duties on both governments and individuals; Pogge's human rights demand no less, despite his rejection of positive human rights. In the abstract, the existence of these rights and duties is compelling. Billions of people in the world suffer severe deprivations of basic human needs while hundreds of millions live well; the deprivations could be radically reduced, if not altogether eliminated, without excessively discomforting the comfortable. To many the juxtaposition is obscene. Yet most beneficiaries of the current order will find the press to change burdensome; reform of current arrangements will therefore encounter enormous resistance.

So the question is how to rearrange the world we now inhabit to reflect the moral imperatives entailed by Shue's and Pogge's views without making demands so onerous as to ensure their failure. This brings us to questions that belong more to psychology than to what might be called moral reality. Perhaps morality *is* very demanding; perhaps it is only reasonable— given how poor the poor are and how rich the rich are, even leaving aside whether the rich have made the poor poor—to expect those who have the capacity to take on great burdens to remedy these awful situations.[38] Even if it is reasonable in some sense to expect people to act accordingly—and it might well be—we still face the question of how to get them to do so when they are not already motivated, and that is a question of psychology. Now it seems to me that there are two different tacks we can take in getting people motivated to do what they ought to do. Broadly speaking, one approach seeks to upgrade their motives, the other seeks to downgrade

---

[37] This idea stands in stark contrast to the libertarian view. "The particular rights over things fill the space of rights, leaving no room for general rights to be in a certain material condition" (Nozick, *Anarchy, State, and Utopia*, p. 238).

[38] Whether demandingness is a factor internal or external to determining moral requirements is an important question. See my "Negative Duties, Positive Duties, and the 'New Harms'" and Robert Goodin, "Demandingness as a Virtue," *Journal of Ethics*, 13 (2009), 1–13.

the demands placed on them. In her chapter in this volume, Neta Crawford investigates the first approach.[39] It is certainly a worthy one, and it could succeed. But here I focus on the second way, which takes human beings as they are rather than as they might become.

How can we downgrade the demands placed on human beings without simply conceding that alleviating others' suffering is no serious business of theirs? The answer is that there are ways to make what might otherwise be strenuous demands on people less strenuous. The clearest route is to get people to act together rather than as isolated individuals. By definition, most human beings are not saintly or heroic. There is a great deal of plasticity in human behavior across cultures, but within a society most people do as others around them do. People can happily get along without all sorts of things that would be considered necessities in a different society, as long as they need not go it alone but can live similarly to those around them.

Several factors explain why well-being is largely relative to what others around one has.[40] One has to do with what economists call networking effects and with the infrastructure of one's community or society. For example, in a city without good public transportation, you need a car to get around; in places where subways and buses are common one can do without. A second factor is salience or availability, in the sense that psychologists use these terms. We want things partly because we see them, and we see them because others around us have them. If I don't see those fancy kitchen gadgets or 5,000-square-foot houses I won't develop a desire for them.

The most complex aspect of the relativity of well-being concerns the status functions of goods. In every society certain goods function as markers of respect and self-respect, or the lack of them: they denote a person's status relations with others. These functions are closely connected with what the economist Fred Hirsch calls "positional goods."[41] The value of a positional good depends on how it compares to what other people have.

---

[39] Chapter 7. See also Robert Goodin, *Motivating Political Morality* (Oxford: Blackwell, 1992). Although Goodin says his aim in the book is to get people "to act from moral motives, to do the right thing for the right reason" (p. 9), the arguments he puts forward often appeal to self-interest.

[40] I have made these arguments at greater length in "Famine, Affluence, and Psychology," in *Singer Under Fire*, ed. Jeffrey Schaler (Chicago: Open Court, 2009), and "Consuming Because Others Consume," *Social Theory and Practice*, 22 (1996), 273–97, reprinted in *Ethics of Consumption and Global Stewardship*, ed. David Crocker and Toby Linden (Lanham, Md.: Rowman and Littlefield, 1997).

[41] Fred Hirsch, *Social Limits to Growth* (Cambridge: Cambridge University Press, 1976), chapter 3; see also Robert Frank, *Choosing the Right Pond: Human Behavior and the Quest for Status* (New York: Oxford University Press, 1985). It would be more accurate to speak of the positional aspects of goods, since many goods have positional as well as nonpositional features.

Positional goods need not be material—in many societies education is as important an example as any. Even non-remunerative activity such as political or philanthropic work has positional aspects. Not only can such work confer status in itself, but the opportunity costs of engaging in it rather than personally remunerative labor decline if "competitors" do likewise. Positionality also applies to institutions. Smaller profits for corporations—as a result of paying higher wages to workers, for example—are less disadvantageous when other firms bear similar burdens, since competitive pressures are not affected. Smaller defense budgets (the savings to be used for social services) do not endanger nations as long as other nations' defense budgets shrink too.

But few people or institutions are sufficiently motivated to change their behavior significantly without assurance that others will too. Coordination is required, and this is partly a matter of institutional design. Coordination matters not only at the supply side but also at the demand side. Discussing the lack of incentives to slow climate change, Jonathan Rauch notes that "There is no market for fuel-cell vehicles because they are expensive; they are expensive because there is no market for them."[42] Solving the chicken-and-egg problem requires coordinating potential buyers—rounding up and guaranteeing orders—and presenting them to suppliers who can then cut costs in view of increased demand. The same logic of organizing markets to achieve economies of scale can be applied to drugs for malaria and other diseases, fertilizer, desalinization equipment, textbooks downloaded on the Internet, and other goods that could improve life for impoverished people in developing countries.[43]

Other means of making the reduction of others' suffering less painful to ourselves do not depend essentially on the need for collective action. Much of human behavior is habitual; once people become routinized in new practices these can become quite painless.[44] Sometimes the virtuous path can even be made fun. Reducing energy consumption can become a game when carmakers install meters on the dashboard alerting drivers to their fuel use (as Toyota does with its hybrid Prius).[45] Experimental psychology

[42] Jonathan Rauch, " 'This Is Not Charity'," *The Atlantic*, October 2007, p. 75. The article describes Bill Clinton's recent ventures that are supposed to "reinvent philanthropy."

[43] Ibid., p. 76.

[44] See Charles Duhigg, "Warning: Habits May Be Good For You," *New York Times*, July 13, 2008, at <http://www.nytimes.com/2008/07/13/business/13habit.html?pagewanted=all>. The article describes the use of advertising strategies in public health campaigns to change habits such as smoking, drug use, and sanitation practices.

[45] For these and other suggestions, see Elke Weber, "Doing the Right Thing Willingly: Behavioral Decision Theory and Environmental Policy," in *Behavioral Foundations of Policy*, ed. Eldar Shafir, forthcoming.

and behavioral economics offer useful lessons—for instance, about the role of default options in influencing what people do. A striking example is organ donation policy. In some countries, including the United States, one must choose to become an organ donor; the default is not to donate. In many European countries, the policy is the reverse: consent to donating one's organs is presumed and one must explicitly opt out to avoid donation. In Austria, France, Hungary, Poland, and Portugal, which all have opt-out policies, effective consent rates are over 99 percent. In countries with opt-in policies, the consent rates are radically lower: Netherlands, 27 percent; United Kingdom, 17 percent; Germany, 12 percent; Denmark, 4 percent.[46]

As Richard Thaler and Cass Sunstein argue, default options can be used to encourage desirable behavior without legal coercion.[47] Although Thaler and Sunstein's aim is to get people to do what is good for themselves (they call it soft paternalism), the same principles apply if the aim is to get people to do what is good for others.

To make the fulfillment of basic or human rights—whether "negative" or "positive"—more likely, we cannot rely on virtue alone, or even primarily. We must capitalize on what we know of human psychology, including the strong tendencies people have to do what others do. We must, therefore, work to bind people together in groups that act collectively. Since both what harms the world's poor and what could benefit them mainly depends on the aggregate effects of the behavior of many people acting within large institutional structures, coordinated action is appropriate not simply for psychological reasons: it offers the only real hope for alleviating global poverty.

Just how guaranteeable and realizable can the duties Shue describes become? By employing approaches of the sort just described (and there are no doubt others as well), we may be able to achieve much gain with relatively little pain. And that, I believe, is essential to success.

---

[46] Eric J. Johnson and Daniel G. Goldstein, "Decisions by Default," in *Behavioral Foundations of Policy*, ed. Shafir. For a general discussion, see Robert Cialdini, *Influence: Science and Practice*, 4th edn. (Boston: Allyn and Bacon, 2001).

[47] Richard H. Thaler and Cass R. Sunstein, *Nudge: Improving Decisions About Health, Wealth, and Happiness* (New Haven, Conn.: Yale University Press, 2008).

5

The Alleged Dichotomy Between Positive and Negative Rights and Duties*

Elizabeth Ashford

Liberty rights are uncontroversially held to be universal human rights. Equally uncontroversially, there can be "special" welfare rights, grounded in special acts or special relationships. But there has been considerable dispute over whether welfare rights can be general human rights, held by every human being simply in virtue of their humanity.

My aim in this chapter is to reinforce from a different angle two of Shue's principal arguments against there being a fundamental distinction between liberty rights and welfare rights such that only the former are genuine human rights. The first argument is that the enjoyment of the right to subsistence is essential to the enjoyment of any other rights, and so has to be acknowledged as a basic human right.[1]

The second argument addresses the duties imposed by welfare rights. Shue points out that the view that welfare rights can only be special rights is underpinned by our inherited picture of the duties imposed by rights as "full of dichotomies," between positive and negative duties, perfect and imperfect duties, and general and special duties. On this inherited picture, liberty rights are held to impose primarily negative duties, whereas welfare rights are taken to impose primarily positive duties.[2] Negative duties are

* I am grateful to Charles Beitz, Simon Caney, Rowan Cruft, Katrin Flikschuh, Pablo Gilabert, Robert Goodin, David Miller, Adina Preda, Henry Shue, Hillel Steiner, Leif Wenar, and the members of a workshop on human rights at the University of Oslo for their extremely helpful comments on previous drafts.

[1] Henry Shue, *Basic Rights: Subsistence, Affluence, and U.S. Foreign Policy*, 2nd edn. (Princeton, N.J.: Princeton University Press, 1996).

[2] Shue also offers a sustained argument against dividing welfare rights and liberty rights into positive and negative rights, respectively, by showing that both kinds of rights impose both positive and negative duties. I will briefly discuss this argument and Onora O'Neill's response to it in section 3.3 of the chapter. The focus of my argument in this chapter is to reinforce Shue's argument against the dichotomies between duties themselves, and show that

taken to be perfect and general, and to be stringent duties of justice that correspond to human rights. Positive duties, by contrast, are held to be either imperfect duties that do not correspond to rights, or special duties that can only correspond to special rights rather than human rights. Shue suggests that these dichotomies present an overly schematic picture of such duties.[3]

Shue's first argument, that the right to subsistence is a basic right, is that enjoyment of subsistence is a necessary precondition for the full enjoyment of other rights, such that it is impossible fully to secure other rights without securing the right to subsistence. My focus, by contrast, is on the substantive interdependence between the right to subsistence and other rights. I argue that while it might be conceptually possible fully to secure other rights in the absence of securing the right to subsistence, it is not possible to achieve the full securing of those rights in a way that can plausibly be held to be in the interests of the right-holder unless the right-holder's access to subsistence has been secured.

Turning to the second argument, I then argue that because of this substantive interdependence, some liberty rights cannot be adequately respected until the right to subsistence has been fulfilled. Until the right to subsistence has been secured, even the primary duties imposed by such liberty rights may be imperfect in nature (in the sense that they are not exceptionless duties that strictly bind agents' conduct at all times, and they are not fully delineated). Thus negative duties of justice corresponding to liberty rights may in fact be imperfect. I conclude that imperfect duties may be general duties of justice owed to every human being, and that the imperfect nature of the positive duties imposed by welfare rights prior to their institutionalization is no reason to deny that they constitute duties of justice. This supports Shue's claim that we should not be straitjacketed by the standard dichotomies between duties that underpin the view that welfare rights cannot be human rights. I therefore aim to reinforce Shue's argument about the interdependence between the right to subsistence and other rights, and in the light of this to reinforce at the same time his argument against our inherited picture of the rigid dichotomies between duties.

I begin in section 1 by discussing Shue's account of the interdependence between the right to subsistence and other rights, and in section 2 I argue

even if we do accept a division of rights into positive and negative rights by distinguishing the primary duties they impose from secondary duties to enforce those primary duties, this does not indicate that welfare rights can only be special rights.

[3] Henry Shue, "Mediating Duties," *Ethics*, 98 (1988), 687–704.

for a substantive interdependence between them. I then turn to the nature of the duties imposed by human rights. In section 3 I analyze the Kantian rationale for the claim that duties of justice must be perfect in nature, and that positive duties, unlike negative duties, cannot be general duties of justice. I focus in particular on Onora O'Neill's Kantian critique of welfare rights and her defense of the Kantian claim that the fundamental duties of justice are perfect, negative duties not to coerce or harm. In section 4 I discuss her account of coercion, and argue that child labor plausibly constitutes coercion on this account. Child labor also constitutes a harm to the children's developmental interests that a Kantian approach will take particularly seriously. In section 5 I argue, however, that because of the interdependence of the right against child labor and the right to subsistence, then unless the right to subsistence has been secured, the right against child labor is more plausibly seen as imposing imperfect duties, and I conclude that the standard dichotomies between positive and negative duties are overly rigid.

1. Shue's Necessary Precondition Argument

Shue argues that enjoyment of the right to subsistence is essential to the enjoyment of any other right. He takes rights to be claims that the object of the right be guaranteed to a reasonable level of security, and argues that until the right to subsistence has been securely established, persons cannot enjoy reasonably secure access to the objects of other rights, including traditional liberty rights. Establishing a right to a reasonable level of security involves protecting the object of the right against standard threats. Lack of subsistence, or a threatened lack, is one of the most common and severe threats to the enjoyment of other rights. First, adequate nutrition is a precondition for enjoyment of any rights involving rational autonomous activity. Second, unless continued enjoyment of subsistence has been guaranteed, people are liable to coercion and intimidation through threats of deprivation "which can paralyse a person and prevent the exercise of any other rights as surely as actual protein or calorie deficiencies can." He concludes that the enjoyment of the right to subsistence is "necessary for enjoying" other rights.[4]

A response that has been given to Shue's argument is that it is possible to guarantee reasonably secure access to the objects of liberty rights in

---

[4] Shue, *Basic Rights*, p. 31.

the absence of guaranteeing the right to subsistence, so that the secure enjoyment of the right to subsistence cannot be said to be literally essential to the secure enjoyment of liberty rights. Shue discusses one such objection, offered by Mark Wicclair.[5] Wicclair's objection is that the right not to be tortured could be secured without securing the right to subsistence through implementing measures to ensure that the duty not to torture was strictly enforced. As the objection runs, while starvation is undoubtedly terrible, the fact remains that starvation without torture is better than starvation with torture. Shue's reply is that unless persons have been guaranteed reasonably secure access to subsistence they could not be said to actually enjoy security against torture, because they would be vulnerable to being drawn into a bargain (with, say, a sadistic millionaire) of undergoing torture in exchange for subsistence.

A riposte to this that has recently been given by Andrew Cohen is that people could be protected against such contracts too, through enforcing a prohibition on them. This could ensure that each person enjoyed freedom from torture to a reasonable level of certainty.[6]

The possibility of prohibiting torture contracts does show that it is conceptually possible to guarantee the right not to be tortured in the absence of guaranteeing the right to subsistence. As I will now argue, however, Shue's example of the torture contract brings out a crucial substantive interdependence between the two rights.

2. The Substantive Interdependence Between the Right to Subsistence and Other Rights

At the root of the interdependence between the right to subsistence and other rights, I suggest, is that the interest in subsistence is so important that it is liable to outweigh the interests protected by any other right, where the two interests come into conflict. As Shue's torture contract case illustrates, given the urgency of the interests protected by the right to subsistence, even extremely harmful and degrading treatment relative to an uncontroversial baseline, such as torture, may constitute a better option than the alternative option of continuing to lack subsistence. The reason a prohibition on the torture contract would be needed in order to guarantee the right against torture in the absence of securing the right to

---

[5] In an endnote in *Basic Rights*, pp. 184–7.
[6] Andrew I. Cohen, "Must Rights Impose Enforceable Positive Duties?" *Journal of Social Philosophy*, 35 (2004), 264–76; Thomas Pogge presents a smailar line of argument, this volume.

subsistence is because in such circumstances, entering into such a contract is likely to be in the overall interests of the destitute individual. This is because the interest in subsistence is likely to outweigh even the interest in freedom from torture. But this means that securing persons' right against torture by preventing such contracts, without at the same time securing their right to subsistence, would not be of benefit to them, but on the contrary would make them worse off, and further reduce their capacity to exercise their autonomy. Since the prohibition of such contracts is the only way in which the right against torture could be guaranteed in the absence of securing the right to subsistence, I conclude that the full securing of the right against torture cannot be achieved in a way that can be plausibly held to be in the interests of the individual right-holder until that right-holder's access to subsistence has been secured.

Suppose, for example, a mother entered into such a contract with a sadistic millionaire as the only way of saving her children from dying of malnutrition, because she judged the mental agony of watching her children preventably die and the permanent marring of her life this would cause to be worse than the physical agony and lasting psychological damage caused by torture, and to be a greater undermining of her autonomy given that her most central goal was to nurture her children. If she were legally prevented from making such a bargain without being given an alternative opportunity to earn a subsistence income, and her children died as a result, she might reasonably complain that the legislators had worsened her suffering and degradation. She might also reasonably complain that they had shown moral hypocrisy, on the ground that they could not claim to have protected her right not to be tortured out of concern for her interests or respect for her dignity as a rational autonomous agent, given that their actions had led to her greater suffering, and had deprived her of her only available opportunity to realize her most important end, of saving her children.

So, while it is conceptually possible fully to secure the right against torture without securing the right to subsistence, this can only be achieved by banning the torture contract, which cannot be plausibly held to be in the interests of the right-holder. This indicates that the right against torture cannot be fully enjoyed in the substantive sense in which the right is worth having unless the right-holder's access to subsistence is secure.

I should stress that I am not appealing to a utilitarian argument about maximizing overall welfare, but am appealing to what is in the best interests of the individual right-holder. Following the standard interest-based account of rights, I am taking rights to be grounded (at least in part) on the importance of certain interests of the individual right-holder. On any interest-based account of rights we need some kind of objective ranking of interests, to work out what interests are important enough to ground rights. My argument is that on a plausible objective ranking of interests, the interest in subsistence is so important that it is liable to outweigh the interests protected by any other right, where those interests come into conflict. That means that if we ban exchanges in which people agree to give up the object of a right in exchange for subsistence, without ensuring the right-holder has other opportunities to earn a subsistence income, this will standardly and predictably worsen the plight of that individual right-holder, which, I suggest, is in tension with claiming that our motivation for securing the right by banning such exchanges is grounded in that right-holder's individual interests. It should also be noted that while the torture contract case is, as Shue notes, rather a bizarre example,[7] in the case of other rights, such as the right against child labor (which I will shortly discuss), the right-holders' interest in the object of the right and their interest in subsistence frequently come into conflict. In such circumstances, attempts to impose a ban on child labor in the absence of other institutional reforms to address the extreme poverty associated with it can standardly have a devastating impact on the interests of the children. It can lead to their starvation or to their taking an even worse form of work such as prostitution.[8]

I should also stress that I am not denying that important and genuine steps can be taken towards protecting other rights such as the right not to be tortured independently of securing the right to subsistence. My claim is that *full* enjoyment of such rights—enjoyment to a reasonable degree of security—cannot be said to have been achieved, in the substantive sense of enjoyment in which such security is worth having, until subsistence has been secured. I am not denying Wicclair's claim that torture heaped *on top of* destitution makes the right-holder worse off. My claim, rather, is

---

[7] Though variations of it are not uncommon, if we consider, for example, that many of the women who are abused in the making of films for the most violent end of the pornography industry are extremely poor prostitutes, often from Latin America.

[8] Kaushik Basu discusses this in "Child Labour: Cause, Consequence and Cure, with Remarks on International Labour Standards," *Journal of Economic Literature*, 37 (1999), 1083–119. Of course the relation between child labor and severe poverty, and the best approach to eradicating child labor, are extremely complex issues. See for example C. Grootaerd and Ravi Kanbur, "Child Labour: an Economic Perspective," *International Labour Review*, 134 (1995), 187–203. For an excellent discussion of the normative issues raised by child labor, see Debra Satz, "Child Labour: A Normative Perspective," *The World Bank Economic Review*, 17 (2003), 297–309.

that any destitute person is potentially benefited by a torture contract, in which the torture is *in exchange for* subsistence. In short, while lack of subsistence without torture is better than lack of subsistence with torture, it is also the case that torture with subsistence may be better than freedom from torture without subsistence. My argument allows, then, that protections against many standard threats to the right against torture will benefit right-holders who are destitute (such as protections against police brutality, and so on). It can therefore accommodate Pogge's objection that Shue's defense of basic rights cannot adequately accommodate the importance of incremental improvements in the degree to which rights are secured:

> Shue's account implies that the enjoyment of basic rights is an all-or-nothing affair: one either enjoys all the basic rights or no rights at all. This account leaves little room for differentiations among those living below the threshold. As far as rights are concerned, their situation cannot be improved incrementally, but only through a shift that would make them enjoy *all* their basic rights.[9]

My argument is that the full securing of the right against torture cannot be said to have been adequately achieved until the right-holder's access to subsistence has been secured, because one very important standard threat will remain: the destitute will always be vulnerable to being drawn into a bargain in which they exchange freedom from torture for subsistence because they are likely to benefit from such exchanges; and responding to this threat by attempting to ban such exchanges is inadequate, for the reasons I have given.

It might be argued that it does not follow from the fact that an individual might be benefited by agreeing to forgo the object of a right in exchange for something else that that individual cannot be said to enjoy the right. However, what is distinctive about the right to subsistence is that the interest in subsistence is so important that on an objective ranking of interests it is standardly and predictably likely to outweigh the interest in other rights should the right-holder be offered an exchange, so that attempts fully to secure those other rights by banning the exchange are standardly and predictably detrimental to the interests of the right-holder. Furthermore, the choice of forgoing a right in exchange for subsistence is in an important respect not a voluntary one. Rather, the right-holder is coerced into forgoing the right. The reason for this is that lacking subsistence is unsustainable, so that the person does not have a

---

[9] Pogge, this volume, ch. 6, section 2.

real choice. The torture contract case, for example, ought to be classified as coercion.

Shue's appeal to the torture contract case can be plausibly read as an illustration of his general claim that if people lack subsistence, they are standardly coerced into forgoing the objects of their other rights, and so cannot be said to have secure enjoyment of the objects of those rights. Pogge's and Cohen's riposte is, in effect, that people can be protected against this coercion, so that they can be said to have secure enjoyment of their other rights even if they lack subsistence. But if we focus on what is involved in securely enjoying those other rights in the substantive sense in which such security is worth having, this riposte lacks plausibility. At the root of the coercion is the fact that until people have subsistence, their plight is completely unsustainable. Responding to such coercion by banning contracts in which the right-holders forgo the objects of those other rights in exchange for subsistence forces them into a situation that they reasonably judge to be the most unsustainable and restricts even further their opportunity to exercise their autonomy. In the torture contract case, for example, it forecloses the only opportunity available to the mother to realize her most important end of saving her children, which she reasonably judges to be the most unbearable outcome of all.

So far I have been offering a substantive argument about the importance of subsistence from the right-holders' point of view. As I will now argue, however, if we think about the relation between destitution and coercion in this kind of case, it also casts doubt on a common conceptual argument against welfare rights such as the right to subsistence that is directed at the nature of the duties they impose. The argument is that unless welfare rights are institutionalized the duties they impose are imperfect in nature, in the sense that they do not bind agents' conduct strictly at all times, and they are not fully delineated. Imperfect duties, it is argued, cannot be duties of justice. Institutionalized positive duties, on the other hand, are perfect duties of justice, but are special duties that correspond to special rights rather than being general duties that correspond to human rights.

I will explain the dichotomies between duties that underpin this argument, and will analyze the Kantian rationale for them, focusing in particular on Onora O'Neill's Kantian argument that welfare rights can only be special rights. I will then argue that in the case of certain liberty rights against coercion and harm that O'Neill acknowledges as genuine human rights, and takes to impose perfect, general, negative duties of justice, the conflict between enjoyment of such rights and enjoyment of the interest in subsistence can be unavoidable, when certain economic conditions are in place. In such cases, I will argue, until the right to subsistence has been secured, to take the duties imposed by such liberty rights to be perfect in nature is implausibly divorced from the interests of right-holders.

3. A Kantian Account of the Dichotomies between Positive and Negative Duties

3.1. The Three Dichotomies

Positive duties are duties to take steps to aid the victim, whereas negative duties are duties "not to do things," that is, duties to refrain from interfering with the victim in various ways.[10]

The second dichotomy, between perfect and imperfect duties, is central to Kant's moral philosophy, and I will follow his account of these terms. There are two central features of perfect duties. The first is that perfect duties are exceptionless duties that strictly bind agents' conduct at all times in their behavior towards every other person. With the possible exception of potentially catastrophic circumstances, perfect duties should always be complied with. As Thomas Hill helpfully puts it, perfect duties have the form "Always one ought" or "One must never," whereas imperfect duties have the form "sometimes, to some extent, one ought."[11] As Hill emphasizes, the scope of perfect duties contains implicit qualifications that accommodate the force of other moral considerations. Perfect duties themselves, though, can and should be completely fulfilled in all circumstances. The second feature of perfect duties is that they are fully delineated: they have a clearly defined content, and they are owed by specific agents to specific recipients. Imperfect duties, by contrast, allow a particular agent latitude over the content of the duty, and, generally, also over the duty's recipient.

The third dichotomy is between special and general duties. As Shue puts it, a special duty is owed to particular individuals "because of an act, event, or relationship of which a causal or historical account can be given." By contrast, "If it is general, it is owed on some ground independent of specific acts, events, and relationships, such as the mere fact that the

---

[10] I am following Jeff McMahan's account of the distinction between positive and negative duties, according to which negative duties are duties not to initiate the threat to the victim, whereas positive duties are duties not to allow a pre-existing threat to continue: McMahan, "Killing, Letting Die, and Withdrawing Aid," *Ethics*, 103 (1993), 250–79.

[11] Thomas E. Hill, Jr., "Meeting Needs and Doing Favours," reprinted in his *Human Welfare and Moral Worth* (Oxford and New York: Oxford University Press, 2002), p. 204.

parties involved are human beings."[12] The duties that correspond to human rights that each person possesses simply in virtue of their humanity are, therefore, general duties.

On the traditional schema, duties are divided into perfect duties of justice and imperfect duties of virtue. Negative duties are taken to be perfect duties of justice, whereas positive duties, unless they are special, are taken to be imperfect duties of virtue. I will now analyze a Kantian rationale for the way in which each of the two principal features of perfect duties may be held to underlie the claim that duties of justice must be perfect.

3.2. Duties of Justice as Exceptionless

First, it may be held that only exceptionless duties can capture the special force of rights, namely, that they can and should be honored in all circumstances. If the duties of justice that correspond to rights are perfect, it follows that their corresponding duties should always be complied with (barring, perhaps, extreme and highly unusual circumstances). There is no need to engage in weighing up of different persons' interests in order to decide whether or not to honor a particular right in a particular situation. As Thomas Nagel points out, only negative rights to non-interference can be universally honored in virtually all circumstances. If rights are taken to impose positive duties to protect the rights, then different persons' rights may need to be weighed against each other in order to decide what conduct is required in a particular case, and the agent may be required to violate one person's rights in order to prevent more serious or more numerous rights violations.[13] On this view, then, the special force of negative rights is that they can and should be honored in virtually all circumstances. Accordingly, the primary and most important moral rights are negative rights.

This Kantian rationale, then, is based on opposition to the claim that rights can be legitimately traded off against each other and against other moral considerations and potentially outweighed. On the Kantian view that the duties imposed by rights are perfect, while there may be limitations in the scope of perfect duties of justice so that they do not apply in certain circumstances, these duties themselves cannot be outweighed.

[12] "Mediating Duties," p. 688.
[13] Thomas Nagel, "Personal Rights and Public Space," *Philosophy and Public Affairs*, 24 (1995), 87–93.

3.3. Duties of Justice as Fully Specified

Second, it may be held that in order for a duty to be a duty of justice corresponding to a right, the right-holder must be entitled to claim the performance of a specific duty by a specific agent that would realize that individual's right. This is the basis of O'Neill's influential argument that welfare rights can only be special rights that depend on institutional structures for their existence, rather than being human rights owed to every person independently of whether or not such rights are institutionally recognized. She takes the primary duties imposed by welfare rights to be positive duties of aid. Duties of aid are imperfect in nature, and therefore, she argues, not claimable, unless institutions are in place that have specified and allocated them:

> Somebody who receives no maternity care may no doubt assert that her rights have been violated, but unless obligations to deliver that care have been established and distributed, she will not know where to press her claim, and it will be systematically obscure whether there is any perpetrator, or who has neglected or violated her rights.[14]

She concludes that welfare rights come into existence only once their corresponding duties of aid have been institutionally specified and distributed. Welfare rights, then, can only be special rights, that exist within a network of institutionally defined special relationships that link specific duty-bearers with specific right-holders. They cannot be human rights held by every human being simply in virtue of their humanity:

> Much writing and rhetoric on rights heedlessly proclaims ... "welfare rights," ... without showing what connects each presumed right-holder to some specified obligation-bearer(s) ... Some advocates of universal economic, social and cultural rights go no further than to emphasize that they *can* be institutionalized, which is true. But the point of difference is that they must be institutionalized: if they are not there is no right.[15]

By contrast, she takes the primary duties imposed by liberty rights to be negative duties that are perfect in nature: regardless of what institutional structures are in place, she argues, these negative duties are fully delineated duties owed by every agent towards everyone else. Accordingly, when such rights are violated, perpetrators can (in principle at least) be identified.

[14] Onora O'Neill, *Bounds of Justice* (Cambridge: Cambridge University Press, 2000), p. 105.
[15] Onora O'Neill, *Towards Justice and Virtue* (New York: Cambridge University Press, 1996), pp. 131–2.

Shue argues against dividing rights into positive welfare rights and negative liberty rights, on the ground that both kinds of rights impose both positive and negative duties. Liberty rights require the implementation of positive duties, involving expensive institutional measures, in order to protect right-holders against violations of such rights and so guarantee actual enjoyment of the rights to a reasonable degree of security. In response to this line of argument, O'Neill concedes that the protection and enforcement of liberty rights requires the implementation of positive duties, but takes the enforcement of rights to be a secondary matter, that can only be addressed after it has been determined which rights exist:

All rights, even liberty rights, can be enforced only by allocating specific owers and obligations to particular agents and institutions ... However, we cannot move on the questions of enforcement until we know what human rights there are. For we would not know what should be enforced.[16]

I take O'Neill to be drawing a distinction here between the *primary* duties imposed by rights—that is, duties to respect rights, the violation of which constitutes a right's violation—and secondary duties, the role of which is to enforce compliance with those primary duties. Her claim, then, is that in order for a right to be genuine the primary duties it imposes must be fully specified. Her worry with welfare rights is that prior to their institutionalization, the primary duties they impose are indeterminate, and so the very content of the rights is unclear. It is "systematically unclear whether one can talk of perpetrators" and unclear what should be enforced. By contrast, she argues that in the case of liberty rights, the primary duties they impose are fully specified prior to the institutionalization of the right. The role of institutions is simply to enforce these antecedently specified duties. O'Neill thus defends a Kantian account of justice according to which the central duties of justice are negative, perfect duties, not to coerce, deceive, or harm: "the central demand of Kantian justice is negative."[17]

Her general line of argument against a rights-based approach to global justice is that it is recipient-focused, and can end up with an inadequate account of the perspective of agency: of who ought to do what to remedy the plight of the global poor. She takes it to be an advantage of the Kantian approach that it is focused on the duty-bearers' perspective rather than the

---

[16] Onora O'Neill, "Hunger, Needs and Rights," in *Problems of International Justice*, ed. Steven Luper-Foy (London: Westview, 1988), pp. 67–83 at pp. 76–7. Cf. O'Neill, *Towards Justice and Virtue*, p. 131.

[17] Onora O'Neill, *Faces of Hunger: An Essay on Poverty, Justice and Development* (London: Allen & Unwin, 1986), p. 141.

perspective of recipience. She offers a striking and compelling account of coercion, according to which pitiful wage bargains are likely to count as coercive. As I will now argue, child labor plausibly constitutes coercion, on this account. (If it is thought to be a problematic example of coercion, because it involves children, another example of coercion involving a pitiful wage bargain could be substituted in my argument.) At any rate, child labor certainly constitutes a harm relative to a fairly uncontroversial baseline, and a harm that a Kantian account will take particularly seriously, given its impact on the developmental interests of the children. The right against child labor thus constitutes a liberty right against harm, and plausibly also against coercion. I will argue, however, that in circumstances in which the child labor is the only feasible alternative to destitution, to take the duties it imposes to be perfect in nature is implausibly divorced from the interests of the children. As I will argue, a serious disadvantage of a Kantian account according to which duties of justice must be perfect is that it gives insufficient weight to the perspective of the recipients.

4. Onora O'Neill's Account of the Duty Not to Coerce

O'Neill focuses on the Universal Law formulation of the Categorical Imperative, according to which rights are attributed when the maxim of a proposed action cannot be conceived as a universal law. Contradictions in conception generate perfect duties and corresponding rights, and these duties are negative. Contradictions in the will, by contrast, generate imperfect duties, which are duties of virtue as opposed to duties of justice. Positive duties are imperfect duties of virtue: while we can conceive of a world in which no one gives aid to those in need, we cannot will such a world. Much of O'Neill's work on a Kantian approach to justice focuses on the negative duty not to coerce, which, in accordance with this first sub-test of the Universal Law formulation, she takes to be a perfect duty corresponding to a right, since the maxim of coercing others cannot be conceived as a universal law.

She develops a particularly rich and nuanced account of coercion according to which certain wage bargains, for example, count as coercive even if accepting them would make the person better off than that person would otherwise have been, measured against the baseline of the person's situation prior to the bargain.[18] (The plausibility of this can be illustrated

---

[18] Onora O'Neill, "Which are the offers *you* can't refuse?" *Bounds of Justice*, pp. 81–96.

with the torture contract case.) She rejects as unpromising the standard attempts to distinguish cases of coercion according to whether they involve threats of harm or offers of benefit, where the former are held to count as coercion. She argues that the same proposal "can often be described equally plausibly *either* as threatening harm *or* as offering benefit."[19] In particular, "the capitalist wage bargain may plausibly be either offer of benefit or threat of harm, and indeed may be coercive in some but not in other contexts."[20] She also points out that most cases of coercion do not involve explicit threats but are presented as offers.

The key criterion for whether or not someone is acting under coercion, she argues, is whether or not their choice of one or other option is a genuine "expression of agency"[21] and this depends on whether or not the alternative options available to the person are sustainable. A genuine offer is one that "can be refused."[22] By contrast, in cases of coercion, the "offer" is unrefusable, because the alternative options are unsustainable, so that the person's acting as they did was not a genuine exercise of choice.

As O'Neill emphasizes, whether or not alternative options are sustainable depends on the particular vulnerabilities of the person. The offer of a particular wage bargain may not be coercive if it is a refusable offer because the worker is in a situation in which refusing it is a genuine option, but in another context, in which the worker is in a vulnerable position because refusing the "offer" would lead to destitution, that same wage bargain might be coercive:

Set in a second context, the same wage bargain might be an option in a coercive "offer": if there is no other work and no welfare state, those without other means must comply with the proffered wage bargain or face destitution.[23]

An important implication of this is that agents must take care to avoid coercion, which requires being alert to others' vulnerabilities:

agents who seek not to coerce have to make sure that they do not inadvertently make unrefusable "offers." Any offers they make others must not link options either overtly or covertly to consequences with which those to whom they make the offer cannot live ... they will therefore need to take account of others' strengths and weaknesses, of their *specific* vulnerabilities and of the *actual* limits of their capabilities. In particular, they will have to be alert to the ease with which the weak can be coerced.[24]

---

[19] Onora O'Neill, ibid., p. 94.   [20] Ibid., p. 95.   [21] Ibid., p. 89.
[22] Ibid., p. 90.   [23] Ibid. p. 95.   [24] Ibid., p. 93

On this account of coercion, if someone accepts a wage bargain only because the alternative is destitution—that is, if they would not have accepted that wage bargain were it not for the fact that they would otherwise face destitution—then the "offer" of the wage bargain is in fact coercive.

This implies that child labor counts as coercion even in circumstances in which the children are not being literally forced to work (by threat of violence, for example), but are "choosing" to work because the alternative would be destitution. If the children would not be choosing to work if it were not for the fact that the option of refusing the "offer" of employment is not sustainable, then the "offer" is unrefusable and constitutes coercion.

5. The Nature of the Duties Imposed by the Right Against Child Labor

As we have seen, what is key to the distinction O'Neill draws between negative duties of justice such as the duty not to coerce, and imperfect duties of aid, is that the former are fully delineated, perfect duties even in the absence of institutional structures. Regardless of what institutional structures are in place, we know who owes exactly what primary duties to whom: every agent is under a clear-cut, exceptionless duty not to coerce or harm anyone else. The role of social institutions is simply to enforce these antecedently specified duties.

The right against child labor is often understood as imposing perfect duties, that is, fully specified duties not to send one's children out to work and not to employ child laborers, that can and should be completely fulfilled in all circumstances, independently of the institutional structures that are in place. Accordingly, the role of social institutions has often been taken to be simply to enforce such duties: the right against child labor has been widely acknowledged, and a common response to this acknowledgement has been to attempt to enforce the duty not to send one's children out to work or to employ child laborers through monitoring and punishing violations of this duty, in isolation from implementing other institutional reforms to tackle the chronic severe poverty that is closely associated with child labor. However, in circumstances in which child labor is the only feasible alternative to destitution, the duties imposed by the right against child labor may have neither of the two principal features of perfect duties.

The torture contract and child labor both plausibly count as coercion, given that in each case the person only accepts the contract because the alternative, of destitution, is unsustainable. They also both constitute harms relative to uncontroversial baselines. However, there is a crucial contrast between them. In the case of the torture contract, the conflict between the right-holder's interest in subsistence and their interest in freedom from torture is entirely avoidable and gratuitous, and results solely from the cruelty of the millionaire. It is therefore perfectly plausible to take the millionaire to be under a strict duty not to torture. In the case of child labor, however, when certain economic conditions are in place, child labor may be the only feasible alternative to destitution. In such circumstances, the conflict between the children's interest in subsistence and their interest in freedom from child labor may be unavoidable. If parents really do face the choice between sending their children out to work as child laborers or allowing them to starve, it is not plausible to take them to be under a strict, exceptionless duty not to send them out to work. This would give insufficient weight to the interests of the children, given that lack of subsistence is likely to have an even more devastating impact on their developmental interests than child labor. Rather, where the conflict between the children's interest in freedom from child labor and their interest in subsistence is unavoidable the parents may have to engage in a tragic trade-off, and their duty not to send their children out to work as child laborers may be outweighed by their duty to provide them with or avoid depriving them of their only available opportunity to attain subsistence. Moreover, it is not only in very rare circumstances that this tragic trade-off between the two duties is liable to occur, but whenever the children's access to subsistence is insecure.

A possible Kantian response to this argument might be to argue that the scope of the right against child labor is limited so that it does not apply in these circumstances.[25] As I mentioned in section 3.1, Kantians have stressed that while perfect duties themselves are exceptionless duties that strictly bind agents' conduct at all times, the scope of such duties has built-in qualifications. It might be argued, then, that one such qualification that is built into the scope of the duty not to employ child laborers is that this duty does not apply in circumstances in which the alternative is destitution. If so, then it is not the case that the duty not to employ child laborers is outweighed, because it does not apply in these circumstances. On this account, then, there is a clear-cut, perfect duty not to employ child

---

[25] This response was suggested to me by Leif Wenar.

laborers, and a corresponding clear-cut negative right, but these do not exist in situations where employing child laborers is the only way for their family to get by.

This response, though, is very much in tension with O'Neill's account of coercion. On O'Neill's account of the duty not to coerce, it is not plausible to limit the scope of the right against child labor and its corresponding duties so that these do not apply in the context of destitution. As she forcefully argues, accepting an option only because the alternative is destitution counts as coercion, because it is not a genuine expression of agency (since the alternative "option" is unsustainable). Moreover, she stresses that destitution is the kind of context in which coercion is most likely and agents must take the greatest care to avoid it.

Turning to the impact of child labor on the developmental interests of the children, it might be argued that the rationale for limiting the scope of the right against child labor so that it does not exist in situations of destitution is that in this context such a right would not be in the overall interests of the children, precisely because it conflicts with their greater interest in subsistence. However, if the right against child labor is grounded on the detrimental impact that child labor has on the children's developmental interests, then it is not plausible that the right would no longer *exist* in situations of destitution. The detrimental impact on the children brought about specifically by child labor is the same in a context in which child labor is the only feasible alternative to destitution as in a context in which the children subjected to child labor are more affluent, even though in the former context this harm is outweighed by the even greater harm posed by lack of subsistence. Therefore to deny that the destitute have the same right against child labor is in tension with acknowledging their equal moral status. Moreover, the logic of the argument would imply that the destitute lack many of the rights possessed by others, given that they would often be likely to benefit from contracts in which they forgo the interests normally protected by rights in exchange for subsistence. This would be a kind of unappealing converse to Shue's argument in defense of the claim that the right to subsistence is a basic right.

On the other hand, however, although it is not plausible to limit the scope of the duty not to coerce so that it does not apply in these circumstances, it may be plausibly argued that the parents cannot be held to be coercing their children given that they are in a desperate position themselves. It might be argued that in order for offers to count as coercive it must be the case both that the alternative options are unsustainable *and* that the agents making the offer are in a position to make a better alternative offer, and are taking advantage of the vulnerabilities of the person they are coercing and of their own position of greater strength. Likewise, it might be plausibly argued that the parents cannot be held to be harming their children if they are acting in their overall best interests in the circumstances. In that case, given that it is not plausible to deny that the children have the right against child labor, then child labor has to be taken to be a systemic harm in these circumstances. If, on the other hand, we do take the parents to be under a duty not to send their children out to work as child laborers,[26] given that this duty is systemically outweighed by the children's interest in subsistence, then child labor again has to be taken to be at least principally a systemic harm in these circumstances; since the parents are trapped and are not in a position to fulfill the duty not to send their children out to work if they have no alternative opportunity to secure their subsistence, then institutional structures under which these alternative opportunities are unavailable have to be seen as playing a constitutive role in deprivations of the right against child labor, and securing such opportunities has be seen as part and parcel of fulfilling the right against child labor. On either view, it is not plausible to take parents to be under a strict, exceptionless duty not to send their children out to work that can be fulfilled regardless of the institutional structures in place, and to take the role of institutional structures as being simply that of enforcing such a duty. Unless institutional structures are in place under which the right to subsistence has been secured, then either parents are not under such a duty, or they are under this duty but are not in a position to fulfill it because it is systemically outweighed. In either case, securing institutional structures under which the right to subsistence has been guaranteed should be seen as essential to fulfilling the right against child labor, and until this has been achieved, child labor has to be seen, either principally or solely, as a systemic harm.

In certain circumstances, it may also be implausible to take individual employers to be under strict duties not to employ child laborers. Of course, the relation between child labor and subsistence is extremely complex. Nevertheless, if the employers are really not in a position to pay wages that are sufficient to enable the parents to support the whole family, and by ending the children's employment would be depriving them of their only available chance of attaining a subsistence income, then it may not be

---

[26] This interpretation might be considered to be supported by the thought that if parents do face a tragic choice in which they opt to send their children out to work to prevent their starvation, this decision will leave a moral residue, and calls for deep regret and, where possible, compensation.

plausible to take them to be under a strict duty not to employ child laborers. Again, it may be much more plausible to take child labor to be principally a structural harm that calls for a coordinated institutional response than to identify specific employers as specifically responsible for particular violations of the right.

Insofar as child labor is a systemic harm, the duties it imposes also lack the second feature of perfect duties: it is not possible to identify specific perpetrators of specific violations of the right, and the content of the duty is not clear-cut. If we were to look for perpetrators of violations of the right against child labor, the parents and employers of child laborers would be the obvious candidates. However, as I have argued, it is not plausible to take parents or employers to be under a strict duty not to send their children out to work, or to employ child laborers, respectively, if fulfilling such a duty unavoidably conflicts with providing the children with or avoiding depriving them of a subsistence income. Rather, in such cases the duty that the right against child labor principally imposes is a duty to seek institutional reform, an integral part of which is to ensure that adequate economic opportunities are in place so that child labor is not the only available alternative to destitution. The duty to seek institutional reform is likely to lie with a huge number of agents, and has not itself been specified and allocated among them. Therefore the content of this duty is not fully defined, and it may not be possible to identify specific agents as the perpetrators of specific rights violations.

It is only if the right to basic necessities has been secured that it is plausible to take parents and employers to be under strict and clearly defined duties not to send their children out to work and not to employ child laborers, and to identify these agents as the perpetrators of specific violations of the right against child labor if they violate such duties. These duties may function in much the same way as perfect duties, given that they are fully delineated and that they can and should always be completely fulfilled. It is important to stress, though, that in a central respect they are not perfect duties in the standard sense, and in the way in which O'Neill is using the term: they are not duties that are fully defined and that strictly bind agents' conduct whatever the circumstances, and, in particular, regardless of the institutional structures that are in place, since the strictness and fully delineated nature of these duties is contingent on the fact that social institutions are in place that have secured the right to subsistence.

I conclude that it is not an essential feature of rights that they impose perfect duties. In order to determine the duties imposed by a right we need to consider the nature of the interests the right is meant to protect and the relation between these interests and other interests that may be threatened, and the nature of the protection all these interests require. In the case of the right against child labor, for example, if we are to give adequate weight to the developmental interests of the children, it follows that securing the right to subsistence is part and parcel of fulfilling the right against child labor, and it is only after the right to subsistence has been secured that the right against child labor imposes perfect duties that can and should be completely fulfilled. Thus, whether the right against child labor imposes perfect duties is contingent on whether the right to subsistence has been secured.

I therefore hope to have reinforced Shue's argument about the interdependence between the right to subsistence and other rights, and in the light of this to have reinforced his argument that in our thinking about welfare rights we should not be strait-jacketed by our inherited picture of the standard dichotomies between duties that underpins the view that welfare rights can only be special rights. As I have argued, there is a crucial substantive interdependence between the right to subsistence and other rights, in that the value to right-holders of enjoying fully secure access to the objects of other rights depends on their enjoying secure access to subsistence. Given the urgency of the interest in subsistence, it may be reasonable to sacrifice the objects of other rights in order to obtain subsistence. It follows that the full securing of other rights cannot be said to have been achieved in a way that can be plausibly held to be in the interests of the individual right-holder unless the right to subsistence has been secured. Furthermore, in the case of certain liberty rights against harm and coercion, when institutional structures are in place under which the right to subsistence is insecure there may be circumstances in which the conflict between enjoyment of the rights and enjoyment of subsistence is unavoidable. In such circumstances, these liberty rights cannot be adequately respected until the right to subsistence has been secured. It is only after the right to subsistence has been secured that these liberty rights impose duties that are fully defined and that can and should be completely fulfilled at all times. This indicates, first, that liberty rights cannot be adequately secured, and in some cases even adequately respected, until institutional structures are in place under which the right to subsistence has been secured, and, second, that in just the same way as with welfare rights, in the absence of just institutional structures, the negative duties imposed by certain liberty rights may be imperfect in nature.

In the light of this we can now finally briefly return to the question of whether the right to subsistence ought to be seen as a special right or a basic human right held by every human being simply in virtue of being human. If the duties imposed by genuine liberty rights can be imperfect, then the imperfect nature of duties of aid that correspond to welfare rights, prior to the institutionalization of such rights, is no reason to deny that these are duties of justice that correspond to human rights. Rather than being constrained by the standard dichotomies between duties we should focus on the interests the right protects, and the relation between these and other interests. The interest in subsistence is as important as the interests protected by any other right and is essential to a minimally decent and autonomous life. Furthermore, the right to subsistence is a basic right in the substantive sense that the value to the right-holder of full enjoyment of other rights is dependent on their secure enjoyment of subsistence. In the case of certain liberty rights, moreover, the right to subsistence is basic in the further sense that these rights cannot be adequately respected until the right to subsistence has been secured.

6

Shue on Rights and Duties*

Thomas Pogge

First published in 1980, Henry Shue's *Basic Rights* has remained influential for an unusually long time.[1] It is still frequently cited today in works on rights, development economics, global ethics, and justice. And it is widely read and referred to also among practitioners in NGOs and governmental foreign aid departments. More than any other, Shue's book has played a significant role in reconceiving in terms of rights, rather than charity, the relationship of affluent countries and their citizens to the poverty-related deprivations still so widespread in poor countries. This shift is of great importance, and I support it wholeheartedly. But I also think that there are other, and perhaps better, ways of supporting it than the argument Shue develops in *Basic Rights*.

Shue's argument starts from the widely accepted premise that human beings have moral rights, specifically claim rights in Hohfeld's sense.[2] This premise leaves open the content of our moral rights as well as their importance relative to one another and relative to other reasons for

---

* It gives me great pleasure to contribute to this celebration of the work of Henry Shue, who has been an inspiration for me as a student and a good personal and intellectual friend for over three decades. I am grateful to Charles Beitz and Robert Goodin for their work in creating this volume, and to them as well as Leif Wenar and two anonymous OUP reviewers for their detailed comments on my draft. Some have said that my chapter is not too critical in a way that suggests that it in fact is. But I know Henry would not want his work to be received in any other way.

[1] Henry Shue, *Basic Rights: Subsistence, Affluence and U.S. Foreign Policy* (Princeton, N.J.: Princeton University Press, 1980; 2nd edn. 1996); page references in parentheses will be to this volume.

[2] Claim rights are rights that impose duties on others and are contrasted by Hohfeld to privileges, which signify the absence of a duty in the right-holder. Thus, one person's claim right to the apples on a certain tree is associated with the rest of us having no privilege to take these apples. See Wesley Newcombe Hohfeld, *Fundamental Legal Conceptions*, ed. Walter Wheeler Cook (New Haven, Conn.: Yale University Press, 1919).

action. Noting that there is considerable disagreement about these matters, Shue proceeds to propose a criterion for identifying the content, or (as he calls it) *substance*, of our most weighty, most important rights.[3] Employing this criterion, he argues that four clusters of rights—security rights, subsistence rights, liberty rights (epitomized by freedom of movement), and political-participation rights—satisfy this criterion. Appealing to the plausibility of this result as well as to the independent plausibility of the criterion that delivered it, Shue concludes that these four rights clusters "are everyone's minimum reasonable demands upon the rest of humanity" (p. 19).

Shue then explores the normative burdens associated with these basic rights: the content of the demands they make on others. He argues that all these rights imply both negative and positive duties—negative duties to refrain from depriving others of the substance of these rights, and positive duties to protect people from such deprivations and to aid them when they nonetheless suffer such deprivations (p. 60). Shue concludes that, because all four clusters of rights impose both negative and positive duties, the common libertarian dismissal of subsistence rights fails. Subsistence rights, no less than security rights, entail negative duties; and security rights, no less than subsistence rights, entail positive duties. A prioritization of security rights over subsistence rights can therefore not be defended by appeal to the supposedly much greater moral weight of negative rights and duties. Both clusters of rights are on a par and thus stand or fall together.

Let us proceed to a critical examination of the stages of Shue's argument.

1. The Definition of a Moral Right

"A moral right provides (1) the rational basis for a justified demand (2) that the actual enjoyment of a substance be (3) socially guaranteed against standard threats" (p. 13). This brief statement makes clear the focus of Shue's account. Leaving aside *legal* rights, whose validity depends on the rules and regulations of an existing legal order, Shue focuses on general moral rights that persons have independently of any legal order.

We can understand what a moral right is, for Shue, by explicating what must be the case for a moral right to some substance X to be fulfilled for

---

[3] "The substance of a right is whatever the right is a right to" (p. 15).

some person P. As I read Shue, he lays down three necessary and jointly sufficient conditions:

(A) P actually enjoys X—formally: A(PX);
(B) P's enjoyment of X is socially guaranteed against standard threats—formally: B(PX);
(C) P enjoys X as a right—formally: C(PX).

Thus, a moral right to X is fulfilled for P at time t if and only if all three conditions are met at t—formally: $ABC(PX)_t$.

We should read all three conditions as implicitly presupposing that P is alive. P's death does not lead to her moral rights being unfulfilled (because P no longer enjoys their substances), but rather to P's no longer being around to have or to lack either moral rights or their substances.[4] To fulfill a destitute smoker's right to vote, his society is not morally required to do whatever it can do (say, to pay for his expensive lung operation) to ensure that he lives to future election days. He may have a moral right to expensive treatment, to be sure. But no such right is entailed by his right to vote. Even if his operation is not paid for and he therefore does not survive to the next election, his right to vote will never have been unfulfilled. His right to vote merely requires that, for any relevant elections he witnesses as an adult, he has a real opportunity to participate.[5] This reasoning suggests that, with respect to a moral "right to life," Condition A is always necessarily met. For either a person is alive, and therefore enjoys the substance of the right, or else the person is not alive, and therefore does not have the moral right. But what is normally meant by a right to life is a right not to be killed and/or allowed to die in certain ways. And once the right is interpreted in this way, then it is indeed possible for the right to be unfulfilled on account of Condition A being unmet: a murderer violates a living person's right not to be killed.

Condition A is straightforward. For P's moral right to be fulfilled, P must actually enjoy what this right is a right to—freedom from assault, for instance, or access to adequate nutrition, freedom of movement, or access to political participation. Here enjoying freedom from assault during some period means not being confronted with physical violence during this period.

---

[4] Though P has no moral rights after P's death, it may still be possible to fulfill or to violate rights P had while P was alive: the right that her last will be honored, for instance, or her right not to have her good name sullied by baseless accusations.

[5] This may require enabling him and others to vote by mail if he and they find it difficult to reach a polling station.

Shue explains Condition B as follows:

a right has not been fulfilled until arrangements are in fact in place for people to enjoy whatever it is to which they have the right. Usually, perhaps, the arrangements will take the form of law, making the rights legal as well as moral ones. But in other cases well-entrenched customs, backed by taboos, might serve better than laws—certainly better than unenforced laws. (p. 16)

Shue clarifies that the required arrangements need not be perfectly effective against all threats to X, but need merely be sufficiently effective against standard threats: the kinds of threats that are foreseeable, remediable, and, if unchecked by adequate arrangements, would render uncertain P's enjoyment of X. It follows that, just as Condition A can be met without Condition B, so Condition B can be met without Condition A: some people are assaulted even when there exist adequate arrangements for suppressing standard threats to the enjoyment of freedom from assault.

Shue does not explain Condition C in detail. When he writes of enjoying something as a right, he occasionally has Condition B in mind: effective arrangements against standard threats to P's enjoyment of X (e.g., p. 76). But his considered view, I think, is that Condition C goes beyond B in three respects. Condition C is met only if the contributions others must make to Conditions A and B being met are understood as *duties* (C_1) that are *owed to P* (C_2); and those contributions and these understandings are culturally anchored (C_3). Let me give three corresponding examples of how Conditions A and B might be met without C. P may enjoy subsistence with social guarantees against standard threats thanks to conduct by others that is understood as mere charity, as when the affluent underwrite poorhouses without recognizing any moral duty to do so; this would leave C_1 unmet. P may enjoy freedom from rape with social guarantees against standard threats thanks to strictly enforced miscegenation laws that forbid those with power over P to have physical contact with her; this would leave C_2 unmet. P may enjoy freedom of expression with social guarantees against standard threats thanks to an enlightened monarch's commitment, which her successors, selected by lot each equinox, may not share; this would leave C_3 unmet.

Let me conceive Condition C narrowly as including only what A and B leave out. Like Conditions A and B, Condition C can then be met even while the other two are not. The aftermath of Hurricane Katrina can perhaps serve as an example: Many residents of New Orleans did not actually enjoy access to clean water, and no social guarantees were in place against standard threats to such access. Nonetheless, Condition C was arguably met: it was widely accepted throughout the U.S. that the state owed a duty to the residents of New Orleans to ensure secure access to clean water for them.

2. The Identification of Certain General Moral Rights as Basic

Shue introduces the notion of a basic right by calling basic rights "the morality of the depths. They specify the line beneath which no one is to be allowed to sink" (p. 18). He then adds this definition: "rights are basic in the sense used here only if enjoyment of them is essential to the enjoyment of all other rights" (p. 19). Parallel passages show that Shue uses the word "essential" as a synonym for "necessary" and that the "only if" can be expanded to "if and only if." By calling a moral right basic in Shue's sense, one is then asserting no more and no less than that the enjoyment of this right is necessary for the enjoyment of all other rights. That R_X is a basic right means that it is impossible to enjoy any right without enjoying R_X.

It is obvious that, if some moral rights were basic in this sense, they would be among the most important rights. Moreover, showing some moral right to be basic would gain it wide support. People differ about what moral rights there are, but few hold that there are no general moral rights at all. By showing that there is some right R_X whose enjoyment is necessary for the enjoyment of *any* right, Shue can hope to convince all those who recognize any general moral rights at all to add R_X to their respective lists. If this strategy succeeds, then he will guide his readers from a rather meaningless agreement to a more substantive one: from a state where people agree that there are some general moral rights, but differ about what these rights are, to a state where these people agree that there are some general moral rights and agree that R_X is among them (p. 31). In fact, Shue wants to qualify several rights as basic and thereby to facilitate an even more substantial agreement.

Further analysis of Shue's definition requires an understanding of what he means by *enjoying a right*. He explains this as follows: "We do sometimes speak simply of someone's 'enjoying a right,' but I take this to be an elliptical way of saying that the person is enjoying something or other which is the substance of a right, and, probably, enjoying it *as* a right" (p. 15). In the formal notation I have introduced, P's enjoying her right to X at some time t is then tantamount to $A(PX)_t$ or—"probably"— something stronger such as $AC(PX)_t$ or even $ABC(PX)_t$. Let us consider these options in order.

On the first interpretation, Shue's definition would identify as *basic* all and only those rights whose substance must be actually enjoyed in order for the substance of any other right to be actually enjoyed. That R_X is a basic right then means that it is impossible, for any person at any time, to enjoy the substance of any right without also enjoying X. Necessarily, for any P, t, and Y, $A(PY)_t$ only if $A(PX)_t$. Are there rights that satisfy this condition?

The most obvious candidate is the right not to be killed. But we have above seen reason to interpret the three conditions as involving the implicit presupposition that P is alive. A killer does bring it about that his victim's right not to be killed is unfulfilled; but he is not thereby bringing it about that all her other rights—to freedom of movement, say, or political participation—are unfulfilled as well. The situation after P's death is not one in which P lacks the substances of her moral rights, but rather one in which she is no longer around to have or lack rights or their substances.

There are, in any case, several other moral rights (beyond the right not to be killed) that Shue seeks to qualify as basic, and they certainly all fail this test. For even if one actually lacks the substance of any one of these rights, one can actually enjoy the substance of some other right. While one lacks freedom of movement, political participation, or adequate nutrition, one may actually be enjoying the substance of some other right, freedom from torture for instance. And, conversely, while one is being tortured one may actually be enjoying the substance of some other right, for instance adequate nutrition. Since the first interpretation so obviously entails a result opposite to Shue's intent, we should set it aside.

On the second interpretation, Shue's definition would identify as basic all and only those rights whose substance must be actually enjoyed as a right in order for the substance of any other right to be actually enjoyed as a right. That R_X is a basic right then means that it is impossible, for any person at any time to enjoy the substance of any right as a right without also enjoying X as a right. Necessarily, for any P, t, and Y, $AC(PY)_t$ only if $AC(PX)_t$.

Adding Condition C before "only if" weakens the requirement for basic-right status: $A(PY)_t$ and $C(PY)_t$ together presuppose more than $A(PY)_t$ alone. But adding Condition C after "only if" strengthens this require-ment: it must be shown that $A(PX)_t$ and $C(PX)_t$ are both presupposed rather than only that $A(PX)_t$ is presupposed.

The upshot is that, on this interpretation as well, Shue's candidates do not qualify as basic rights. For example, P can enjoy participation in periodic elections, and can enjoy such participation as a right, even while

P enjoys neither personal security nor subsistence as a right. This is a plausible scenario in a feudal society, for instance. The nobles are in power and they periodically elect a monarch from among themselves. They recognize one another's moral claim to partake in the elections and would fiercely resist any effort to disenfranchise any from among themselves. Yet, they recognize no claim to contribute to one another's personal security; in this regard they each depend on their own resources and expect one another to do so. Nor do they recognize any claim to contribute to one another's subsistence, again depending on their own resources and expecting one another to do so. As elections pass without a hitch, each of the nobles enjoys political participation, and enjoys it as a right, while also enjoying personal security and subsistence, but not enjoying these as rights. The example shows that the rights to personal security and subsistence are not basic on the second interpretation of Shue's definition: it is possible to enjoy some right's substance as a right without enjoying either personal security or subsistence as a right.

Seeking to qualify subsistence rights as basic, Shue writes: "Could there actually be a right not to be tortured in the absence of a right to subsistence? The difficulty is that a person who ... was in fact deprived of food might, without other recourse, be willing to submit to limited torture in exchange for food" (p. 185)—and would then, so the implication, not be enjoying freedom from torture as a right. This remark will not help on the second interpretation of Shue's definition. Even if there is some case in which not enjoying subsistence as a right makes it impossible to enjoy freedom from torture as a right, it does not follow that this impossibility holds generally. In fact, as my feudalism example illustrates, this impossibility does not hold generally. The noblemen do not enjoy security and subsistence as rights. But they do enjoy them both and have no reason at all to refrain from voting, or to submit to limited torture, in exchange for food. Shue's difficulty does not extend to them, and their case shows that it is possible to enjoy political participation as a right even without enjoying personal security and subsistence as rights.

It is evidently unwise to interpret Shue's definition so that the kind of difficulty he poses becomes decisive. On this third interpretation, a basic right would be defined as one whose enjoyment as a right may *in some cases* be necessary for the enjoyment of any other right as a right (so that it is *sometimes* impossible to enjoy R_Y without enjoying R_X). Far too many rights would then qualify as basic. For instance, the right to a gas mask is basic, because enjoying this right as a right may sometimes be essential to enjoying other rights as rights. In a context of dangerous pollution, a person without a gas mask may be willing to trade away the substance of any of her other rights to obtain one. As Shue would agree, the mere possibility of this scenario—or even its actual occurrence—is insufficient to qualify the right to a gas mask as basic. So rights to personal security or adequate nutrition cannot by qualified as basic by outlining some scenario in which someone might be willing to trade away the substance of her other rights for personal security or food. I conclude that, for the definition of a basic right to function as Shue intends it to, the terms "P" and "t" must be bound by universal rather than existential quantifiers. For enjoyment of one right to be necessary for enjoyment of another it must *never* be possible to enjoy the latter without enjoying the former.

There may be a way of rescuing Shue's definition from coming up empty even while retaining the universal quantifiers. Suggested by our discussion of the first two interpretations, this way involves introducing an asymmetry by putting more *before* the "only if" than *after*. Let us consider a fourth interpretation that does just that: Basic are all and only those rights whose substance must be actually enjoyed in order for any right to be fully enjoyed.[6] By a right being *fully enjoyed*, I mean that the substance of the right is actually enjoyed and socially guaranteed and enjoyed as a right. My proposed fourth interpretation of Shue's definition would then identify as basic all and only those rights whose substance must be actually enjoyed in order for any right to be fully enjoyed. That R_X is a basic right then means that it is impossible, for any person and any time and any right R_Y, fully to enjoy R_Y without also enjoying X. Necessarily, for any P, t, and Y, $ABC(PY)_t$ only if $A(PX)_t$.

This fourth interpretation still captures Shue's central concern: to identify the most important rights by asking whether a right is such that a person must have its substance in order fully to enjoy any rights at all. And this fourth interpretation also gets us closer to actually identifying some rights that qualify as basic. This is so because, for any specific P and t and R_Y, we have now as it were seven ways of showing that R_X is basic: we can try to show that $A(PY)_t$ or $B(PY)_t$ or $C(PY)_t$ singly presupposes $A(PX)_t$; failing that, we can try to show that any two of them—$AB(PY)_t$ or $AC(PY)_t$ or $BC(PY)_t$—together presuppose $A(PX)_t$; and, should we fail once more, we can still try to show, finally, that all three of them together, $ABC(PY)_t$, presuppose $A(PX)_t$.

---

[6] There is textual evidence for this "asymmetrical" interpretation. Explicating his claim that "security and subsistence are basic rights," Shue writes for instance: "Other rights could not be enjoyed in the absence of security or subsistence" (p. 30; rather than "without enjoying rights to security and subsistence").

As far as I can see, even on this fourth interpretation of Shue's definition, no rights qualify as basic. To show this, let R_Y be the right not to be arbitrarily deprived of one's nationality. Is there any other right R_X such that, for any person P and any time t, if P lacks X at t then P cannot fully enjoy R_Y at t?

I think there is no such R_X. Suppose that the right not to be arbitrarily deprived of one's nationality is prominently guaranteed in the constitution of P's country, vigorously enforced by the national courts, strongly affirmed by the population as owed to every citizen, reaffirmed in international treaties this country has ratified, and overseen by international courts and tribunals with punitive powers. Suppose further that all this has been so for a very long time during which not a single national of P's country has ever been arbitrarily deprived of her or his nationality. Given all this, one would be inclined to say that P fully enjoys R_Y: P enjoys the substance of the right, socially guaranteed and as a right.

Seeking to vindicate his candidate rights as basic rights on the fourth interpretation of his definition, Shue would have to disagree and to assert instead that it is never possible fully to enjoy R_Y without enjoying both personal security and subsistence. But this assertion is incorrect. Suppose P has been kidnapped for ransom and has been starved by his kidnappers and roughed up. P enjoys neither freedom of movement nor adequate nutrition nor personal security nor political participation. He'd be most willing to give up his nationality to end his ordeal. But this outcome is so evidently of no interest to his captors that it does not even occur to P to offer to renounce his citizenship. In this situation, I see no reason to doubt that P continues fully to enjoy his right not to be arbitrarily deprived of his nationality. And the situation demonstrates then that it is possible fully to enjoy some rights even while one lacks the substances of all the rights that Shue deems basic.[7]

Parallel arguments can be devised to reinforce the conclusion. The right not to be convicted under a retroactive law, for example, is another instantiation of R_Y that would support the same points: It is not always necessary for the full enjoyment of this right that one have the substance of any of the rights Shue picks as basic. Hunger, personal insecurity, disenfranchisement, confinement—none of these are standard threats to the right not to be convicted under a retroactive law. And rights to

---

[7] I think that this example escapes the charge of being "quite contorted and exotic" with which Shue dismisses a rather less plausible counterexample he poses against himself (p. 187).

subsistence, personal security, political participation, and freedom of movement are then unqualified to be basic rights also according to Shue's definitional remark that "the substance of a basic right is something the deprivation of which is one standard threat to rights generally" (p. 34).

From a practical, political standpoint, the failure of Shue's strategy is perhaps not to be regretted. Had it succeeded, the language of moral rights might have become a rather blunt instrument. At least on the more straightforward first and second interpretations, Shue's account implies that the enjoyment of basic rights is an all-or-nothing affair: one either enjoys all the basic rights or no rights at all. This account leaves little room for differentiations among those living below the threshold. As far as rights are concerned, their situation cannot be improved incrementally, but only through a shift that would make them enjoy *all* their basic rights (cf. p. 191 n. 23, 200 n. 14).

Such all-or-nothing thinking is, I believe, counterproductive in the political struggle Shue wants to support: the struggle to empower the global poor. This struggle requires incremental thinking. We must be ready to exploit any opportunities for expanding and better protecting the rights of the poor, especially when such marginal improvements, typically by enhancing the capacity of the poor to fend for themselves, bring further marginal improvements within reach. For example, it can be meaningful and important to fight—on both the global and the national levels—for the recognition and implementation of poor people's right to have access, when they fall ill with malaria, to an advanced, artemisinin-based combination therapy. Winning this fight can be hugely important for poor people in malaria-infested regions even if these same people do not enjoy their right of access to a secure food supply. This point, which I am confident Shue would agree with, would be undermined by his account, which would make it impossible to secure any rights at all for the poor without securing at least the substances of all their basic rights.

I conclude that Shue's definition of basic rights, at least on the interpretations I have considered, fails to support a plausible identification of the most important moral rights. More broadly, my analysis also suggests that his key idea for achieving such an identification through an exploration of the concept of a right and of presuppositional relations among rights is unlikely to succeed and likely to be politically counterproductive.

Nonetheless, there is no denying that the rights Shue identifies as basic are indeed very important rights, and it is quite possible that his identification could be justified in some other, perhaps less formalistic way.[8] In what follows, I will then keep using the expression "basic rights," but now as a convenient group label for the important rights Shue has singled out.

3. The Account of Moral Rights and Their Correlative Duties

Following Shue's own order of exposition, I have thus far discussed moral rights in terms of what they secure for the right-holder, without much thought of the normative burdens they impose upon other agents.[9] Shue's exposition here reflects an important and unexamined decision on his part about how to conceive rights and their substances.

Broadly speaking, rights can be conceived in personal or impersonal terms. Conceived in personal terms, a right (*in personam*) addresses another agent and, more specifically, the conduct of this other agent. The right divides this other agent's conduct options into right-compatible and right-incompatible ones, and it constrains this agent to avoid the right-incompatible conduct options. So conceived, a right—or claim right in Hohfeld's sense—is then a three-place predicate relating a right-holder (H), a duty-bearer (D), and a behavioral substance (Q): H has a right against D that D shape her conduct so that it instantiates Q (or, equivalently, so that it does not instantiate $-Q$).

Conceived in impersonal terms, a right (*in rem*) addresses the way the world goes and divides alternative histories into ones compatible with this right and ones incompatible with it. So conceived, a right is a two-place predicate relating a right holder (H) to states of the world (Z): R has a right that the world be such that it instantiates Z or such that it does not instantiate $-Z$.

---

[8] Shue is at his more formalistic when he writes that his argument:

is based upon what it normally means for anything to be a right or, in other words, upon the concept of a right. So, if the argument to establish the substances of basic rights is summarized by saying that these substances are the "other things ... necessary" for enjoying any other right, it is essential to interpret "necessary" in the restricted sense of "made essential by the very concept of a right." The "other things" do not include whatever would be convenient or useful, but only whatever is indispensable to anything else's being enjoyed as a right. Nothing will turn out to be necessary, in this sense, for the enjoyment of any right unless it is also necessary for the enjoyment of every right. (p. 31)

In this volume, Elizabeth Ashford makes an effort to adapt Shue's account in a way that downplays its conceptualist elements in favor of greater concern with empirical facts about human needs and political realities.

[9] Beyond Shue's quoted remark that basic rights "are everyone's minimum reasonable demands upon the rest of humanity" (p. 19).

Any account that conceives rights in personal terms can easily be translated into impersonal terms. This translation employs a very simple manual: the world instantiates Z just in case D shapes her conduct so that this conduct instantiates Q. But an account that conceives rights in impersonal terms can be translated into personal terms only in the very special case where all the Z-predicates the former account involves are of the form "D shapes her conduct so that it instantiates Q." The rights Shue discusses are not of this form. They specify what H ought to be enjoying not in terms of other agents' conduct, but in terms of H's own capacities for well-being and agency. Let us call an account like his—formulated in impersonal terms and not readily translatable into personal terms—a *programmatic account of rights*.

We can further appreciate how different Shue's programmatic account is from the Hohfeldian way of conceiving rights in personal terms by looking at the individuation of rights.[10] What Shue postulates as *one* right to a secure food supply, Hohfeld would decompose into a large number of diverse rights that H has against specific other agents with regard to their conduct relevant to H's food supply. H might have one specific food-related claim against her government's conduct, a separate and possibly different such claim against her mother, plus separate and possibly diverse such claims against the local rice cooperative, her neighbor, and the local UNICEF team.

By stressing the differences, I am not suggesting that there is anything wrong with conceiving rights programmatically. This is the language of national constitutions and of many international documents such as the *Universal Declaration of Human Rights*, the two UN Covenants, and various regional human rights conventions. Yet, to be meaningful, a programmatic account of rights needs to be cashed out in personal terms. If we want morally unacceptable states of the world—like −Z, incompatible with a programmatic right of H—to be avoided, then we need reasonably precise duties to be laid upon specific other agents such that they are likely to comply with these duties and that their compliance is likely to avoid −Z. Shue fully accepts this desideratum, and he tries to meet it with his account of correlative duties.

Such duties, as we have seen, require specification in two dimensions: regarding their addressee or duty bearer, and regarding their content or behavioral substance. In the latter dimension, Shue offers the following typology of duties (p. 60), which has laid the foundation for the "respect,

---

[10] Shue himself cites Hohfeld (p. 183 n. 3, p. 184 n. 4) but uses Hohfeld's term *claim right* without recognizing that for Hohfeld each claim right contains essential reference to an addressee.

protect, fulfill" mantra that has become widespread in the discourse of international agencies and many governments:[11]

I. to avoid depriving
II. to protect from deprivation
    1. by enforcing duty I
    2. by designing institutions that avoid the creation of strong incentives to violate duty I
III. to aid the deprived
    1. who are one's special responsibility
    2. who are victims of social failures in the performance of duties I, II-1, II-2
    3. who are victims of natural disasters

Which agents have which of these duties? As far as basic rights are concerned, Shue holds that *all* agents have duty III-2 up to the point where doing even more to fulfill this duty would endanger the enjoyment of their own basic rights (or, presumably, basic rights of their dependents). We are required to sacrifice all of our preferences, all our opportunities for cultural enrichment, and all substances of our non-basic rights insofar as this is necessary and useful for helping others gain access to substances of their basic rights (pp. 114–19).

In response to the worry that such a duty to aid the deprived is extremely demanding, Shue points out that this requirement "is specifically about duties to aid people whose rights have already been violated,

---

[11] Crucial in this development was General Comment 12 <http://www.fao.org/legal/rtf/cescr-e.htm>, adopted by the UN Committee on Economic, Social and Cultural Rights in 1999, whose Article 15 reads as follows:

The right to adequate food, like any other human right, imposes three types or levels of obligations on States parties: the obligations to *respect*, to *protect* and to *fulfil*. In turn, the obligation to *fulfil* incorporates both an obligation to *facilitate* and an obligation to *provide*. The obligation to *respect* existing access to adequate food requires States parties not to take any measures that result in preventing such access. The obligation to *protect* requires measures by the State to ensure that enterprises or individuals do not deprive individuals of their access to adequate food. The obligation to *fulfil* (*facilitate*) means the State must pro-actively engage in activities intended to strengthen people's access to and utilization of resources and means to ensure their livelihood, including food security. Finally, whenever an individual or group is unable, for reasons beyond their control, to enjoy the right to adequate food by the means at their disposal, States have the obligation to *fulfil* (*provide*) that right directly. This obligation also applies for persons who are victims of natural or other disasters.

This typology is most directly due to Philip Alston and Asbjorn Eide. They in turn were both influenced by Henry Shue's *Basic Rights*, as is well-documented in Philip Alston and Katarina Tomaševski, eds., *The Right to Food* (Dordrecht: Martinus Nijhoff, 1984) and in Asbjorn Eide, Wenche Barth Eide, Susantha Goonatilake, and Joan Gussow, eds., *Food as a Human Right* (Tokyo: United Nations University, 1984), esp. pp. 169–74.

which, I believe, makes the position embodied in it less extreme than it may otherwise seem" (p. 159). But Shue does not explain why duties III-3 (to aid victims of natural disasters) should be less stringent or less demanding than duties III-2 (to aid victims of social failures in the performance of duties I, II-1, II-2). Such an explanation is straightforward in cases where the addressee of the duty to aid bears some responsibility for the social failures in question. But no such responsibility is assumed in Shue's definition of duties III-2. And Shue does then owe an explanation for the asymmetry he suggests: when people—through no fault of theirs or ours— are deprived of the substance of their basic rights, why should they have a stronger moral claim on us when this deprivation is due to duty violations by third parties? I can see no rationale for this asymmetry.

But even if we set duties III-3 aside, Shue's position is still extremely demanding. In our world, well over a billion human beings lack secure access to adequate food and clean water. Most of these subsistence deprivations are due to social failures in the performance of duties I, II-1, and/or II-2.[12] Some dedicated but under-funded governmental agencies and non-governmental organizations are successfully helping very poor people gain access to such basic means of subsistence. We other, not-so-poor people can support such organized efforts with our time and money. In this and other ways, each of us has practically inexhaustible opportunities effectively to devote his or her resources to basic-rights fulfillment. This is true especially for the super-rich who can fund clean-water and sanitation systems, and for the poor in affluent countries, who can donate money to UNICEF or Oxfam or Doctors Without Borders for ready-to-use therapeutic food or urgently needed medicines and safe drinking water. Though we may be at the tail end of a sequence of "successive waves of duty" (p. 156), we are still morally required to renounce all of our preferences, all of our opportunities for cultural enrichment, and all substances of our non-basic rights in order to help fulfill the basic rights of others.[13]

Shue's postulate of such a moral requirement may seem implausible— especially when we attend to two intuitively relevant factors that Shue

[12] For evidence, see Thomas Pogge: *World Poverty and Human Rights: Cosmopolitan Responsibilities and Reforms*, 2nd edn. (Cambridge: Polity Press, 2008), General Introduction and chs. 4 and 5.

[13] To be sure, it is only so long as most of us do nothing or very little toward redressing socially caused basic-rights deficits that each of us can find ways of increasing his or her effective contribution to this end by devoting more resources to it. But this, unfortunately, has been the actual situation for a very long time. It is unlikely, then, that our duties III-2 will be mitigated by "limits upon the absorptive capacity of recipient nations and individuals" (p. 104). And even if our efforts, collectively, reached such limits, it is very likely that, with creative intelligence, these limits could be bypassed, shifted, or overcome.

disregards. One is the factor of involvement in deprivation. Disregarding this factor, Shue assigns the same stringent and demanding duties III-2 to us even when we are wholly disconnected from the wrongs that sustain the deprivations we are asked to mitigate, that is, when we have made no causal contributions to these wrongs and have not benefited from them in any way. The other factor is the cost-benefit ratio. Disregarding this factor, Shue assigns the same stringent and demanding duties III-2 to us regardless of how much or how little our renunciation of all discretionary resources could achieve toward reducing socially caused basic-rights deficits.

Most readers will find this view implausibly demanding. Even if our III-3 duties (left unspecified by Shue) regarding basic-rights deficits due to natural disasters are not very demanding, it is quite clear that, in the world as it is, our III-2 duties require us to give up all but our own basic rights for the sake of fulfilling basic rights of others. Seeing how much socially caused deprivation there is, and how little others are doing toward the fulfillment of basic rights, everyone is morally required to give up everything except the substances of one's own basic rights in order to help fulfill the basic rights of others.

Shue is not unaware of the implausibility of the requirement he postulates, explicitly asking:

> which allocations of right-grounded duties would be fair to individual duty-bearers? I intend to invoke this perspective when I say that we should not forget that for the duty-bearers too this is the only life they will live, by which I mean that, however terrible the prospects from the point of view of potential right-bearers if certain rights are not acknowledged and implemented, the point of view of the bearers of the duties implicated by those rights also should be taken into account before one decides whether those rights should, all things considered, be acknowledged. (p. 165)

But in the end, Shue does endorse the basic rights he had identified, despite the huge burdens their correlative duties III-2 impose in the present world. The implication is that nearly all of us more privileged people, who are enjoying our basic rights with resources to spare, are massively non-compliant with our most important moral duty when we fail to devote our spare resources to reducing socially caused basic-rights deficits.[14]

---

[14] In later work, Shue points out that our duties to aid would be manageable if they were appropriately organized through institutional mechanisms whose costs are fairly shared worldwide. This is true. But in our world, where adequate such institutional mechanisms are lacking, Shue's point can only add to the workload of those who recognize their duties to aid. See Henry Shue, "Mediating Duties," *Ethics*, 98 (1988), 687–704.

Shue's judgment makes sense when one accepts his account of general moral rights and their correlative duties. We must then either accept these hugely demanding duties III-2 or else deny the corresponding basic right. But one need not accept Shue's account, and one might challenge, in particular, his central claim that any basic right is "an inseparable mixture of positive and negative elements" (p. 192). Why should this "mixture" be so inseparable on the basic-rights side, given that Shue has managed to separate things so neatly on the correlative-duties side? Using the helpful differentiations Shue has introduced on the side of duties—distinguishing duties to avoid depriving, duties to protect from deprivation, and duties to aid the deprived—one might draw matching distinctions on the side of rights, between

I. one general moral right not to be deprived of X
II. two distinct general moral rights to be protected against being deprived of X, and
III. three distinct general moral rights to be aided when one lacks access to X.

One might then ask about each of these candidate rights whether it exists at all and, if so, against whom it is held, in what formulation, and with what stringency.

This move helps avoid a false dichotomy. We are not forced *either* to deny a basic right to X *or* to accept extremely demanding duties III-2 toward those who suffer socially caused deprivation of X. Instead, we can disassemble Shue's basic right to X and then perhaps postulate very weighty moral rights, against every other agent, not to be deprived of X and perhaps less weighty and less wide-ranging moral rights to be protected against, and aided in the event of, deprivation of X.

This move also resurrects the moral significance of the distinction between negative and positive rights which Shue had sought to bury for good. But it draws this distinction in a way that is orthogonal to the traditional way that Shue was right to criticize. It does not present security rights as negative and subsistence rights as positive. Instead, this challenge characterizes as negative one's rights against others that they not actively deprive one of one's security and subsistence. And it characterizes as positive one's rights against others that they should actively protect one against such deprivations and should aid one when one nonetheless ends up so deprived.

Actually, matters are even a little more complex than this once we attend to the morally relevant factor of involvement, which Shue disregards. Two standard modes of involvement in deprivation are contribution and benefit. Those who are contributing to depriving others of the substances of their rights have a duty, of course, to discontinue this contribution. But they also have more stringent duties (than uninvolved bystanders similarly placed) to protect and to aid the deprived. The man who has, in a fit of jealous rage, sent poisoned chocolates to his rival has a more stringent duty to intercept the package, and a more stringent duty also to aid the victim (if the harm has already been done), than some uninvolved third person who also knows about the attack. And likewise for those who are, however innocently, benefiting from deprivations suffered by others—as we all often do when we buy products that are cheap thanks to the use of bonded labor, child labor, and unjust restrictions of educational opportunities and of labor mobility.

When contribution or benefit is in play, the rights and duties of protection and aid are, on the surface, still straightforwardly positive. But at a deeper level, the rationale for these duties has a negative element: we have a general duty, insofar as we reasonably can, to avoid making uncompensated contributions to the deprivation of others and also to avoid receiving uncompensated benefits from such deprivation. Often, it is not reasonably possible to avoid benefiting from deprivations or to stop contributing to them (e.g., through unjust foreign policies our government is pursuing with our tax monies in our behalf). In such cases, it is typically still possible to compensate for such contributions and benefits through actions that protect or aid the deprived and thereby reduce the deprivations we will have contributed to or benefited from.

The proposed disaggregation of rights makes it easier also to attend to the other morally relevant factor Shue disregards, the relation of cost and benefit. This factor is straightforwardly relevant to the stringency of duties. The moral reason one has to contribute a sum of money to a safe-water initiative in Africa is more stringent the more money one has (reducing the cost of the contribution to oneself) and the more deprivation this initiative would avoid (increasing the benefit one's contribution would bring). This factor is also highly relevant to the prioritization of duties: other things equal, we ought to focus our protection and aid efforts to where they can be most cost-effective.

Finally, this factor is also relevant to the allocation of duties in the absence of effective institutional arrangements. When the question is who, among many similarly placed agents, ought to take the initiative in a morally important protection or aid effort, then the salient solution surely is that this should be the agent or agents who can do so in the most cost-effective way.[15] I would think that one morally relevant dimension in which agents may not be similarly placed is that of involvement. Those who are contributing to, or benefiting from, deprivations may have stronger moral reasons to protect and aid the deprived than others who can protect and aid at lower cost. But discussing these matters further here would clearly lead us too far afield. The important point for the present discussion is that the complexities I have briefly canvassed—the differentiations among diverse rights that deprived people may have against various others and consideration of various factors that seem relevant to establishing the existence and strength of any such right against a specific such agent—are needed for a full appreciation of our moral situation and also helpful in addressing the allocation of duties in the absence of suitable institutional arrangements.

The last few paragraphs are not unrelated to how I have tried to structure the discussion of human rights in my own work. They document how my own thinking has been greatly enriched by my long engagement with Shue's work, especially with *Basic Rights*, which I have been discussing in many courses and writings. Yes, I have found some aspects of this book frustrating and have come to disagree with several of its central claims and distinctions. But it has also been a great inspiration for me that has shaped my thinking like few others.

[15] See Leif Wenar, "Responsibility and Severe Poverty," in *Freedom from Poverty as a Human Right: Who Owes What to the Very Poor?*, ed. Thomas Pogge (Oxford: Oxford University Press, 2007), pp. 255–74.

7

No Borders, No Bystanders: Developing Individual and Institutional Capacities for Global Moral Responsibility*

Neta C. Crawford

For most of the world's inhabitants, security and subsistence are rights precariously secured, if they are enjoyed at all. Indeed, the facts of existence are harsh. The lives of billions of the world's poor are more miserable and shortened compared to the lives of those with means in wealthier countries. The number living in "extreme" poverty, on less than $1.25 per day, grew in India and Africa between 1981 and 2005. Thousands of children die each day for lack of safe drinking water. The global rise of sea levels will, all too soon, inundate several low-lying islands and coastal areas, eliminating the homes and farmlands of thousands of people. Millions suffer and die annually from multi-drug-resistant tuberculosis and other curable illnesses. Civilian deaths in war are often excused if those deaths are understood as a "necessary" and unintended consequence of military actions that are undertaken for a legitimate military end.

Should we see these facts as something to care about? And if I am saddened by these situations, am I obliged to do anything about them? These brutal conditions existed before my birth and will likely persist for the foreseeable future absent any fundamental change in the organization

* I am deeply grateful to Henry Shue for inspiration and example. I thank Charles Beitz, Robert Goodin, Ann Ferguson, and Toni Erskine, whose work has also inspired over the years, for comments on early drafts. I also thank anonymous readers and perceptive members of workshops and seminars at the University of Wales, Aberystwyth in July 2007, at the University of Toronto in September 2007, at Cornell University in October 2007, and at Stanford University in February 2008 including Emanuel Adler, Matthew Evangelista, Jeremy Weinstein, and Joshua Cohen.

of the world economy, in the resources the world's rich send to the world's poor, or in the norms of war. In a sense, are we not all bystanders to forces and situations beyond our immediate circumstance?

In other words, what do we owe each other as humans living on the same planet? For centuries the answer was quite simple—not much. The dominant understanding of obligation in world politics was that moral boundaries were coterminous with state borders. States were moral containers and intervention across borders was supposed to be exceptional, reserved for cases where the intervening state's security or sovereignty was at risk.

Yet, it is becoming increasingly difficult to say that we are unconnected to others. Specifically, as Henry Shue argues, while it was previously possible to sharply delimit our moral obligations to others, humans now "lack sufficient reason to think that once we leave behind the intimates to whom we have special duties, as well as the inner circle of genuine friends and meaningful acquaintances, duties to strangers decline progressively with their distance from us."[1] Shue thus rejects the notion that our duties to others diminish as we move outward in concentric circles.

It was not so long ago that if you really wanted to have much effect in a distant place, you had to go there in order to have it ... But now the concentric-circle image is no more accurate a representation of causality than it is of responsibility ... Perhaps the nearest thing to an accurate representation of the real circumstances now is one of those irregular spider webs with some very short strands and some very long strands, such that if something touches one strand it may send a shock to the farthest side of the web, while if it touches a different strand its effects may quickly fade away.[2]

Shue thus suggests that because humans are causally tied to others in the globe as never before, there is no reason, other than limited individual resources, to circumscribe our moral concern to compatriots. What is different over the last 150 or so years is that the causal stories we tell increasingly include distant others. As Onora O'Neill argues,

We live with and by the complex interlock of agents which global trade, communications, and densely connected institutions have produced. For us distance is no guarantee of lack of interaction, and we constantly assume that many distant others are every bit as much agents and subjects as nearby or familiar others, and hence are beings whose claim to just treatment (and perhaps to other forms of moral concern) we cannot reasonably settle merely by arbitrary exclusion.[3]

---

[1] Henry Shue, "Mediating Duties," *Ethics*, 98 (1988), 687–704 at p. 693.   [2] Ibid.
[3] Onora O'Neill, *Bounds of Justice* (Cambridge: Cambridge University Press, 2000), p. 196.

This increasing but incomplete globalization of the world economy, and our increasing but incomplete political and cultural connection to distant others, thus potentially poses moral dilemmas of both an everyday sort, such as what kind of coffee to buy or whether to donate to Oxfam or Save the Children, and the exceptional variety, for instance how to respond to what might be an unfolding genocide. If we cannot draw *arbitrary* boundaries around our moral responsibilities, what are we to do?

Humans today thus live at a crossroads of moral concern and action: we can't go back, but it is often unclear how to go forward. If there are hard physical boundaries, I can remain a bystander to the suffering of those beyond the border. If boundaries are not so hard I am no longer so clearly a bystander. Individuals and states might limit their moral concern and action to citizens within borders, or we might care about and act with equal concern toward (at least some) outsiders. Where until recently humanitarian intervention was considered a rare benevolent act we might today blame ourselves, and others, when we don't help distant strangers in great distress. Intervention may saves lives, but it can also be self-interested, paternalistic, and a violation of others' rights.

To greatly simplify, these dilemmas reflect three intertwined discourses. The first is an argument over *whether* we are obliged to act to help distant others, and if so, just exactly what we owe them.[4] Shue articulates the core issue of the first discourse when he says: "The world is full of foreigners. Most of them are strangers to me, and I have every reason to doubt that most of them have ever given me a thought. Is there some reason I should give thought to them?"[5] One side in this discourse asserts that individuals live in states and political communities and that states are obliged to provide for their own security in a context of anarchy. Realists argue that not only do individuals care about themselves and members of their in-group first, but that is how it ought to be. Humans are not obliged to care for outsiders. At the root of this argument is a view of "human nature" as basically self-interested.

The other side in the first discourse argues for an essential human connection to others that goes beyond narrow definitions of self and community. This side argues that we should care about even distant others, even if we aren't causally connected to them, and has documented the

---

[4] A powerful exposition and intervention in this discourse is Charles R. Beitz, *Political Theory and International Relations*, rev. edn. (Princeton, N.J.: Princeton University Press, 1999).

[5] Shue, "Mediating Duties," p. 687.

consequences of the failure to do so. For example, cosmopolitans such as Onora O'Neill suggest that, "Today we have moved so far beyond the earliest State of Nature that there can be few, if any, distant strangers whom we can coherently see as living beyond the pale or *limes* of justice (and perhaps some other forms of moral concern)."[6] Many scholars and human rights activists on this side of the first discourse have focused on enumerating rights and corresponding duties, such as Immanuel Kant's duty to "universal hospitality." Henry Shue argues that certain rights are basic in the sense that when those rights—security and subsistence—are guaranteed, other rights can be enjoyed. When basic rights are not guaranteed, other rights can be enjoyed only precariously.[7]

In the second discourse, the argument is no longer whether we can or ought to care about others, or what we specifically owe them, but the procedures for enacting our responsibilities. In other words, the second discourse is about *how* to act: what arrangements and procedures could produce more just outcomes? Interlocutors acknowledge that even if one wants to exercise moral responsibility in a global context, there are trade-offs and difficult dilemmas to be faced, and it is not always clear what to do in any one instance. What are the most effective interventions? Discourse at this level is also concerned with the problems of moral hazard and paternalism. Specifically, how can individuals, governments, international institutions, and NGOs act while preserving others' autonomy and agency?

Shue intervenes in the second discourse when he argues that because individuals cannot provide for all others in need, we must design institutions that do so. Shue focuses on institutions in part for efficiency reasons. "Such duty-respecting institutions can at least partly coordinate the activities of those claiming their rights and those doing their duties. There is no reason this cannot be done across national borders."[8] Shue also wants to allow for individuals to have some respite from what would be burdensome duties. "[W]e are all entitled to some off-duty time whether it improves performance on the job or not ... I am only invoking the familiar point that the duties of ordinary people must be less demanding than the performance of saints and heroes because duty bearers are themselves right-bearers too and may justifiably choose not to be heroes."[9] The second

---

[6] O'Neill, *Bounds of Justice*, p. 197.

[7] Henry Shue, *Basic Rights: Subsistence, Affluence and U.S. Foreign Policy* (Princeton, N.J.: Princeton University Press, 1980), p. 30.

[8] Shue, "Mediating Duties," p. 703.   [9] Ibid., p. 697.

discourse is thus focused on building responsible international institutions and repairing broken ones.[10] Shue acknowledges this problem when he says: "among the most important duties of individual persons will be indirect duties for the design and creation of positive-duty-performing institutions that do not yet exist and for the modification or transformation of existing institutions that now ignore rights and the positive duties that all rights involve."[11] Scholars have suggested ways to democratize international institutions so that they become more transparent, inclusive, and accountable.

The trouble is that individual humans all too often fail to see others' needs, or if they do see those needs they may consider themselves helpless bystanders. Many of the institutions that ought to foster the promotion of moral responsibility beyond borders do so inadequately, and institutions are often structured so that moral deliberation and action are difficult. Once we recognize that something is required of us, we also have to overcome the hurdle of *akrasia*, any weakness of will, to act. Two relatively recent books document the failure of the world's most powerful bystander to either see or act to address grave human rights violations. Samantha Power's *A Problem From Hell* documents American inaction in the face of genocide during the twentieth century and John Shattuck's *Freedom On Fire* is an insider's account of the difficulty in getting the Clinton Administration to act to halt human rights abuses abroad.[12]

The third discourse is provoked by the frustration occasioned by specific cases and conditions. Why is desperate human need not manifest and political will to help others all too frequently lacking? Why is it that people of good will often let others' indifference or greed determine policies? How can humans with resources be transformed from bystanders to heroes, albeit ordinary heroes who can see others as deserving of empathetic and respectful care? How can actions designed to help others be designed so that it really does so? In sum, how shall humans increase our capacities so that we know when to act, how to act, and when to stop

---

[10] See Toni Erskine, ed., *Can Institutions Have Responsibilities? Collective Moral Agency and International Relations* (New York: Palgrave, 2003); Michael Barnett, *Eyewitness to a Genocide: The United Nations and Rwanda* (Ithaca, N.Y.: Cornell University Press, 2002); Peter Uvin, *Aiding Violence: The Development Enterprise in Rwanda* (West Hartford, Conn.: Kumarian Press, 1998); Joseph E. Stiglitz, *Globalization and its Discontents* (New York: Norton, 2002).

[11] Shue, "Mediating Duties," p. 703.

[12] Samantha Power, *A Problem from Hell: America and the Age of Genocide* (New York: Basic Books, 2002); John Shattuck, *Freedom on Fire: Human Rights Wars and America's Response* (Cambridge, Mass.: Harvard University Press, 2003).

acting to promote global basic rights? Put differently, as Robert Goodin asks, how can we "motivate political morality?"[13]

Goodin suggests several strategies for getting people to act morally, even if their first impulse is to act self-interestedly or in ways that harm others. He admits however that his strategies "start from the fact that people have certain firmly held moral intuitions."[14] Indeed, "All of those strategies ... implicitly assume that there is already something in people's motivational make-up—a 'sense of morality'—to which we can appeal when trying to motivate moral beliefs and moral behavior."[15]

My intervention in the third discourse argues that individuals and institutions all too often assume the role of moral bystanders because individual and institutional moral capacities are underdeveloped. I am thus concerned less with specific moral responsibilities than with how to enhance the capacities for individuals and institutions to discover, understand, and act on those responsibilities in particular situations. In other words, while agreement that we have moral responsibilities to distant others (the first discourse) and that appropriate institutional arrangements can help us enact them (the second discourse) are essential, I argue that more fundamental work must occur at the individual and institutional level before individuals will be able to see distant others as deserving of their attention and before institutions will be capable of promoting global basic rights. The bulk of this chapter thus offers an outline of individual and institutional prerequisites for enhancing global moral responsibility.

Before turning to arguments about enhancing individual and institutional capacities, I first describe how discourse in world politics has moved, in an incomplete and halting way, from the first to the second discourse. I then suggest a parallel set of capacities as prerequisites for building more responsible individual actors and social institutions: individuals and institutions must be able to see clearly how their actions affect others, they must be able to empathize, they must be able to reason or deliberate, and they must be able to act. These prerequisites are dispositions (to see, empathize, and act), embedded in general and particular knowledge (of moral language and about historical relations of self and other), supported by procedures for deliberation. I am not saying that individuals and institutions currently entirely lack these capacities; rather I am arguing that these prerequisite capacities can and should be deliberately enhanced.

[13] Robert E. Goodin, *Motivating Political Morality* (Oxford: Blackwell, 1992).
[14] Ibid., p. 153.   [15] Ibid., p. 156.

1. The Rise and Fall of Bystandership

For much of recent history, humans have thought of themselves as citizens of states: many still do. Outside state borders, it was argued, is anarchy and future war. If sovereignty was to be protected, self-help was necessary. In the era of the Treaty of Westphalia, the invocation of sovereignty was also a call and license for bystandership, where bystanders were understood to be neutral, uninvolved, and above all not responsible. Responsible states refrained from intervening in the affairs of other states. Humanitarian assistance was a voluntary act of benevolence.[16] Non-intervention was a virtue.

Yet, only a decade after the end of the Cold War, the notion of legally justified intervention as a self-interested act to preserve international peace and security had given way to the idea of intervention as a moral obligation to others. Domestic political responsibility, defined as democracy and respect for human rights, is now understood by many as a prerequisite of sovereignty. This is most clearly seen in the language of the International Commission on Intervention and State Sovereignty report, *The Responsibility to Protect*: "sovereignty implies a dual responsibility: externally—to respect the sovereignty of other states, and internally, to respect the dignity and basic rights of all the people within the state. In international human rights covenants, in UN practice, and in state practice itself, sovereignty is now understood as embracing this dual responsibility. Sovereignty as responsibility has become the minimum content of good international citizenship."[17] *The Responsibility to Protect* was thus a watershed articulation of a view suggested much earlier by the work of many political theorists and international relations scholars, including Henry Shue and Charles Beitz, working in the cosmopolitan tradition.

Thinking of sovereignty as responsibility, in a way that is being increasingly recognized in state practice, has a threefold significance. First, it implies that the state authorities are responsible for the functions of protecting the safety and lives of citizens and promotion of their welfare. Secondly, it suggests that the national

---

[16] Of course "benevolent" interventions were long part of the discourse of the "civilized" about the "uncivilized." See Gerrit W. Gong, *The Standard of "Civilization" in International Society* (Oxford: Oxford University Press, 1984); Neta C. Crawford, *Argument and Change in World Politics: Ethics, Decolonization and Humanitarian Intervention* (Cambridge: Cambridge University Press, 2002); William Bain, *Between Anarchy and Society: Trusteeship and the Obligations of Power* (Oxford: Oxford University Press, 2003).

[17] International Commission on Intervention and State Sovereignty (ICISS), *The Responsibility to Protect* (Ottawa: International Development Research Centre, 2001), p. 8.

political authorities are responsible to the citizens internally and to the international community through the UN. And thirdly, it means that the agents of state are responsible for their actions; that is to say, they are accountable for their acts of commission and omission.[18]

This view of responsibility implies an obligation to intervene: "sovereign states have a responsibility to protect their own citizens from avoidable catastrophe—from mass murder and rape, from starvation—but ... when they are unwilling or unable to do so, that responsibility must be borne by the broader community of states."[19] In 2004, the UN Secretary-General's High-level Panel on Threats, Challenges and Change articulated a more comprehensive right to intervene. The report's title, *A More Secure World: Our Shared Responsibility*, emphasized global responsibility.

In signing the Charter of the United Nations, States not only benefit from the privileges of sovereignty but also accept its responsibilities. Whatever perceptions may have prevailed when the Westphalian system first gave rise to the notion of State sovereignty, today it clearly carries with it the obligation of a State to protect the welfare of its own peoples and meet its obligations to the wider international community. But history teaches us all too clearly that it cannot be assumed that every State will always be able, or willing, to meet its responsibilities to protect its own people and avoid harming its neighbours.

The responsibility to protect devolves on to multilateral institutions when individual states fail to act to prevent or halt ongoing abuse.

And in those circumstances, the principles of collective security mean that some portion of those responsibilities should be taken up by the international community, acting in accordance with the Charter of the United Nations and the Universal Declaration of Human Rights, to help build the necessary capacity or supply the necessary protection, as the case may be.[20]

Both the High Level Panel and the International Commission articulate procedures for determining resort to humanitarian interventions that echo the "Just War" approach.

In this way, the debate moved from the first discourse about whether, to the second of when and how we are responsible to distant others. When states or international institutions, such as the United Nations or NATO, fail to act to prevent or halt genocide, prevent famine, or rectify gross

---

[18] Ibid., p. 13.   [19] Ibid., p. viii.

[20] United Nations Report of the Secretary-General's High-level Panel on Threats, Challenges and Change, *A More Secure World: Our Shared Responsibility* (New York: United Nations, 2004), p. 17.

inequality we say they have failed, and policy-makers sometimes apologize. The United States, under the Bush Doctrine, also asserted a duty to promote democracy in distant lands—by force if necessary—not only to promote U.S. security, but as a way to better the lives of others. Similarly, social movement activists exhort individuals to take actions that have positive consequences across borders.

2. Developing Both Individual and Institutional Capacities

There is now, arguably, a political consensus on a vision for an obligation to help distant others, articulated most clearly in *The Responsibility to Protect*, and a view about which international institutions should act. Moreover, there is also, arguably, an emerging consensus on the responsibility to prevent injustice and to help repair after harm has been done. Yet it is still unclear how to increase the likelihood that global moral responsibility will be exercised in a timely way and in a manner that is responsive and respectful of those the protectors and promoters of rights aim to help.

Political theorists often separate discussions of how to promote individual and institutional moral responsibility.[21] Christian Barry, for instance, distinguishes between moral responsibilities "held directly to other agents" and responsibilities of justice, "such as those to institute and uphold just institutions, to ensure that they are complied with, or to bring remedy to hardships when they are lacking, are held only indirectly to other agents insofar as they are affected by social rules."[22] For Barry, appeals to justice call on agents to change the rules, while appeals to moral responsibility call on actors to change their behavior within existing rules.

I agree with Barry that individual agents have moral responsibilities and that one must also be concerned with how institutions might or might not be just or create the conditions that foster justice. Nevertheless, agency and structure cannot be easily separated. Unjust institutions and practices are more likely to produce unjust outcomes no matter the best intentions of individuals or collective agents. Conversely, agents with well-developed moral capacities are more likely to produce institutions and develop social practices that are just. As Martha Nussbaum suggests, "institutions do not

---

[21] For a summary, see Toni Erskine, "Introduction: Making Sense of 'Responsibility' in International Relations—Key Questions and Concepts," in *Can Institutions Have Responsibilities?*, ed. Erskine, pp. 1–16.

[22] Christian Barry, "Global Justice: Aims, Arrangements, and Responsibilities," in *Can Institutions Have Responsibilities?*, ed. Toni Erskine, pp. 218–37 at p. 220.

come into being unless people want them, and they can cease to be if people stop wanting them."[23] Thus, while the recent attention to the institutional design of international organizations is appropriate, scholars of world politics should also attend to individual capacities for moral vision and deliberation, and the ways institutions can enhance individual capacities.

The prerequisites for enacting global responsibility at an individual level include dispositions for empathy, respect, critical awareness, and action, and knowledge—both substantive (about moral principles and historical context) and procedural (about how to engage in respectful dialogue and deliberation). At the institutional level, I identify the ways that institutions should support the development of individual capacities and discuss some procedures that could enhance moral deliberation. Only individuals can see the needs of other humans. Whether or not individuals can see others depends a great deal on whether and how institutions inculcate the dispositions necessary for action, systematically acquire and produce the information necessary for deliberation, and provide the space for encounter and deliberation. These individual and institutional capacities for promoting global basic rights must be enhanced in parallel.

3. Enhancing Individual Capacities

By stressing the importance of and potential for enhancing individual capacities for moral vision and action, I am challenging the dominant view that humans have fixed moral capacities. Specifically, the first discourse presumes limited human capacities for empathy and emphasizes a view of humans as self-interested rational actors. The question becomes, how humans define their "self" and their "interests." Narrow definitions of self and interests lead to a harsh Hobbesian world that recreates, in some respects, the state of nature. Communitarianism assumes that humans are primarily moved to act kindly, or at a minimum justly, toward one another because of their pre-existing affective ties. Membership in a particular community is constitutive of their identity and moral obligations. Many stop here and say that since human nature is "fixed" in ways described above, there is no hope for increasing human capacity to care for others.

---

[23] Martha Nussbaum, *Frontiers of Justice: Disability, Nationality, Species Membership* (Cambridge, Mass.: Harvard University Press, 2006), pp. 409–10.

The second discourse also presumes limited human capacities but turns to exhortation and institutional design to ameliorate the effects of those limits. Specifically, cosmopolitans want to overcome barriers by appeals to conscience, or alternatively, to the argument that helping others is in our long-term interest. Others suggest that we might overcome limitations on human capacities—granting the tendency to look after oneself and one's kin first—by essentially blindfolding ourselves. Thus, John Rawls argued, the way to determine what is just is to assume an "original position" where one is blind to one's own particular circumstances and interests. In the original position, according to Rawls, without any knowledge of their starting point or certainty about where they will end up, individuals are likely to choose a social rule or arrangement that is the most just. This is an operationalization of Kant's categorical imperative—to treat others as ends and to enact only those laws to which you yourself could be bound.[24]

The chief complaint of communitarians against cosmopolitans is the abstracted nature of the individuals supposed in this view.[25] Critics of Rawls and the cosmopolitans who rely on his model sometimes stop there, asserting that because it is neither possible nor desirable to forget the self and one's community, *global* justice is therefore impossible.

Toni Erskine responds to these criticisms by suggesting a model of "embedded" cosmopolitanism. We cannot ignore that people are born into and live in communities, but they are also members of many communities, "a web of intersecting and overlapping morally relevant ties."[26] I agree that it is impossible to completely abstract the self from one's circumstances and to assume an original position. And neither is such abstraction desirable. Like Erskine, I think pre-existing ties matter; in any case, they cannot be avoided and there are many of them. But why do these ties and our actual position in the world matter? What do we get from those ties other than (potential) relations of affection and material interests we might like to self-interestedly protect and enlarge? The pre-existing

---

[24] John Rawls, *A Theory of Justice* (Cambridge, Mass.: Harvard University Press, 1971); John Rawls, *The Law of Peoples* (Cambridge, Mass.: Harvard University Press, 1999); Beitz, *Political Theory and International Relations*.

[25] For a summary and discussion of this complaint see O'Neill, *Bounds of Justice*, pp. 120–1 and Toni Erskine, " 'Citizen of Nowhere' or the 'Point Where Circles Intersect'? Impartialist and Embedded Cosmopolitanisms," *Review of International Studies*, 28 (2002), 457–78.

[26] Erskine, " '*Citizen* of Nowhere' or the 'Point Where Circles Intersect'?", p. 474. Sidney Tarrow observes that "What is 'rooted' in this conception is that, as cosmopolitans move physically and cognitively outside their origins, they continue to be linked to place, to the social networks that inhabit that space, and to the resources, experiences, and opportunities that place provides them with"; Sidney Tarrow, *The New Transnational Activism* (Cambridge: Cambridge University Press, 2005), p. 42.

social world that individuals are born into and live in not only entails webs of more or less dense interaction, but it is the nursery of our moral knowledge, moral language, and emotional capacity.

As Barbara Herman notes, "The tendency in modern moral philosophy to think about the developed system of moral motivation as if it were just a robust minimal moral capacity has made it hard to see how central moral learning is to a system of moral motives, or to appreciate the active or normative role moral theory should play in our view of moral development."[27] Participants in the first and second discourses of international ethics also often implicitly assume that adult humans come as fully formed moral agents and/or that after adolescence our capacities for moral reasoning, our "moral development," is fixed at one "level" or another.[28]

But it is important to ask, as Herman does, how our understanding is different if we don't take moral development and moral capacity as a given. Herman suggests that humans develop "moral literacy" which she describes as "a capacity to read and respond to the basic elements of the moral world."[29] We can be more or less literate, and this moral literacy is a prerequisite to moral responsibility. If Herman is right, then we had better start explicitly attending to the development of our moral capacities.

> The formation of motives and motivational structures is the business of morality, of what we might call its "department of education." Its clientele is not restricted to children. If we think of moral education as finished with primary skills acquisition, it can be hard to see that it is part of the nature of moral character that it remains open to change.[30]

I am not saying that we have to substantially change human "nature": most humans have all the raw ingredients we need to become better protectors and promoters of basic rights. I am arguing that it is possible to deliberately enhance features of our already existing, if underdeveloped, human capacities. Individuals with more fully developed moral capacities, who are *skilled* in the dispositions and knowledge required for the promotion of basic rights, will have a better chance of creating more just institutions. There are two aspects of individual capacities that should be

---

[27] Barbara Herman, *Moral Literacy* (Cambridge, Mass.: Harvard University Press, 2007), p. 104.

[28] On theories of moral development see Lawrence Kohlberg, *Essays on Moral Development* (San Francisco: Harper and Row, 1981) and Carol Gilligan, *In a Different Voice* (Cambridge, Mass.: Harvard University Press, 1982).

[29] Herman, *Moral Literacy*, p. 97.   [30] Ibid., p. 104.

deliberately cultivated: *dispositions* for empathy, respect, critical awareness, and action; and substantive and procedural *knowledge*, respectively about moral principles and historical context and about how to engage in respectful dialogue.

3.1. Dispositions

As Herman argues, "Moral education, where it is something beyond inculcating a list of 'dos and don't's,' involves the creation of a sense of self and other that makes shared moral life possible."[31] Scholars talk about the sense of self and other, feelings of respect and compassion, in various ways. Jürgen Habermas emphasizes empathy and moral feeling. "Moral feeling," Habermas argues, plays a role in the "constitution" or understanding of moral phenomena: humans would not understand what is moral without such feelings. "We would not experience certain conflicts of action as morally relevant at all unless we *felt* that the integrity of a person is threatened or violated. Feelings form the basis of our *perception* of something as moral." Habermas argues that a lack of moral feeling is an incapacity, while those who have moral feeling are able to engage in moral reasoning. "Someone who is blind to moral phenomena is blind to feeling. He lacks a sense, as we say, for the suffering of a vulnerable creature who has a claim to have its integrity, both personal and bodily, protected. And this sense is manifestly closely related to sympathy or compassion."[32] Moral feelings help us judge when someone has been harmed or when they need our caring attention. Arne Vetlesen emphasizes the cultivation of "concern" and "attentiveness." Like Habermas, Vetlesen believes that the "sequence of moral performance is set in motion by an act of moral perception."[33] Vetlesen argues that "The empathy at work in moral perception not only turns on the ability to see; it also requires an ability to listen. Both seeing and listening mean paying attention to. They are the characteristics of what might generally be called attentiveness."[34]

Geographic distance is not the primary reason that borders sometimes hinder the ability to see others and to listen empathetically: emotional and

---

[31] Ibid., p. 130.

[32] Jürgen Habermas, "Morality, Society, and Ethics: An Interview with Torben Hviid Nielsen," in *Justification and Application: Remarks on Discourse Ethics* (Cambridge, Mass.: MIT Press, 1993), pp. 147–76 at p. 174.

[33] Arne Johan Vetlesen, *Perception, Empathy and Judgment: An Inquiry into the Preconditions of Moral Performance* (University Park, Pa.: Penn State University Press, 1994), p. 5.

[34] Vetlesen, *Perception, Empathy and Judgment*, p. 8.

cognitive distance create borders and bystanders. Ideologies and mythologies of otherness including racism and social Darwinism, technologies that ease our own labors and distance us from the immediate suffering of others, and bureaucracies that allow the work of helping and harming to be divided among many hands, make it difficult sometimes to see the other and sometimes easy to harm the other without thinking. The tasks are thus first to see how we are related to and affect others, and then to feel. As Robert Lifton's research on Nazi doctors and other perpetrators of atrocities shows, those who harm, or permit such harm to occur, often cut themselves off from their feelings and experience "psychic numbing" and dissociation.[35]

Brain research and everyday experience suggests just how hard it is to empathize with those whom we fear. Human biology (and current institutions) are in some ways optimized to both detect threats and increase our vigilance toward others. The areas of our brains that engage in complex moral reasoning (specifically the pre-frontal cortex) can be overridden when the areas of our brain that process and moderate fear (the amygdala and hippocampus) are overwhelmed by that emotion.[36] Traumatized individuals and groups find it difficult to be empathetic toward those who are perceived as different. Fear reduction is thus an essential element in promoting individual empathy and other-regarding attentiveness.[37]

Closely related to moral feeling and empathy is the capacity that Habermas, borrowing from G. H. Mead, calls ideal role-taking: actors should be able to step out of their own perspective in order to see the world from another person's perspective. This form of reason is not divorced from feeling.[38]

Ideal role taking has come to signify a procedural type of justification. The cognitive operations it requires are demanding. Those operations in turn are internally linked with motives and emotional dispositions and attitudes like empathy. Where socio-cultural distance is a factor, concern for the fate of one's neighbor—who more

---

[35] See Robert J. Lifton, *The Nazi Doctors: Medical Killing and the Psychology of Genocide* (London: Macmillan, 1986); Robert J. Lifton and Eric Markusen, *The Genocidal Mentality: Nazi Holocaust and Nuclear Threat* (New York: Basic Books, 1990).

[36] On the biology of fear and empathy, see Donald W. Pfaff, *The Neuroscience of Fair Play: Why We (Usually) Follow the Golden Rule* (New York: Dana Press, 2007); Bruce S. McEwen, "Protective and Damaging Effects of Stress Mediators," in *Foundations in Social Neuroscience*, ed. John T. Cacioppo et al. (Cambridge, Mass.: MIT Press, 2002), pp. 1127–40.

[37] On the other hand, neuroscience demonstrates how flexible our brains are—although all things are not possible, we can literally re-wire our brains on a cellular level, not simply through traumatic experiences, but through learning, and even meditation.

[38] In *Moral Literacy*, Herman argues that Kant should be read this way as well.

often than not is anything but close by—is a necessary emotional prerequisite for the cognitive operations expected of participants in discourse.[39]

3.2. Substantive and Procedural Knowledge

Of course a disposition toward empathy and respect may not, alone, facilitate a leap from indifferent bystandership. Substantive and procedural knowledge is also required. The lifeworld, or "horizon of shared, unpro_blematic beliefs," of every culture has a moral language and procedures for moral reasoning.[40] By substantive knowledge I mean both an understanding of moral language and moral traditions of one's own lifeworld, and concrete historical knowledge. Procedural knowledge is an understanding of how to engage in moral deliberation with others, including those from different lifeworlds. These moral structures include the values individuals hold, the roles they adopt, and the practices they consider appropriate. The question is how well individuals understand this background discourse and how well prepared they are to engage in moral reasoning.

The first step in developing the substantive knowledge that complements dispositions to empathy and ideal role-taking is an education in the moral traditions of one's culture, specifically in the vocabulary and structures of belief that comprise a moral language—the values and principles that people in communities use to make their moral world. These are the normative moral structures within which individuals exist and from which they reason. It is also important that this knowledge include a critical perspective on one's own "lifeworld"—a self-reflectiveness of one's causal, identity, and normative beliefs. In this way, moral literacy is destabilized and disoriented in the sense that the "normal" is not taken for granted: the moral world could be otherwise.

Thus, the second step in developing substantive moral knowledge is an education in other moral traditions. This comparative perspective serves two functions—enhancing understanding and empathy. Since private and public moral reasoning depends on comprehensible and meaningful communication within and across communities, including across different lifeworld assumptions, respectful engagement with those from different moral traditions indeed depends on learning the moral language of others.

---

[39] Jürgen Habermas, "Moral Consciousness and Communicative Action," in *Moral Consciousness and Communicative Action* (Cambridge, Mass.: MIT Press, 1990), pp. 116–94 at p. 182.

[40] See Jürgen Habermas, *Between Facts and Norms: Contributions to a Discourse Theory of Law and Democracy* (Cambridge, Mass.: MIT Press, 1996), p. 22.

The emotional distance that sometimes hinders empathetic understanding may be a function of the clash of actual or perceived differences in moral language. In this way, specific moral knowledge can help foster the development of empathy.

Individuals also need specific historical knowledge of how the present world came to be arranged as it is. Substantive knowledge should thus also include an education in history. Such historical perspective will not only show how relationships became the way they are but will facilitate the development of a critical self-understanding—a realization that the material world could be otherwise. An individual's particular situation is not simply the outcome of their efforts, but is also both accidental and structurally produced. Historical structures of wealth provided or denied certain endowments to individuals with which they could act, while contemporary relationships can exacerbate or ameliorate inequalities. As Shue suggests, "it is groundless to think that whatever international distribution turns up over the course of history is fully just." Indeed, Shue argues, "we have lots of good reasons to think that the existing distributions of wealth and resources are morally arbitrary at best and the result of systematic exploitation at worst."[41]

The self-conscious individual, who is critically aware not only of their normative beliefs but of their social position, is more likely to be aware of the inequalities that made their present position more or less powerful and which gives them greater or lesser advantages in ongoing and future interactions. Self-conscious individuals will also know that a contemporary agreement or set of relations may appear to be fair yet may be rooted in background circumstances that are unjust. As Shue highlights,

[I]t is perfectly possible for an instance of internal injustice to be the result of background injustice: someone may in fact accept unconscionable terms in an agreement because an independent background injustice has, for example, left her with no good alternatives to the agreement. Without the agreement she will be even worse off than she will be with the agreement ... but the reasons she will be worse off without the agreement is a prior injustice, independent of the agreement in question.[42]

In sum, like Rawls, I want individuals to imagine that their social, economic, and political position could be otherwise. Unlike Rawls, I want

---

[41] Henry Shue, "The Unavoidability of Justice," in *The International Politics of the Environment: Actors, Interests and Institutions*, ed. Andrew Hurrell and Benedict Kingsbury (Oxford: Oxford University Press, 1992), pp. 373–97 at p. 386.

[42] Shue, "The Unavoidability of Justice," p. 387.

individuals to know their personal position and to understand how their situation, and those around them, was made possible. How was wealth accumulated? How was social capital acquired? Who suffered and suffers so that others live well? How do historically specific structures produce current dispositions, assets, and starting points. In other words, humans ought to be able to tell causal stories about their relation to others and envision alternative outcomes.[43]

Substantive moral knowledge must be supplemented by procedural knowledge. Humans must not only be able to put chains of reasons together for themselves and to be self-conscious about why and how they value what they do, they must be able to listen to and make moral arguments, and form collective judgments. This capacity can be nurtured through an examination of case studies, so that individuals have systematic exposure to moral reasoning, and also by training individuals in Habermasian "discourse ethics."

Discourse ethics is a formal "procedure for testing the validity of norms that are being proposed and hypothetically considered for adoption."[44] In this ideal speech situation, actors eschew strategic action (coercion) and come to an uncoerced understanding with others. One tries to convince the other through the "force of the better argument." For Habermas, the key to legitimacy is rational argumentation:

[T]he claim that a norm lies equally in the interest of everyone has the sense of rational acceptability: all those possibly affected should be able to accept the norm on the basis of good reasons. But this can become clear only under the pragmatic conditions of rational discourses in which the only thing that counts is the compelling force of the better argument based upon the relevant information.[45]

But humans do not come into the world knowing how to engage in discourse ethics: individuals must be taught how to engage in moral argument.

The dispositions and substantive knowledge that I have argued should be cultivated enable the use of discourse ethical procedures, while the use of discourse ethical procedures enables the acquisition of substantive

---

[43] Narratives about commodity production and exchange may emphasize free markets and equal exchange or histories can include narratives of unequal exchange, extraction by theft, and brutal exploitation of labor.

[44] Jürgen Habermas, "Discourse Ethics: Notes on a Program of Philosophical Justification," in *Moral Consciousness and Communicative Action* (Cambridge, Mass.: MIT Press, 1990), pp. 43–115 at p. 103. Richard Shapcott argues in *Justice, Community and Dialogue in International Relations* (Cambridge: Cambridge University Press, 2001) that hermeneutics is a better approach than discourse ethics.

[45] Habermas, *Between Facts and Norms*, p. 103.

knowledge and the cultivation of the dispositions. Ideal role-taking, adopting another person's perspective, is essential for discourse ethics because otherwise we cannot know whether the norms we claim as valid for all those who are affected by them are actually valid (justification). Ideal role-taking enables empathy: "the continued existence of this communication community ... demands of all its members an act of selfless empathy through ideal role taking."[46] Habermas argues that "at the very least, empathy—the ability to project oneself across cultural distances into alien and at first sight incomprehensible conditions of life, behavioral predispositions, and interpretive perspectives—is an emotional prerequisite for ideal role taking, which requires everyone to take the perspective of all others."[47] Self-reflectiveness about the moral and material world aids in ideal role-taking:

To view something from the moral point of view means that we do not elevate our own self-understanding and world view to the standard by which we universalize a mode of action but instead test its generalizability also from the perspective of others. It is unlikely that one would be able to perform this demanding cognitive feat without generalized compassion, sublimated into the capacity to empathize with others, that points beyond affective ties to immediate reference persons and opens our eyes to "difference," to the uniqueness and inalienable otherness of the other.[48]

In this way, the ideal speech situation is not between individuals who are blind to their position and interests. Indeed, it is just the opposite. Individuals should be critically self-conscious of their own beliefs and position, at the same time they are able to listen to and argue with others.

The dispositions for empathy and respect, the substantive knowledge of different moral traditions and causal relationships, and the knowledge of procedures for moral deliberation are not enough to promote global basic rights if individuals fail to use their capacities. The final dispositional prerequisite at the individual level is thus the ability and willingness to act. This ability to act could be rooted in habits but it must also be a cultivated disposition to stand up against moral wrongs. If more of us are educated in the necessity of action, "heroism" would be less exceptional.

In sum, the prerequisites of moral responsibility at the individual level include the ability to see, feel, think, and act in relation to another no

---

[46] Habermas, "Morality, Society, and Ethics," p. 154.
[47] Ibid., p. 174.   [48] Ibid., pp. 174–5.

matter their distance from us. In *Moral Boundaries*, Joan Tronto writes about four elements of care: "caring about, noticing the need to care in the first place; taking care of, assuming responsibility for care; care-giving, the actual work of care that needs to be done; and care receiving, the response of that which is cared for to the care."[49] Tronto then articulates four ethical elements of care: attentiveness, responsibility, competence, and responsiveness. The cultivation of dispositions of empathy, respect, and action, and substantive and procedural knowledge of moral traditions and discourse ethics, support and amplify Tronto's ethic of care.

4. Social Capacity: Institutional Prerequisites

Three aspects of social institutions relevant for increasing moral capacities are emphasized—structural, developmental, and supportive. The first aspect is structural: is the institution organized to provide relevant information, foster deliberation, and include wide participation? Scholars of world politics have paid significant attention to these organizational and procedural aspects of institutional structure, with the aim of producing organizations that are not only more efficient but also understood to be legitimate. Specifically, there are case studies and proposals for democratizing deliberative institutions and international organizations by promoting transparency, accountability, and wide participation as organizational norms.[50]

I agree with the emphasis on organization and procedure. Almost all organizations systematically acquire and produce the information necessary for decision-making, and provide a space for encounter and deliberation. It is vital that the moral dimensions of these latter activities be made explicit and enhanced. This is in part because in complex and interdependent systems, such as the contemporary political and economic world, it is extremely difficult for humans, by themselves, to figure out the scope of their negative and positive moral responsibilities and how to enact them. Moreover, humans must determine their moral responsibilities in

---

[49] Joan Tronto, *Moral Boundaries: A Political Argument for an Ethic of Care* (New York: Routledge, 1993), p. 127.

[50] See, for instance, Barry, "Global Justice"; Rodger A. Paine and Nayef H. Samhat, *Democratizing Global Politics: Discourse Norms, International Regimes, and Political Community* (New York: SUNY Press, 2004); Ann Florini, *The Coming Democracy: New Rules for Running a New World* (Washington, D.C.: Brookings Institution Press, 2005); Heikki Patomäki and Teivo Teivainen, *A Possible World: Democratic Transformations of Global Institutions* (London: Zed Books, 2004).

dialogue with others who will be, in some instances, participants in the co-creation of a just world, and at other times, the beneficiaries of benevolence. Further, we are concerned with accountability and fairness—namely whether the institution is organized to act in ways that are both fair for the members of the institution and respectful of those who are the potential beneficiaries of action. Are burdens distributed fairly? Is there a way for those affected by a decision to give testimony about its impact?

The second, developmental, aspect is much less the focus of contemporary scholarship. It focuses specifically on how institutions help us care for our basic human needs and socialize us into our roles as moral agents. Institutions inculcate the dispositions and knowledge necessary for moral deliberation and action. "Attentiveness ... does not rise in a vacuum; it needs to be learned, cultivated, maintained."[51] Scholars of world politics have not yet adequately examined how to ensure that the institutions which care for and educate us enable individuals to become better moral actors. Indeed the discussion of individual capacity above assumed that institutions foster and sustain individual moral capacity and make their exercise more or less possible. But unless we focus more specifically on how this is done, there is no guarantee that institutions will reliably perform this role.

How can institutions help individuals enhance their capacities to see how their actions affect others, empathize, reason, and deliberate, and ultimately act in ways that are morally responsible? Before and during our earliest socialization humans must have their basic biological and emotional needs met. Our brains, including the capacity for reasoning, cannot fully develop without nutrition and basic education.[52] Our ability to connect and empathize cannot fully develop without love and examples of empathy. The development of individual moral capacities is stunted in conditions of poverty and traumatic fear. Thus, the care of children, from pre-natal nutrition to early childhood education and through late adolescence, is an essential step for the formation of individual moral capacity. As these children and their parents cannot create the conditions for quality care on their own, the provision of basic child welfare and medical care becomes an institutional responsibility. Socialization can only "stick" if

---

[51] Vetlesen, *Perception, Empathy and Judgment*, p. 9.

[52] Amartya Sen and Martha Nussbaum have written eloquently about the capabilities required for full human flourishing. These include the physical capacities as well as emotional and reasoning capabilities. See Amartya Sen, *Development as Freedom* (New York: Knopf, 1999) and Martha Nussbaum, *Women and Human Development: The Capabilities Approach* (Cambridge: Cambridge University Press, 2000).

there is a human with basic capacities to stick to. Thus, Joan Tronto's emphasis on care-*giving* is vital not only in and of itself, but because it is important for enhancing the capacities essential for the development of moral responsibility: only the cared for can be capable of fully participating in responsible moral deliberation.

The institutions that care for and socialize humans are first our families and then, depending on the social setting, our extended family, schools, religious institutions, and public and private associations.[53] These institutions often reinforce communitarian identities and narrow notions of relations to self and other, but they are also sometimes the incubators of cosmopolitan identity and moral literacy broadly conceived. Educational and cultural institutions set the deliberative context long before publics and elites ever get to respond to a particular crisis. Thus, as Nussbaum argues, "a society aspiring to justice ... must devote sustained attention to the moral sentiments and their cultivation—in child development, in public education, in public rhetoric, in the arts."[54] So, our institutions should provide for the basic needs of individuals and then help citizens learn the dispositions and substantive and procedural knowledge that will enable them to become attentive to others and morally responsible actors.

The institutions within which we conduct our lives can be more or less supportive of moral vision and moral deliberation.[55] Institutions can help us see the other, or blind us; they can help us hear the other, or silence us and thereby make us deaf or at least hard of hearing; institutions can provide space to reason, or they can shut down opportunities for discussion; they can help us organize and act, or they can constrain our action. The third, supportive, aspect of enhancing institutional capacity thus focuses on how institutions can support the full use of individual capacities.

Most advocates of democratizing institutions argue that institutions should be structured so that collective *deliberation* (not simply vote-counting) occurs, so that decisions are open to wide participation, and so that institutional procedures and decisions are transparent and accountable.[56] It must be admitted, however, that most institutions are designed to allow a minimum of deliberation: we should simply follow the rules and hew to standard operating procedures. Rationality of a narrow instrumental

---

[53] This web of institutions is thus wider than but inclusive of civil society.

[54] Nussbaum, *Frontiers of Justice*, p. 414.

[55] See Stephen L. Elkin and Karol Edward Soltan, *Citizen Competence and Democratic Institutions* (University Park, Pa.: Pennsylvania State University Press, 1999).

[56] See Iris Marion Young, *Inclusion and Democracy* (Oxford: Oxford University Press, 2000).

sort is prized. Individual agency, including moral agency, is often highly circumscribed. Public institutions and the public sphere, locally and globally, ought to be venues not simply for bargaining or voting, but for moral discourse and deliberation. Institutions ought also to be structured so that it is possible for individuals to give testimony about the effects of actions and systems. Inclusion is also about including other forms of communication beyond "rational" argumentation, as much as it about who is allowed to speak.[57] Institutions should be venues for both telling and hearing "sad and sentimental" stories.[58] The more robust institutions are in this respect, allowing all aspects of human expression, the more likely that moral responsibility will be understood and practiced. Specific historical knowledge and contemporary testimony can help shrink the distance between us and them, so that it is not possible to tell a simple story of laziness, corruption, or incompetence. If deliberative venues are open to the testimony of those affected, it might not be so easy to endorse solutions that prescribe "austerity," "belt-tightening" or the "private sector."

Contemporary institutional design often assumes that individual agents enjoy equal starting points despite the fact that institutions and individuals have unequal endowments and starting points due to pre-existing inequality in historical and contemporary relations of injustice. Historically disadvantaged groups are disadvantaged for historical reasons—wealth (resources and labor) was taken without due compensation so that others might become rich. As Shue argues in *Basic Rights*, systemic deprivations are caused by economic policies and plans that are designed to produce wealth for some and these deprivations can only be eliminated by "eliminating the strategy that requires them."[59] Once we grant that not everyone has the same starting point, and moreover, that our unequal starting points are the result of systemic deprivation, we would be obliged to alter practices that yield ongoing exploitation and make repairs that begin to ameliorate past harm. An eye toward inclusiveness and Barry's "responsibilities of justice" suggests that resources be redirected to those whose labors made contemporary institutions as rich and powerful as they are.

It may take a long time to repair these underlying inequalities, so institutions should be designed to help individuals who currently lack

---

[57] Young, *Inclusion and Democracy*.

[58] Richard Rorty, "Human Rights, Rationality, and Sentimentality," in *On Human Rights: The Oxford Amnesty Lectures 1993*, ed. Stephen Shute and Susan Hurley (New York: Basic Books, 1993), pp. 111–34.

[59] Shue, *Basic Rights*, p. 47.

the capacity to engage with equal resources. I have in mind something like the notion of the "reasonable accommodation" to disabilities called for in the Americans with Disabilities Act or the sliding scales that we see in some fees for lower-income individuals. In other words, at the same time that individual capacities are enhanced, the structural barriers to individual participation should be lowered, for example by increasing investment in public education and social services so that individuals who are members of groups that are historically disadvantaged can have the capacity and opportunity to participate. But more than that, rather like how ramps for wheelchair access can make a public building accessible not only to those in wheelchairs, but also to small children and those pushing strollers, regulations requiring open meetings, and accessible public forums can make the public sphere more accessible to non-elites.

5. Toward Global Responsibility

When we recall systems of great injustice, or practices which were intended to and succeeded in creating great harm—such as the Holocaust, apartheid, and racial slavery—we often wonder how it is that people could have done what they did. How could the individuals and institutions that could have acted to halt the Holocaust or the genocide in Rwanda not have done more? What was wrong with those people or those institutions? How could bystanders who failed to speak and act in the days before a crisis not be complicit? We assume that humans could have done otherwise and chose not to.

Indeed, we know that some individuals do act responsibly and we can name some of them—William Wilberforce worked to end the British slave trade; Oskar Schindler saved Jews during the Holocaust; Mother Theresa worked to alleviate poverty; and Roméo Dallaire tried to halt the Rwandan genocide. Highlighting their exceptional status, Samantha Power calls those who act in contexts of brutality "upstanders," and Ervin Staub calls them, "heroic helpers." Staub, himself a Holocaust survivor, argues that "We cannot expect bystanders to sacrifice their lives for others. But we can expect individuals, groups, and nations to act early along a continuum of destruction, when danger to themselves is limited, and the potential exists for inhibiting the evolution of increasing destructiveness." Staub wants passive bystanders to become active bystanders—indeed, if we heed him, there would be no moral bystanders.

This will happen if people—children, adults, whole societies—develop an awareness of their common humanity with other people, as well as of the psychological processes in themselves that turn them against others. Institutions and modes of functioning can develop that embody a shared humanity and make exclusion from the moral realm more difficult. Healing from past victimization, building systems of positive reciprocity, creating cross-cultural relations between groups, and developing joint projects and superordinate goals can promote the evolution of caring and nonaggressive persons and societies.[60]

There are cases where more than a few "heroic helpers" acted together. There were *movements* to end slavery, ameliorate the conditions of colonialism, and end apartheid. There are international institutions that coordinate sometimes generous responses to famines and the plight of refugees displaced by armed conflict; there are non-governmental organizations focused on ameliorating poverty, hunger, and ill health. Our human natures do not have to change. The capacity to make manifest our latent moral concern is always nascent.

Staub writes that, "Heroic helpers are not born."[61] Nor is the everyday capacity for moral reflection and responsibility of the sort that obviates the need for heroism. Our capacities for recognizing human suffering, for acting responsibly, and for structuring responsible institutions must be deliberately developed and nurtured.

There are many reasons why attentiveness to others is difficult to achieve, one of which is the sense that we are not causally responsible for the situations of others. After all, much of what happened to make "them" how they are was put into a chain of causality long ago, sometimes so long ago, it is hard to remember why things are the way they are. As Rachel Manley writes, "Time shrinks time. Old time becomes simply a number of things we know, a set of images that are one horizon, like the entire world reduced to a map and the years to one day."[62] Distance and difference may also flatten the others' features and obscure our connection to them. In being critically aware of ourselves and in listening to others, it is possible to fill in the time and the distance that creates borders and bystanders; one is able to make close what is distant, and to make concrete and specific what is abstract.

---

[60] Ervin Staub, *The Psychology of Good and Evil: Why Children, Adults, and Groups Help and Harm Others* (Cambridge: Cambridge University Press, 2003), p. 318.

[61] Staub, *The Psychology of Good and Evil*, p. 315.

[62] Rachel Manley, *Slipstream: A Daughter Remembers* (Toronto: Random House, 2000), p. 68.

The prerequisites for developing global moral responsibility that I have outlined are intended to increase the likelihood that we will act to promote global basic rights and the quality of mercy and care individuals and institutions will display. I emphasized the importance of deliberately cultivating dispositions and knowledge at the individual level. At the institutional level, I underscored the importance of designing institutions that are capable of truly democratic deliberation and that are able to support individual participants in deliberation and action.

I also emphasized the important role of institutions in providing for individual basic needs—basic welfare, security, and socialization. These needs must be met for individuals to be able to care about others; it is institutions that reliably create the context for the broad provision of those needs. In stressing the role of institutions in developing prerequisites for individual moral capacity, I have thus, in a way, returned to my starting point, Shue's argument that basic rights—security and subsistence—are essential prerequisites for the protection of other rights. Does that mean we are in a vicious circle—that we cannot make the good, understood as the guarantee of basic rights, without already having the good, the provision of basic needs? No. Rather, the necessity of a context of subsistence and security for promoting the development of individual moral capacity suggests the possibility of gradually ratcheting upward spirals of security, subsistence, empathy, and caring. Conversely, there is the potential for downward spirals of fear and indifference if we fail to cultivate individual and institutional capacities.

8

Global Power and Economic Justice

Richard W. Miller

The story of the last three decades of philosophical discussion of global poverty could be told as a quest narrative. The Holy Grail, Golden Fleece, and Ithaka is the establishment of a vast, demanding, as yet unmet responsibility of people in developed countries to give up advantages in the interest of needy people in developing countries. Moral reasons are to be found showing that there is a transnational duty whose fulfillment would transform people's lives for the better throughout the developing world and would require doing much more than is done now to improve their prospects, including measures with substantial costs, if these are needed to achieve the global transformation.

Henry Shue's *Basic Rights* is an especially influential, enduring, and insightful effort to reach this goal, notable for resourceful arguments that appeal to deep humane concerns, forthrightness about the potential demands of the duties it imposes, and cogent interweaving of the institutional and personal aspects of suffering. Yet, despite admiration of the resourcefulness and insight of Shue and other leaders of the quest, some of us questers have lost faith in this and other established expeditions. I will sketch some reasons for discouragement, and then lay out another approach, which could reach the goal if the old paths are blocked. The old paths tend to avoid all but the most obvious and generic characterizations of transnational relationships. The new approach relies on specific characterizations, established through empirical scrutiny of current transnational activity, in arguing that people in developed countries have a demanding responsibility to transform their current relationships to people in developing countries in order to avoid taking advantage of them. This is how to bridge the gap between the sadness of the fact that so many suffer from unmet desperate needs and a demanding duty, pervasive in developed countries, to help foreigners to meet them.

1. Paths and Obstacles

While a route through general beneficence was certainly worth exploring, the duty of responsiveness to neediness as such, apart from specific relationships, seems too moderate and flexible to sustain a vast, demanding responsibility to the global poor. On one moderate account, which I have defended, one must display an underlying concern for neediness sufficiently great that more concern would impose a significant risk of worsening one's life if one met one's other responsibilities. But there is no duty to have any greater concern, and one has a broad prerogative to contribute to worthy causes close to one's heart that do not provide the most relief of the world's gravest needs. Deep background facts of human action and vulnerability generate an additional duty to rescue those in imminent physical peril encountered close at hand. Peter Singer's drowning toddler must be saved. But this duty of nearby rescue is a morally compelling policy for pursuing the general task of beneficence in specific circumstances, owing to considerations of coordination, motivation, and solidarity specially linked to close encounter; it is not a guide to our responsibility to help people in peril near and far.[1]

On a different route, worldwide economic interdependence has been used as a basis for extending demanding duties toward disadvantaged compatriots to the disadvantaged of the world at large. But the mere fact of commerce had no such moral impact on relations among Bronze Age tribes. Why should it among us now? In general, the mere fact of commerce seems to generate strong obligations of honesty and mild obligations to accept delayed payment from someone going through a rough patch, but not demanding duties of concern.[2]

[1] See Richard W. Miller, "Beneficence, Duty and Distance," *Philosophy & Public Affairs*, 32 (2004), 357–83, for detailed arguments in support of these limits to general beneficence. In "The Possibility of Special Duties," *Canadian Journal of Philosophy*, 16 (1986), 651–76, Philip Pettit and Robert Goodin emphasize the coordinative benefits of shared norms allocating special responsibilities, including duties of rescue. Singer's powerful argument from the obligation to rescue the drowning toddler was first presented in "Famine, Affluence and Morality," *Philosophy & Public Affairs*, 1 (1972), 229–43 at p. 235.

[2] Charles R. Beitz, *Political Theory and International Relations*, rev. edn. (Princeton, N.J.: Princeton University Press 1999; 1st edn. 1979), pt III, and Thomas Pogge, *Realizing Rawls* (Ithaca, N.Y.: Cornell University Press, 1989), pt III, are incisive, influential examples of the extrapolation of demanding obligations toward compatriots to all associates in global economic cooperation.

Basic Rights includes a notable effort to respond to this doubt, connecting the mere fact of global commerce with a potentially stringent duty of concern. The protection of property from those who come to take it is an essential part of commerce. But, Shue notes, a desperately needy person has no duty to let himself deteriorate and die out of respect for a set of social institutions that prohibits him from taking what he needs to survive. Shue treats this claim about morally acceptable conduct by a have-not as reason to condemn haves for maintaining social protection of property without supporting social guarantees of subsistence—even if those guarantees would require them to sacrifice all goals less fundamental than the fulfillment of basic rights.[3] But it is not clear that the moral permission to try to take is enough to make any such effort to keep immoral. In previous eras, pastoral nomads have coped with recurrent famines through raids on more prosperous, settled agrarian societies, and perhaps this was not wrong. Still, the farmers do not seem to have been wrong to have resisted tribute that would have reduced their higher standard of living, so that they could no longer use fruits of their labor to successfully and enjoyably pursue worthwhile goals with which they identified. By the same token, people in developed countries need not be wrong to refuse to make significant sacrifices to satisfy subsistence needs in Bangladesh just because Bangladeshis would not be wrong to launch an expeditionary force to extract this concession, if, miraculously, they could hope for successful taking without excessive violence.

Disappointment with these arguments for obligations to help creates hope for guidance by the sign-post, "negative responsibility." In this guidance, people in developed countries are said to impose severe poverty on people in developing countries, acquiring a vast, unmet responsibility to repair the harm and avoid further imposition. The looming obstacle here is the need to explain how poverty is imposed in a way that generates the responsibility. The imposition is sometimes identified with participation in global institutions under which dire poverty foreseeably persists and could be eliminated by institutional change. But if the earlier route through general beneficence was blocked, it is not clear why the foreseeable persistence of the burden should generate the duty to lift it. Duties not to make matters worse for others might seem to provide an alternative route to the violated negative responsibility. But the question, "Worse than what?", stands in the way. "Worse than what we affluent people

---

[3] See Henry Shue, *Basic Rights: Subsistence, Affluence and U.S. Foreign Policy*, 2nd edn. (Princeton, N.J.: Princeton University Press, 1996; 1st edn. 1980), pp. 24, 118, 125.

could have provided" gets us back to general beneficence. "Worse than what would have happened otherwise" often leads to a swamp of inconclusive speculations, without identifying a sufficient basis for moral condemnation. That Zambia's copper-based economy was much worse off than it would have been on account of the development of fiber optics did not make that development wrong. "Worse than what moral responsibility requires" certainly describes negligence that ought to be avoided, but provides no distinctive guidance as to how a vast, unmet, transnational responsibility is to be established.[4]

Such doubts put giving up and going home on the questers' agenda. But moral common sense offers some hope. In ordinary moral thinking, demanding duties of concern are responsibilities to others in specific relationships, for example, children, parents, friends, compatriots, and promisees. Extremely diverse in the nature of the underlying relationship, the values expressed, and the kind of concern owed, none of these duties is, as a whole, a responsibility to avoid worsening. Perhaps the quest will succeed through multiple expeditions that establish the existence of specific current transnational relationships and duties to live up to them.

Three types of interaction among developed and developing countries seem especially promising terrain for this multiple quest. They involve ways in which individuals, firms, or governments in developed countries currently take advantage of people in developing countries, and ought, instead, to pursue interactions based on genuine cooperation. In taking

---

[4] The turn to negative responsibility has been powerfully advocated by Thomas Pogge, in work including: "A Global Resources Dividend," in *The Ethics of Consumption*, ed. David Crocker and Toby Linden (New York: Rowman and Littlefield, 1998); *World Poverty and Human Rights* (Cambridge: Polity Press, 2002), especially chapter 8; and "Severe Poverty as a Violation of Negative Duties," *Ethics and International Affairs*, 19 (2005), 55–83. Along with the generic charge that dire poverty foreseeably persists under current institutions and would be dramatically less under different arrangements, his trenchant indictments include specific charges of current violations of negative responsibility, appealing to such obvious facts as developed countries' past engagement in bloody conquests, the unequal distribution of the natural resources over which governments claim sovereign control, and the lucrative support that tyrannies derive from sales of natural resources. These specific charges of immoral worsening inspire further questions about processes and benchmarks, for example: "Is it wrong to make good use of advantages due to old wrongs of conquest committed by long dead people from one's country?"; "How different would the current global distribution of advantages and disadvantages be in the absence of those old wrongs?"; "Why should the full current value of a natural resource be equally shared among people whose technologies and activities make very different contributions to its value?"; "When is the monitoring of external commerce to influence poor countries' governance an excessive demand on external agents, or an excessive intrusion into local political processes?"; and "How much better off would resource-rich poor countries be if they were bereft of lucrative resources?" While some currently unmet duties of limited scope, such as a commitment not to purchase natural resources from ferociously predatory tyrannies, might well survive such scrutiny, it is by no means clear that a duty to lift pervasive burdens of global destitution would emerge.

advantage of someone, one derives a benefit from her inferior capacity to pursue her interests in the relevant interaction, in a way that shows inadequate regard for her autonomy and equal worth. The proviso about disregard is important, since using another's weakness to get one's way, while always in need of justification, can be justified by further considerations. Sometimes the costs of governing one's conduct by a prohibition against using others' weaknesses, in the case at hand or similar cases in general, would be too great. A firm that strives never to take advantage of special pressures on others to obtain concessions will probably sink under the burden of both competitive loss and the distraction of monitoring its commitment. Sometimes, a rule forbidding the use of others' weakness would interfere with efficiencies on which weaker parties depend, or infantilize them. Ordinarily, condemning the stronger tennis-player for taking advantage of a weakness in the backhand at the other side of the net shows contempt for the autonomy of the weaker player. In addition, manipulating weakness is sometimes the only way, given other parties' short-sightedness or moral insensitivity, to establish arrangements that would result from responsible deliberation based on shared values.

However, all of these reasons to permit some to use others' weaknesses can be blocked in transnational economic and political interaction. The prosperity and power of people, governments, and firms in developed countries block claims that their losses would be excessive. Relevant alternatives to the current manipulation of weaknesses of the global poor advance their interests and respect their autonomy. The global power structure creates outcomes utterly different from respectful coming-to-terms. In the three crucial forms of transnational interaction, the concern not to use weakness is decisive. Enormous unmet responsibilities to help the global poor are generated by activities that go well beyond the mere existence of global commerce yet are not well-characterized as imposing poverty on the global poor.

The first is a current feature of transnational production and exchange, giving substance to a charge of exploitation. People in developed countries take advantage of people in developing countries by deriving benefits from bargaining weakness due to their desperate neediness. To express appreciation of their equal worth and respect for their autonomy, people in developed countries must be willing to use the benefits to relieve the destitution that underlies the weakness.

In the second type of interaction, governments reach agreements over the institutional framework of global commerce in ways that justify a charge of inequity. The major developed countries, led by the United

States, take advantage of bargaining weaknesses of the citizenries of developing countries in order to shape arrangements far more advantageous to developed countries than reasonable deliberations would sustain. This creates a duty of a citizen of one of the countries that take advantage (especially pressing in the United States) to support measures that reasonable deliberations would yield.

Finally, some developed countries have foreign power far exceeding the shaping of a few international agreements. Above all, the United States exerts influence that makes "the American empire" an apt metaphor, taking advantage of other countries' difficulties in going against its will. This "imperial" process generates demanding responsibilities to foreigners whose lives are shaped, responsibilities reflecting both resemblances to and differences from the shaping of citizens' lives by a modern state.[5]

2. Globalization and Exploitation

First, for all its ambiguities, "exploitation" points to substantial, unmet responsibilities in global commerce. In some interactions, one party extracts a benefit from another because of the other's inferior bargaining power due to desperate need, extracting the benefit in a way that displays inadequate regard for her equal worth and inadequate appreciation of her capacity for choice. Then, in one strong, especially morally freighted sense of the term, he exploits her. The moralizing rider, specifying disrespect, is not redundant, because of the possibilities of further justification previously noted. Presumably, Nike in Thailand extracts a benefit from the desperation of women escaping rural poverty. Both self-respect and pressing responsibilities toward children or parents make the escape from dire into lesser poverty urgent for many of these sellers of labor, weakening the bargaining power of each. But perhaps if Nike did not take advantage of bargaining weakness due to desperate neediness to some significant extent, the interests of the desperately needy would be undermined, through slower growth of employment opportunities. Consideration of this countervailing reason might show that Nike's taking advantage of the bargaining weakness of its Thai stitchers (to some significant extent) does not disregard the worth of their lives and of their capacity for choice. Perhaps Nike takes advantage of their weakness without taking advantage of them.

---

[5] The derivation of responsibilities from these and other transnational relationships is developed in much greater detail in my *Globalizing Justice: The Ethics of Poverty and Power*, forthcoming.

Other considerations can provide an effective rebuttal of the charge of wrongful exploitation. But there are familiar defenses—especially familiar in debates over globalization—that are not valid even if their factual premises are true. Most importantly, people can be wrongfully exploited even if they are better off than they would be in the absence of interaction with the exploiter. The desert-dweller who saves a lost traveler from dying of thirst in exchange for an effective agreement to be his menial servant for life wrongfully exploits the wanderer while bettering him. Similarly, in other spheres in which advantage is taken, benefit is compatible with wrong. The militarily brilliant despot who saves subjects from chaotic disorder and extracts harsh tribute to sustain a luxurious court and the Victorian husband who provides his wife with valued options of tranquil family life but relies on sexist limits in divorce and employment to insure her self-abnegating deference take advantage of people by taking advantage of an incapacity for effective self-assertion, wronging while bettering. This is not to say that disengagement is the moral cure. Leaving someone in the lurch when continued engagement could benefit you and save him from disaster is normally terribly wrong, even if the wrong is not exploitive. This does not make it right to extract every last ounce of benefit from his compelling neediness.

Another familiar bad excuse is the exaggeration of the truth that restrictions on profit-seeking can slow commercial growth into a reason for doing nothing about transnational exploitation. Granted, a firm's unilateral compunctions about taking advantage of bargaining weakness can have costs that hurt the unemployed or pointlessly or unfairly burden the firm. While uniform minimal labor standards reduce burdens of unilateral compunction, they, too, are limited by morally important dangers of inhibiting growth, dangers that would be serious even if developing countries coordinated their standards. Still, these problems at the sites of exploitation merely transfer burdens of responsibility to typical affluent people living in developed countries. As a consumer and investor, such a person benefits on balance from bargaining weakness due to desperate neediness in developing countries and helps to sustain continuing exploitation. To express appreciation of the autonomy and interests of people in developing countries, he should support measures that would use those benefits to reduce the underlying desperate neediness. This endeavor should aim at relief of desperation among the global poor as a whole, since desperate neediness that is not currently exploited gives substance to the threat to the exploited, "If your wages get too high, we will move elsewhere."

The stupendous growth in benefits of people in developed countries from manufacturing in developing countries derives, to a significant extent, from bargaining weakness due to desperate neediness. The current dollar value of manufactured goods exported from low- and middle-income countries to high-income, OECD countries in 2000 was 3.7 times the value in 1990 (as compared to a ratio of 1.7 for high-income country imports as a whole.) In that decade, it rose from 7 to 16 percent of total high-income-country merchandise imports, further increasing to 21 percent in 2006.[6] To some extent, the low wages paid for work in manufacturing in developing countries reflect low productivity, but this is hardly the whole story. At the end of the twentieth century, the ratio of labor cost per worker per year in manufacturing in the United States to value added per worker per year was .36, significantly greater than in a number of developing countries playing a large role in U.S. imports and investments, for example .19 in Thailand, .23 in the Philippines, .25 in China, .27 in Malaysia and .29 in Mexico.[7] Moreover, ratios for manufacturing as a whole vastly underestimate transnational benefits, since globalized manufacturing favors especially labor-intensive processes that do not depend on elaborate and advanced technology. From 1990 to 2005, while foreign direct investment in high-income countries quadrupled, it grew elevenfold in low- and middle-income countries, nearly thirteenfold in lower-middle-income countries.[8] These steep increases reflected appreciation of exceptional opportunities to make money, not the view that low wages barely balanced difficulties of production.

The duty not to take advantage of partners in commerce is, then, one important source of responsibilities of people in developed countries to help relieve desperate neediness in developing countries. Much more must be done to fulfill this duty, even though transnational manufacturing does not "impose poverty" but makes poor people somewhat less poor than they would have been. But help which fulfills the duty not to wrongfully exploit would fall far short of eliminating that desperate neediness. In seeking not to take advantage of others' bargaining weaknesses, one may still favor those with more to offer over those with less. And employment in the sites of desperate neediness often does have less to offer, at a

---

[6] See World Bank, *World Development Indicators 2002* (Washington, D.C.: World Bank, 2002), Tables 4.6, 6.3; *World Development Indicators 2007* (Washington, D.C.: World Bank, 2007), Tables 4.5, 6.4; *World Development Indicators 2008* (Washington, D.C.: World Bank, 2008), Tables 4.5, 6.4.

[7] World Bank, *World Development Indicators 2006* (Washington, D.C.: World Bank, 2006), Table 2.6.

[8] See World Bank, *World Development Indicators 2007*, Table 6.8.

given wage, on account of local deficiencies in skills, supplies, equipment, repair, coordination, infrastructure, access to the best markets, and the rule of law.

This limitation is a reason to pursue a second route as well. It moves through a different sphere of global economic life in which outcomes are pervasively affected by participants' power: the shaping of the international institutional framework for commerce.

3. Bullying Negotiations and Reasonable Deliberations

This process is now epitomized in the Uruguay Round of negotiations, leading to the trade, investment, and property-rights regime administered by the World Trade Organization. In its thirteen years, a joint commitment of governments to restrict their exercise of legitimate prerogatives was shaped by threats—above all, threats by the United States to permit less access to its vast markets from countries that got in its way. Though usually implicit and rarely carried out, the threats were sometimes proclaimed—flamboyantly, as when Carla Hills, the most important U.S. Trade Representative, warned that resistance would start "trade wars over all sorts of silly things,"[9] or in measured tones of ominous intimation, as in Secretary of State James Baker's declaration that less liberalization than desired would lead the U.S. to "explore a 'market liberalization club' approach, through minilateral arrangements or a series of bilateral agreements."[10] It was no bluff when Hills announced that she would be the "USTR with a crowbar ... prying open markets ... so that our private sector can take advantage of them"[11] and decorated her office with a crowbar in a frame.[12]

The raw material for the crowbars wielded by trade representatives of the United States and other developed countries includes the especially urgent needs of people in developing countries for access to developed countries' markets. The threats of reduced access take advantage of the consequent inferior capacity to hold out. So there is cause for concern that

[9] See Jarrod Wiener, *Making Rules in the Uruguay Round of the GATT* (Aldershot: Dartmouth Publishing Company, 1995), p. 186.

[10] See Ernest Preeg, *Traders in a Brave New World* (Chicago: University of Chicago Press, 1995), p. 80.

[11] Testimony at her nomination hearing at the Senate Finance Committee, in Steve Dryden, *Trade Warriors* (New York: Oxford University Press, 1995), p. 355.

[12] See Clyde Farnsworth, "New U.S. Trade Chief Is Set to Use a Big Stick Against Any Barriers," *New York Times*, April 14, 1989, p. A20.

the threat-process shaping the current trade framework takes advantage of people in developing countries. Granted, ordinary threats in day-to-day commerce to take one's business elsewhere are not wrong. But they do not have a foreseeable grave impact if carried out and are an essential part of a way of doing business that expands people's capacity to pursue freely chosen goals by free and self-reliant choices. In contrast, threats that manipulate desperate needs in trade negotiations have grave impacts on some vulnerable people's lives if carried out and subject the people of developing countries to increased control by the will of others, in arrangements shaping the terms and prospects of their self-advancement.

The steering of negotiations by threats that manipulate needs might still be justifiable as the only feasible way of achieving a morally urgent goal: the arrangement to which all would agree in reasonable deliberations, in which each government fulfilled its responsibilities both to its own citizenry and to the other participants in the negotiations. However, by the same token, if citizens actually benefit from uses of threat-advantage that depart from this standard, they must express a proper valuing of others' lives and autonomy by supporting change to the different division of benefits and burdens that reasonableness would have yielded. Even the channeling of gains from the status quo to genuinely needy compatriots will not justify the current framework: no one has a right to gain from political injustice. So a specification of how governments would proceed in reasonable deliberations further specifies the duty not to take advantage of others.

Fully reasonable deliberations over the international framework would be deliberations in which all relevant responsibilities are fulfilled by all involved. These include responsibilities to bargain in good faith, responsibilities to those at home who are represented, and responsibilities to seek arrangements by which each party can fulfill these domestic responsibilities. If observed by all governments, these interacting constraints would produce a trade regime much more beneficial to the global poor than the one that has resulted from the actual process of transnational bullying.

3.1. Good Faith and Reciprocal Reasoning

First of all, to deliberate in good faith, responsible deliberators must observe reciprocity in their reasoning: they must justify their proposals on the basis of considerations that they recognize as relevant when offered by others, according similar considerations strength determined by the degree to which they obtain, not by the identity of who offers them.

That is why the current selective attention to the needs of farmers when they live in rich countries shows appalling bad faith. Whatever the severity of the disruptions that rich-country farm subsidies are meant to prevent, it is much less than the severity of similar disruptions which they cause in developing countries. Similarly, the combination of insistence that developing countries accept disruption of local ways of life and job security through openness to flows of goods and investment with refusal to open borders to the flow of labor from developing countries where this is no more disruptive shows bad faith, and imposes even graver losses.

3.2. Domestic Responsibility and International Equity

The citizens represented in negotiations over the international framework have a responsibility to compatriots to do what domestic justice requires in the way of help for the needy. This national responsibility generates further international responsibilities of good faith. On the one hand, this duty of self-reliance generates a sliding scale in special exemptions from jointly imposed constraints, in which countries lose privileges as they move from Cambodian to Indonesian to Brazilian capacities for self-help. On the other hand, showing international good faith in accepting national responsibility rules out tempting complaints from rich countries about costs of economic displacement: one must not put costs of domestic injustice on foreign shoulders by supporting arrangements that are worse for needy foreigners in order to save vulnerable compatriots from costs that they would not endure if social justice were secured. For example, costs of injustice in the United States should not be put on Chinese shoulders by instituting trade protection instead of the protection of displaced American workers by a safety net that domestic justice requires.

Apart from its impact on requirements of good faith, governments' special responsibilities toward their citizens shape the basic pattern of global distributive justice in reasonable deliberations over a trade arrangement. Insofar as the outcome of the trade arrangement itself is the relevant moral concern, the reasonable outcome must benefit every citizenry taken as a whole, since a responsible government will not restrict its legitimate means of advancing the well-being of its citizens except in expectation of benefit to its citizens.[13] To avoid irrelevant counterfactual speculations

---

[13] In addition, trade agreements can implement responsibilities external to the joint trade-regulative process itself, as when trade sanctions are penalties for violating anti-pollution commitments. Since these further responsibilities require separate investigation, I will put this extension of trade deliberations to one side.

while grounding mutual trust, the governments would take as their benchmark for benefit the status quo corrected for serious recent departures from the constraints of reasonableness that I have begun to describe. (As these injustices fade into the past, current correction ceases to be a prerequisite for trust and becomes a sort of enslavement to others' bad choices.)

In choosing among the broad range of alternatives that would benefit each citizenry as a whole, the pursuit of an arrangement compatible with all governments' responsibilities as representatives requires special sensitivity to the needs of people in developing countries. Unless further, especially morally serious considerations come into play, a government cannot responsibly justify to its citizens willing acceptance of a system of trade injunctions and permissions if another system, giving it greater access to other economies, greater freedom to regulate the national economy, or greater compensation for burdens produced by the agreement would substantially reduce their suffering overall. Such an agreement to forgo opportunities for relief could only be justified to those who endure the consequences as acquiescence to threats. Of course, a government appealing to these trade-related needs must accept the overriding force of stronger reasons of the same kind offered by other governments, to show good faith in deliberations. But the mere fact that the citizens of a developed country could do even better if their government held out for more would not make it irresponsible for their representative to accept less. In the absence of further, morally serious reasons, this representative can responsibly explain to its citizens, "We could have held out for even more, but the resulting system of injunctions and permissions would have involved substantial suffering in other participating countries that the agreement avoids." So, responsible trade deliberations will tend to give priority to satisfaction of the most important trade-related needs, taking into account acuteness of needs, numbers of the needy, and impact of concessions.

3.3. Special Protections Constrained by Good Faith

When life prospects of some citizens are seriously threatened by arrangements that would benefit the citizenry as a whole, this default position of global need may be overridden: a responsible government—even of a generally prosperous developed country—may seek protection, if this is compatible with transnational good faith. But this special regard for interests within the borders will be extremely hard to reconcile with transnational good faith by a government with vast economic resources that tolerates considerable economic displacement within its borders or expects such tolerance from others in advancing the trade regime. For example, in choices among domestic policies, the United States often treats lay-offs, firings, and bankruptcies as creative destruction, accepting displacement as a means to efficiency and long-term growth. If the same trade-off of limited displacement for overall benefit is afforded by a trade arrangement, the United States is in no position to insist that other countries bear burdens to protect against American displacement that would be quite acceptable if it were due to competition within its borders. Similarly, in asking other countries to bear costs of protecting Americans from disruptions due to trade liberalization, the United States should, reciprocally, be willing to bear costs of protecting foreigners vulnerable to liberalization, costs that are more serious concerns the greater the harm and the less the local capacity to relieve it. Such reciprocity would require a strong commitment to cushion burdens in developing countries, where such displacement is much more extensive, more painful, and harder to mitigate using local resources.

The outcome of deliberations that are reasonable in all these ways would be the adoption of general standards like those that have been proclaimed and flouted for decades by the framework institutions. For example, deliberations over the international framework for the flow of goods and services would (as they supposedly now do) pursue a general reduction in transnational restrictions accompanied by measures needed to mitigate disruptions that are a special burden for people in developing countries, by especially broad openness to inflows from developing countries that create escapes from dire poverty, and by special exemptions from policy constraints to permit people in developing countries to find their own way out of national destitution.

The faithful pursuit of these institutional goals is a substantial, largely unmet responsibility. Developing countries' goods face trade barriers in high-income countries that are three times greater on a value-weighted basis than the barriers faced by goods from other high-income countries. (The ratio of U.S. trade barriers faced by the least developed countries to those confronted by high-income countries is ten to one.)[14] The one exception to the general sharp increase in transnational openness to inflows of factors of production has been the most important factor,

<hr>

[14] See Kevin Watkins et al., *Human Development Report 2005* (New York: United Nations, 2005), p. 127.

whose free flow is urgently sought by people in developing countries, namely, labor. Restrictions on protective tariffs, export subsidies, and special rules for foreign investors, together with global regimentation of patent rights, exclude strategies of development that have succeeded in the past. When "social funds" were finally set up to cushion the disruptive impact of trade liberalization on the lives of vulnerable people in developing countries, annual expenditure from funds that were mostly externally financed averaged less than $8 per poor person.[15]

Still, the scope of this responsibility to improve equity is limited by its topic. The underlying moral concern is that participating governments provide one another with adequate reasons to agree to long-term restrictions of legitimate prerogatives. Benefits and burdens of such agreements are at issue, not success and failure in economic life as a whole. Suppose that governments of developing countries were exempted from barriers to their exports on an appropriate sliding scale of economic capacity, that their resort to protection, subsidy, and reverse engineering was much less constrained, that barriers faced by would-be immigrants from developing countries were lowered, and that governments of developing countries were provided with substantial help in coping with disruptive liberalization. This might achieve the goal of deliberative responsibility in shaping the trade framework, but enormous suffering would endure. Extending the scope of responsibility seems to depend on extending the quest from particular imposed economic arrangements to transnational influence whose impact extends beyond any particular agreement or institution.

4. "Imperial" Obligation

In our post-colonial era, the systematic influence of great powers crosses borders unaccompanied by appeals to political allegiance or legitimacy. This lack hardly entails the absence of a duty of concern for those whose lives are shaped. A tyrant who dispenses with such appeals in the frank use of power to sustain a life of luxury at his court does not abolish his duty of concern. Still, although no one should mourn the passing of old hypocrisies about colonial authority and concern for subject peoples, the post-colonial silence makes inferences from transnational political power to

---

[15] See Giovanni Andrea Cornia and Sanjay Reddy, "The Impact of Adjustment-Related Social Funds on Income Distribution and Poverty," in *Inequality, Growth and Poverty in an Era of Liberalization and Globalization*, ed. Giovanni Andrea Cornia (New York: Oxford University Press, 2004), pp. 275, 281.

transnational responsibilities unfamiliar terrain. In exploring it, I will concentrate on the most important case. What responsibilities to poor foreigners do citizens of the United States have, as a result of the power structure that might be called "the American empire"?

The American empire, as I will use the term, involves the global superiority of the U.S. government in three mutually reinforcing types of domineering influence, i.e., influence that pushes in directions determined by the interests of the United States as perceived by the United States government or politically important American groups, rather than the willing support of the foreigners whose lives are affected. In the first place, the United States far exceeds other countries in the global impact of its exercise of prerogatives, capacities to pursue interests regardless of costs to others on account of America's importance in joint arrangements which, as a whole, answer to shared needs. Prime examples are U.S. credit and trade prerogatives due to the pervasive use of the dollar and American financial instruments. In the second place, helped by these prerogatives, the United States influences lives abroad through threat power, influencing choices because people have reason to fear what the U.S. will do if it does not get its way, in American conduct partly motivated by an interest in maintaining such fears. For example, in the Uruguay Round, manipulation of these fears opened up trade and investment and clamped down patent rights in ways that benefited the United States. The third element in imperial power, namely, the exercise of destructive power, makes threats credible, and does more besides. As in Iraq, it endeavors to destroy others' contrary threat power and to forcibly gain access to resources at others' expense.

In part, the phrase "the American empire" labels the global fact that each type of American domineering influence has substantial impact throughout the world, much more so than any other power's. In part, it labels a fact of territorial dominance: American domineering influence is deep, asymmetrical, and superior to competing outside influences in many developing countries.

Often, U.S. domineering influence on developing countries is exerted at one remove and without resort to fears of physical violence. The United States shapes the course of conduct of international institutions, which, then, affect the terms of life in developing countries through decisions about the offering and withholding of resources. The World Bank's and IMF's use of loan conditions to shift over seventy countries toward greater reliance on market forces and away from state-directed development is a fit emblem of American imperial power. Those multilateral institutions implemented Ronald Reagan's insistence on "the magic of the market-place" in his 1983 address to the Bank and IMF much more effectively than the U.S. could have on its own. The benefits to developing countries are, to put it mildly, subject to dispute. In an extensive comparison of IMF-adjusted with otherwise similar non-adjusted countries, Adam Przeworski and James Vreeland estimate that being under an IMF structural adjustment program lowered growth by 1.5 percent on average.[16] But there is not much dispute that the broad trends pushed by the United States promoted American wealth and power. The switch from state-directed development, the privatization of state enterprises, the abolition of barriers to foreign commodities, investment, and ownership, and the reduction of tax-financed social services vastly expanded the global opportunities of transnational corporations based in the United States and other important developed economies. Despite inevitable backlash, the shift in the course of development reduced prospects for defiant independence of governments of developing countries, which no longer occupied the commanding heights of their own economies.

What responsibilities come with this power? It would create a duty of egalitarian justice, if the following, attractively simple view were right: those whose exercise of power, direct or indirect, affects life prospects of a group of people have a joint responsibility to sustain arrangements that make the prospects of the worst off as good as possible—or in any case, that maximally, impartially advance the interests of all enmeshed in the network of power. But closer scrutiny deprives power of this moral magic. If farming households in an ungoverned valley set up a minimal state apparatus, just to protect against banditry and cheating on market days, they may (as even Robert Nozick would have conceded) take on a responsibility to provide free protection for destitute people subjected to this minimal sovereign power.[17] But this responsibility does not mushroom into a duty to make the worst off among their compatriots as well off as possible (or as well off as they would be if well-being were impartially promoted to the fullest extent).

Of course, anything like the modern state is utterly different from this minimal state. Three interacting differences are especially important in generating political duties of concern. First, compatriots rely on their shared, potentially demanding loyalty to a political order that settles

---

[16] See Adam Przeworski and James Vreeland, "The Effect of IMF Programs on Economic Growth," *Journal of Development Economics*, 62 (2000), 385–421 at pp. 397, 399–402.
[17] See Robert Nozick, *Anarchy, State and Utopia* (New York: Basic Books, 1974), pp. 113–15.

many vital questions in contentious ways: reliance on their institutional loyalty generates a correspondingly strong duty of loyalty to compatriots. Second, the types of public provision by the modern state that serve every compatriot's legitimate interests extend far beyond the protection of natural rights in the farmers' republic: fair public provision must show equal regard for the interests of all. Third, the joint imposition of terms of self-advancement by modern compatriots acting through their government extends far beyond the enforcement of natural rights and, along with the process of provision, deeply affects both chances of getting ahead and the nature of success; to reconcile their imposition of these terms with respect for those on whom they are imposed, compatriots must be willing to use consequent benefits of advantage to relieve burdens of imposed disadvantage.

In these and other ways, the interactions that underlie the extensive responsibilities toward worse-off compatriots within the borders of any modern state do not produce the same responsibilities across borders, despite what the U.S. does in exercising transnational domineering influence. Loyal commitment to the American political order is not expected, transnationally shared public provision is not a major basis for self-advancement, and local political processes play a major independent role—usually, the most important—in shaping people's prospects of self-advancement.

Two initial simplifications are useful in investigating the unfamiliar territory of political responsibility that *is* acquired through transnational power. First, suppose that the United States were the only outside power independently exercising substantial, asymmetrical domineering influence over developing countries. Second, suppose that the only process of domineering influence is structural-adjustment-like: it involves steering countries' courses of development by setting conditions on access to resources and opportunities which their governments could not responsibly reject, on account of urgent needs.

This process creates a duty of concern, as a matter of justice, not beneficence. Choices among national courses of development ought to be politically responsible. Those in charge have a duty to act as agents of those whose ways of life are steered. A reasonable fee for the labor of governing may rightly be expected. But otherwise, people's autonomy is dishonored when control over their terms of self-advancement is used for profit. This is clear in the case of a local government. Even if the only alternative to governance by the local political elite is destructive anarchy, they should not choose laws and policies with their own profit in view. To do so would be to treat the people of the territory as assets, not as persons. When the United States changes the local course of development by manipulating local incapacities, it inherits this duty to act as an agent of those whose lives are shaped. Beyond administrative expenses, benefits of its initiatives should be treated as *their* resources. Otherwise, in taking advantage of people's weakness in order to steer the course of development of their society, the United States takes advantage of them.

This duty to avoid political exploitation makes extensive resources available to help people in the countries whose development is shaped. But further considerations limit this help to provision for their basic needs to an extent that does not intrude on their duties of self-reliance.

One aspect of the limit is the residual character of the imperial responsibility. The power that steers the course of development is only morally required to do what the people of the subordinate territory cannot in providing for relevant needs. This location of primary responsibility avoids disrespect. Self-respecting people in a territory prefer self-reliance, individual and collective, to outside help. Their preference for collective self-reliance expresses their valuing of relationships in which they take part in which enduring mutual obligations are recognized—relationships that largely bind people within borders. Not to expect Nicaraguans to do what they can to provide for Nicaraguan needs is to show contempt for them, not respectful concern.

The object of the residual responsibility is to meet basic needs. By this, I mean the goal of providing access to an autonomous life, i.e., a life in which energy and attention are devoted to the meaningful and enjoyed pursuit of valuable, intelligently chosen life goals, which exercise a reasonably broad range of capacities. As Joseph Raz has noted, any other sort of life for a person is not truly her own.[18] These needs will certainly include needs for subsistence, basic healthcare, and physical security. But meeting basic needs requires more than help directed toward those below these thresholds to get them up to threshold. For one thing, the point of a meaningful life is not mere survival. Someone lacks access to a life truly her own if she must devote nearly all of her attention and energy to gathering fallen branches to sell as firewood, to keep her and her dependent children safe and sound. Also, social prerequisites of basic needs extend the demands of the imperial goal. For example, if most people think that their political order does not advance their interests, then

[18] See Joseph Raz, *The Morality of Freedom* (Oxford: Oxford University Press, 1986), especially ch. 14.

alienation, instability, or repression will undermine basic needs for security. So the discontent inspired by neglect of the material well-being of those whose mere subsistence is not in peril would thwart a basic need. The American empire would not be absolved of responsibilities if the people of the Philippines could eliminate destitution in their country by measures that left most Filipinos just a bit above destitution.

Despite the extensive demands of basic needs, their fulfillment would not, remotely, advance all worthwhile and important human goals. For example, worthwhile aspirations to educational enrichment, personal acquaintance with diverse places and ways of life, and effective informed political activity lead beyond the minimum needed to live some life that is truly one's own. Still, basic needs are properly the focus of this imperial responsibility because of the process that creates it. In this process, an outside agency steers policies directed at meeting basic needs by setting conditions to which the local government must yield in order to deal responsibly with a crisis jeopardizing those needs. Otherwise, the acceptance of the conditions would be a relevantly free choice, influenced by local lacks but not forced by bargaining weakness, as when a government takes on a loan with strings attached to fund a first-rate national university. So the agency's obligation to avoid taking advantage will be fully discharged once the local people have sufficient power, acting through their government, to provide for local basic needs. By this means, the agency restores the autonomy it has diminished. Because subsistence, health, and physical security are of fundamental value in every culture, outside help in providing for this core of basic needs is also less liable to interfere with processes of shaping the way of life in a territory that are properly the joint project of those who live there.

Granted, in receiving outside help, the people of a developing country are not wholly self-reliant. But the pursuit of self-reliance entails openness to indispensable help in overcoming enduring obstacles, frequently encountered, to meeting basic needs. Until those needs are served, one's life is not truly one's own. So at the threshold of basic needs requiring assistance, help from others and the commitment to take responsibility for one's own life are reconciled.

This special moral role for certain lacks is paralleled by the role of urgent needs in exploitation and of suffering in trade equity—and, also, by the distinction between the basic and non-basic that is a hallmark of *Basic Rights*. But Shue's criterion, what someone must enjoy to enjoy any right, has proved to be a slippery instrument for marking the threshold of the duty to provide, as Charles Beitz, Robert Goodin, and Thomas Pogge note in this volume. Pogge shows that it invites interpretations that either exclude everything from the sphere of basic rights or require provision far in excess of what Shue intends. Shue's own apt observation that there is no duty to provide pediatric open-heart surgery as a matter of basic right is hard to reconcile with reliance on the functional role of a threatened need in an individual's life as the criterion for basic status.[19] The relational perspective that I have adopted may be a better way to establish thresholds of duty-generating need like those that *Basic Rights* illuminated.

It is time to cancel the fictions through which I have simplified the initial account of imperial responsibility. Since the network of domineering influence emanating from the District of Columbia is complicated enough, I simplified by supposing that the United States is the only ultimately independent exerter of domineering influence on developing countries. Of course, this is not true. France has its own metaphorical empire in Africa. EU countries and Japan are independent forces in world trade negotiations, even if basically allied with the United States. In the World Bank and the IMF, the U.S. is the leader in a dominant coalition of developed countries, but coalition partners provide resources and play a role in shaping policies.

Because of this multiplicity, the citizens of a single developed country, however powerful, only owe a share of the total obligations that are generated by domineering influence. Two comparisons among governments are especially important in determining fair shares. One is effective initiative: the greater the extent to which the distinctive activities and goals of a government shape terms of self-advancement in developing countries, the greater its contributions should be to further activities needed to discharge responsibilities of power. In addition, relative burden is relevant, when domination is a shared activity: among those joined in an activity generating further responsibilities, some have reason to complain if the burdens of meeting the responsibilities fall more heavily on them than on others. (Within borders, this leads to complaints of disproportionate tax burdens.) In principle, there could be a serious conflict between these two dimensions of comparison, say, because the leading dominator is militarily powerful but poor. In fact, the leader in initiative does least, in proportion to its resources, to help meet basic needs in developing countries. The United States owes the greatest share of the unmet responsibilities of empire.

The other simplification was an extreme idealization. I have only considered ways in which a great power derives advantages from pressures,

---

[19] See *Basic Rights*, p. 22.

due to neediness, to yield to conditions in offers, conditions which, under the circumstances, a government would be wrong to reject. But domineering influence also involves the exercise of destructive power (directly and through sponsored violence), the propping up of client regimes, and the use of local injustice to acquire transnational benefits. These interactions generate further responsibilities, which can exceed residual provision for basic needs. In the case of client regimes, the United States shares in the overall responsibilities of the repressive regimes it sponsors. Limiting the American residual responsibility to basic needs would neglect people (in Egypt, for example) whose autonomy is thwarted through repression. Similarly, destruction due to U.S. foreign policy in Iraq and Afghanistan over the last several decades creates a duty of repair to Iraqis and Afghans in general, not just a duty to poor Afghans and Iraqis to help meet basic needs.

5. The Global Project

Quick and incomplete though it is, this tour has surveyed relationships generating unmet responsibilities in all developing countries. Those countries that are not shaped by asymmetrical domineering influence tend to have strengths that make transnational exploitation lucrative and, hence, common, as in China. These strengths may lead to a larger role in world trade, but they convey no immunity to burdensome unreasonableness in the world trade regime. Countries without much to exploit in transnational manufacturing are often useful sites for client regimes or for exemplary projects of structural adjustment, or provide cheap access to raw materials through arrangements taking advantage of local political weakness. Lacking large internal markets, developing countries that are relatively weak economically tend to be deeply affected by the shaping of global trade and finance. (In 2005, imports and exports of goods and services amounted to 72 percent of Senegal's GDP and 60 percent of Guatemala's, as compared to 28 percent of U.S. GDP.)[20] In addition to their dispersal over many places, obligations to stop taking advantage are accompanied by moral debts extending back in time, reflecting duties to become worthy of trust by making good on negligence in at least the fairly recent past.

[20] See *World Development Indicators 2008*, Table 6.1.

If there are any utterly isolated, destitute countries, unaffected by the web of exploitation, subordination, and inequity, and they could be helped by developed countries, the small group of people in those countries would fall within the limited scope of a political duty of beneficence. While concern to help the neediest does not monopolize the beneficence of those who are adequately responsive to human need, it is the default position, a proper concern of all, whatever other particular concerns are dear to them. This is a source of a genuine, if limited, political responsibility, not just a personal one. The global poor need projects whose scale requires funding by governments. Politically enforced measures are needed to protect them from negligent unconcern, and, also, to protect those who live up to their responsibilities from competitive loss to those who have greater resources because of their inadequate beneficence.

Assuming no limit to the sacrifices that would help, the fulfillment of these duties would far exceed what is remotely politically feasible. Within the bounds of the politically feasible, partisans of global justice will need to find an equitable way to balance the urgency of the various unmet demands of justice. In choosing among means of redress for victims of global negligence, special concern should be devoted to those who currently suffer more, to those who can be helped more, and to the provision of relief that would benefit more people who are seriously deprived. These concerns can conflict. What is better for great numbers of poor people in China may not be better for far fewer, poorer people in the least developed countries. Here, the device of choice behind a global veil of ignorance of one's situation has an important use, as a fair way of assigning urgency among the unmet responsibilities.

6. The Question of Efficacy

Despite these advances, the Grail/Fleece/Ithaka has not yet been found. The goal was to describe a duty whose fulfillment would involve doing much more than is done now in developed countries—if need be, taking on substantial sacrifices—and substantially improving lives for the better throughout the developing world. No one is interested in a penitential duty to make sacrifices regardless of whether they help, and no such duty has emerged from scrutiny of transnational interactions. If, beyond a small effort, requiring no significant sacrifice, the endeavor to help will not relieve pervasive severe unmet needs, the quest ends in disappointment. So the question of efficacy must be faced.

The question poses a new obstacle because of evidence of the limited efficacy of philosophers' favorite way of helping, foreign aid. The most compelling statistical arguments for aid efficacy—as in the work of Michael Clemens, Steven Radelet, and Rikhil Bhavnani and of Henrik Hansen and Finn Tarp—are accompanied by warnings of diminishing returns that would typically dwindle to nothing in the current upper range of aid dependence.[21] One important factor seems to be the tendency of large quantities of aid to interfere with the formation of the transformative leadership, effective bureaucracy, and national network of political demands and responsibilities on which successful development depends. Worse yet, in the case of corrupt and repressive regimes, aid tends to nourish the underlying infection. Even those, such as Jeffrey Sachs and the UN Millennium Project, who claim to have found strategies for over-coming current limits to efficacy, seek increases that only loom large on the tiny scale of current aid. In 2006, official development assistance amounted to $115 per person in developed countries.[22] No one proposes even quadrupling this figure. So far, what people in developed countries must do is very little, not because it is so easy to relieve foreign depriv-ations, but because it is so disappointingly hard.

But these people are not off the hook of large, extremely productive yet demanding responsibilities to give up advantages to advance the interests of the global poor. The transfer of funds, credit, goods, and services by governments (or, for that matter, beneficent individuals) is just one way of helping. If, as Andrew Charlton and Joseph Stiglitz propose, every WTO member would provide free market access to goods from any developing country with a smaller economy than its own, as measured by GDP, and less prosperity, as measured by per capita GDP, this would do a lot for the world's poor, without a cent of foreign aid.[23] If the developed countries were to open their borders to people from developing countries of all levels of skill, this would do a lot for immigrants and for those they leave behind, who would benefit directly from remittances and indirectly from a more seller-friendly labor market. Granted, these changes would do relatively little for the poor of the poorest countries, who have relatively little to

---

[21] See Michael Clemens, Steven Radelet, and Rikhil Bhavnani, "Counting Chickens When They Hatch: The Short Term Effect of Aid on Growth" (Center for Global Development, 2004), available at <http://www.cgdev.org/content/publications/detail/2744>; Henrik Hansen and Finn Tarp, "Aid Effectiveness Disputed," in *Foreign Aid and Development*, ed. Finn Tarp (London: Routledge, 2000), pp. 103–28.

[22] *World Development Indicators 2008*, Table 6.12. The per capita U.S. contribution was $76.

[23] See Joseph Stiglitz and Andrew Charlton, *Fair Trade for All* (Oxford: Oxford University Press, 2005), pp. 94–102.

offer in the world economy. But here, the weather has intervened. The damage that would be done to countries by Business As Usual in greenhouse gas emissions is tightly correlated with their current poverty. It would be an enormous help to the world's poor, including the poorest, if developed countries would bear the brunt of reducing greenhouse gas emissions, leaving people in developing countries to spew more carbon dioxide as they escape from destitution.

These measures would have significant costs to economically vulnerable people in developed countries. This is a powerful reason for social-democratic protection of the disadvantaged in these countries, to mitigate domestic costs of global justice as well as to fulfill purely domestic responsibilities. But the opening of borders and the stifling of emissions should be sought without illusions that serious costs of economic displacement can be avoided.

7. A Second Quest

None of these alternatives to foreign aid will be fully implemented. For example, an adequate greenhouse gas regime suitably providing for development needs of poor people in China would be too offensive to the desire of political and corporate elites in the United States to postpone imperial displacement by a Chinese superpower. Neither will the goal of a highly productive upscaling of aid be achieved, on account of political realities in donors as well as limits to aid absorbency in recipients. The many bilateral flows of aid, which constitute three-quarters of official development assistance, guarantee bad coordination and channel nearly as much aid to middle-income as to low-income countries—a clumsy method of betterment but an effective means of advancing national political and commercial interests.[24] The volatile fluctuation of aid severely limits its effectiveness in development. In 2000–2003, aid volatility was forty-five times greater than the volatility of government revenue in recipient countries.[25] Yet volatility is an outcome of insightful agility of donors, especially the largest donor, the United States, using aid effectively in pursuit of changing national foreign policy objectives. In both the promotion of foreign aid that helps the foreign poor and the pursuit of alternatives to

---

[24] See *World Development Indicators 2008*, Tables 6.12, 6.15.
[25] See Ales Bulir and Javier Hamann, "Volatility of Development Aid," *IMF Working Paper No. 06/65* (Washington, D.C.: IMF, 2006), pp. 10, 12, 13.

foreign aid, the relationships of power that generate the most demanding responsibilities resist their fulfillment.

Finding the Holy Grail of a vast, demanding, as yet unmet duty is one thing. The political task of bringing a bit of this bounty home to the world's poor is another matter, much more difficult. In this harder quest, those inside established institutions and those outside, planners of imperial policy and those who seek to hem in the excesses of empire have productive roles to play. In the face of conflicts between the global power structure and global justice, social movements can make a vital contribution, changing the calculus of power by increasing reputational costs of transnational irresponsibility. Such movements advance through diverse, mutually reinforcing processes. Tumultuous protests can change the public agenda and challenge legitimacy. Focused campaigns bring limited reforms and higher standards of good conduct. And books help to shape and strengthen new communities of outlook with outposts in all the sites of change. No book has done more than *Basic Rights* to advance this quest.

9

Unthinking the Ticking Bomb[*]

David Luban

1. Torture and the Ticking Bomb Scenario

Although the novelty of *Basic Rights* lies in the powerful case it makes for subsistence rights, Henry Shue is equally concerned about basic rights to physical security. The paradigmatic security right is that against torture, and Shue focused on torture in an important pair of papers spanning a quarter century.[1] When Shue wrote his now-classic paper on torture in the late 1970s, he had important real-world examples in mind—mostly Latin American dictatorships such as the Pinochet regime, which used torture as a device for terrorizing citizens into submission. The United States bore some responsibility for supporting and propping up several anti-communist authoritarianisms that indulged in terroristic torture; and, as we learned in 1996, the School of the Americas in Fort Benning, Georgia had actually helped train Latin American security forces, using instruction manuals that advocated torture.[2] But the United States was not itself a state that tortured. By the 1990s, in fact, the U.S. had joined the international Convention Against Torture, which declares that torture is always illegal even in times of war or national emergency; and, in compliance with the CAT, the U.S. has enacted stringent anti-torture laws.

---

[*] Since this paper went to the publisher, U.S. torture policy has changed significantly, and is still changing. I have not attempted to update the paper, which was written during the administration of President George W. Bush, to reflect these changes.

[1] Henry Shue, "Torture," *Philosophy & Public Affairs*, 7 (1978), 124–43; Shue, "Torture in Dreamland: Disposing of the Ticking Bomb," *Case Western Reserve Journal of International Law*, 37 (2006), 231–9.

[2] Dana Priest, "U.S. Instructed Latins on Executions, Torture," *Washington Post*, Sept. 21, 1996.

By the time Shue wrote his second torture paper in 2005, the dictatorships that formed his primary illustrations had disappeared. The chief example was now quite different, and it was probably one that Shue did not anticipate in 1978. Now, the issue was torture by the U.S. The chief motivation is intelligence-gathering rather than terrorizing populations into obedience. Until the final hours of the Bush administration, no U.S. official ever admitted that the government tortured detainees, and that administration indignantly insisted that the United States does not torture.[3] But, as is well known, this statement turns out to mean only that, under strained legal interpretations of the anti-torture laws, the government's harsh interrogation tactics do not technically qualify as torture.[4] This is a result that few analysts outside the U.S. government accept.

The United States has also enacted a law prohibiting so-called "CID"— cruel, inhuman, or degrading treatment that falls short of torture. This law was enacted over the objections of the Bush administration. After it was enacted, President Bush appended a signing statement suggesting that he considers it an unconstitutional encroachment on his authority, so that he is not bound by it. In any event, however, the Department of Justice contrived an interpretation of the law under which conduct does not count as cruel, inhuman, or degrading if it advances a legitimate governmental interest such as intelligence-gathering.[5] Apparently, the United States government has a strong commitment to its freedom to use cruel techniques in interrogations, strong enough that it will use every legal argument its lawyers can think of to preserve that freedom. The top

---

[3] In January, 2009, Susan Crawford announced that one Guantánamo detainee, Muhammed Al-Qahtani, had been tortured by U.S. interrogators. Crawford is the top Bush administration official overseeing the military commissions set up to try terror suspects, and she added that she had refused to allow charges to go forward against Al-Qahtani because of his torture (Bob Woodward, "Detainee Tortured, Says U.S. Official," *Washington Post*, January 14, 2009, p. A1). Crawford is the only Bush administration official to concede that abusive treatment amounts to torture, and she conceded it only in the single case. As I write this note in January, 2009, incoming Obama administration officials have stated that some treatment of detainees is torture.

[4] See David Luban, "The Torture Lawyers of Washington," in *Legal Ethics and Human Dignity* (Cambridge: Cambridge University Press, 2007), and "Liberalism, Torture, and the Ticking Bomb," in *The Torture Debate in America*, ed. Karen J. Greenberg (New York: Cambridge University Press, 2006), pp. 55–68.

[5] The interpretation appears in a letter of April 4, 2005 from Assistant Attorney General William E. Moschella to Senator Patrick Leahy. The letter is available at <http://www.scotusblog.com/movabletype/archives/CAT%20Article%2016.Leahy-Feinstein-Feingold%20Letters.pdf>. For discussion, including a demonstration that the interpretation depends on misrepresented Supreme Court precedent, see David Luban, "Torture and the Professions," *Criminal Justice Ethics*, 26 (Summer/Fall 2007), 2–66 at pp. 59–60.

officials of the Bush administration met dozens of times to approve "enhanced" interrogation plans for detainees, and President Bush admits that he was aware of the meetings.[6]

Parallel with U.S. government enthusiasm for harsh interrogation practices, the American public has become increasingly tolerant of torture, provided that the subjects are described as terrorists.[7] When President Bush admitted in summer 2006 that the CIA was indeed using "enhanced interrogation techniques," little public outrage was heard, and the U.S. Congress—a reliable weather-vane of public opinion—responded by augmenting the President's authority to interpret the Geneva Conventions' protections against cruel treatment as he sees fit. Similarly, when September 11 planner Khalid Sheikh Mohammed declared—as part of his March 2007 confession—that he had been tortured, American media expressed no interest, except when commentators fretted that it might make it hard to try KSM because of pesky evidentiary rules against admitting tortured testimony.

Of course, one can only speculate why poll-respondents answer as they do. It may indicate a kind of collective callousness, or reveal that brutality has always had a much larger following than elites like to deceive themselves into thinking. But one guess about why Americans are so well disposed to torture is the steady and (in my view) astonishing popularity of the "ticking bomb scenario" (or, as I shall abbreviate it, TBS). In the TBS, you have captured someone involved in a bomb plot. He is your only source of information about where the bomb is located, and you have only a few hours before the bomb goes off, killing hundreds of innocent people. (On some versions of the TBS, it is a nuclear bomb in a large city.) He won't talk. Do you torture him or not?

The TBS is, among other things, a remarkably effective propaganda device. For one thing, it is nearly ubiquitous in discussions of torture. More importantly, it is simple, easy to grasp, emotionally powerful,

---

[6] Jan Crawford Greenburg, Harold L. Rosenberg, and Ariane de Vogue, "Sources: Top Bush Advisors Approved 'Enhanced Interrogations'," ABC News, April 9, 2008, available at <http://abcnews.go.com/TheLaw/LawPolitics/Story?id=4583256&page=1>; Greenburg, Rosenberg, and de Vogue, "Bush Aware of Advisors' Interrogation Talks," ABC News, April 11, 2008, available at <http://abcnews.go.com/TheLaw/LawPolitics/story?id=4635175&page=1>.

[7] A June 2008 poll found 44 percent of Americans agreeing that "Terrorists now pose such an extreme threat that governments should now be allowed to use some degree of torture if it may gain information that saves innocent lives"—up from 36 percent two years earlier. See <http://www.worldpublicopinion.org/pipa/pdf/jun08/WPO_Torture_Jun08_packet.pdf>, p. 3. The latter survey was conducted in nineteen countries. The United States was in the top third for pro-torture sentiment and in the bottom third for sentiment favoring an absolute prohibition on torture (ibid., p. 2).

and—above all—it seems to have only one right answer, the pro-torture answer. Thus, Charles Krauthammer writes:

Let's take the textbook case. Ethics 101: A terrorist has planted a nuclear bomb in New York City. It will go off in one hour. A million people will die. You capture the terrorist. He knows where it is. He's not talking.

Question: If you have the slightest belief that hanging this man by his thumbs will get you the information to save a million people, are you permitted to do it? Now, on most issues regarding torture, I confess tentativeness and uncertainty. But on this issue, there can be no uncertainty: Not only is it permissible to hang this miscreant by his thumbs. It is a moral duty.[8]

I note in passing that there are actually two different argumentative routes to reach this conclusion in the TBS. One is that *anyone* would be permitted (or obligated?) to torture under these circumstances. The other, more subtle and circumspect, version of the argument is that only government officials have a special public obligation to dirty their hands if the public welfare demands it. Some philosophers have suggested that public officials must be guided by a largely consequentialist public morality that would be unacceptable as private morality.[9] At several points Krauthammer suggests that he holds the latter interpretation, that regardless of whether everyone must take a rigorously consequentialist point of view, public officials who fail to do so are irresponsible and feckless. In the same vein, Jean Bethke Elshtain writes, "Far greater moral guilt falls on a person in authority who permits the deaths of hundreds of innocents rather than choosing to 'torture' one guilty or complicit person."[10]

Promiscuous invocation of the TBS has real-life consequences. In November, 2006, Gen. William Finnegan, the dean of the United States Military Academy, flew to Hollywood to meet with the producers and writers of the popular television series *24*, in which heroic agent Jack Bauer routinely tortures terrorists in various incarnations of the TBS. Gen. Finnegan's mission was to persuade *24*'s makers to stop dramatizing

---

[8] Charles Krauthammer, "The Truth About Torture: It's Time to be Honest About Doing Terrible Things," *The Weekly Standard*, Dec. 5, 2006, available at <http://www.weeklystandard.com/Content/Public/Articles/000/000/006/400rhqav.asp>.

[9] See, e.g., Stuart Hampshire's two papers in his collection *Public and Private Morality* (New York: Cambridge University Press, 1978); or Thomas Nagel's "The Fragmentation of Value," in *Mortal Questions* (Cambridge: Cambridge University Press, 1991), pp. 128–41.

[10] Jean Bethke Elshtain, "Reflection on the Problem of 'Dirty Hands'," in *Torture: A Collection*, ed. Sanford Levinson (New York: Oxford University Press, 2004), pp. 77–90 at p. 87. It is not clear why Elshtain puts scare-quotes around the word "torture"; perhaps because she doubts that the kind of techniques used by the U.S. government really are torture? Perhaps because "torture" is such a disagreeable word?

the TBS, because the show—wildly popular among U.S. military forces—was leading to abuse and mistreatment of detainees, as the TBS overrode the careful training that the soldiers had in how to treat captives.[11] He brought along experienced interrogators to explain why the scripts are preposterous. Such is the power and the peril of the TBS: it can even override military training backed by threats of court-martial and prison. The meeting was to no avail: the show's producer is a friend and ideological soul-mate of pro-torture politicians, and the next season of *24* included at least as much torture.

In 2007, I attended a conference of anti-torture NGOs who had come to the unhappy conclusion that they were losing the fight against torture, because their arguments about torture's illegality, its worldwide condemnation, and its horrors simply have no traction in the face of the TBS; the purpose of the conference was to produce a response. All participants agreed that doing so is devilishly hard. Not that anyone among the anti-torture organizations thought the TBS actually does establish the justifiability of torture. Responding to it is hard in the same way, and for some of the same reasons, that epistemologists find it hard to respond to brain-in-the-vat Cartesian hypotheses that seem to establish the truth of radical skepticism. The question-begging assumptions built into Cartesian hypotheses are built in in subtle ways, and it takes patient, delicate argumentation to show this.[12] The Cartesian hypotheses, on the other hand, seem simple, powerful, and irrefutable on their surface. A child can understand them; many children have discovered them on their own. The power of the example seems more direct, more visceral, and (therefore) more convincing than hyper-intellectualized responses. The same is true with the TBS.

The disanalogy between Cartesian hypotheses and the TBS is that nobody takes Cartesian examples as practical threats to common sense; it is not even clear what taking them seriously would amount to. Opponents of torture, unfortunately, need to respond in the public

---

[11] Jane Mayer, "Letter from Hollywood: Whatever It Takes," *The New Yorker*, Feb. 19, 2007, available at <http://www.newyorker.com/fact/content/articles/070219fa_fact_mayer>. A Pentagon survey reveals that one-third of U.S. troops deployed in Iraq believe that torture should be allowed if it reveals information about insurgents; 40 percent approve of it if it would save the life of a fellow soldier; and 10 percent admitted to abusing detainees themselves: Thomas E. Ricks and Ann Scott Tyson, "Troops at Odds With Ethical Standards," *Washington Post*, May 5, 2007, p. A1.

[12] See, e.g., Michael Williams, *Unnatural Doubts* (Princeton, N.J.: Princeton University Press, 1995) and *The Problems of Knowledge: A Critical Introduction to Epistemology* (Oxford: Oxford University Press, 2001).

forum to the friends of torture; they need to meet the TBS sound bite with something equally short and equally pithy. That is nearly impossible to do.

2. Myth and Fact in the TBS

The first thing to notice about the TBS is that it rests on a number of assumptions, each of which is improbable, and which taken together are vanishingly unlikely. It assumes that an attack is about to take place, and that "the authorities" somehow know this; that the attack is imminent; that it will kill a large number of innocent people; that the authorities have captured a perpetrator of the attack who knows where the time-bomb is planted; that the authorities know that they have the right man, and know that he knows; that means other than torture will not suffice to make him talk; that torture will make him talk—he will be unable to resist or mislead long enough for the attack to succeed, even though it is mere hours away; that alternative sources of information are unavailable; that no other means (such as evacuation) will work to save lives; that the sole motive for the torture is intelligence-gathering (as opposed to revenge, punishment, extracting confessions, or the sheer victor's pleasure in torturing the defeated enemy); and that the torture is an exceptional expedient rather than a routinized practice.[13] Some of these assumptions can be dropped or modified, of course. But in its pure form, the TBS assumes them all.

That makes the TBS highly unlikely. For the authorities to know that an attack is going to take place, and that their captive knows where the bomb has been planted, will normally require substantial human intelligence ("Humint")—informants or infiltrators of the enemy organization. That is rare; Israel's is most likely the only national intelligence service that has first-rate Humint on its adversaries. Rarer still are cases where the Humint exists but is unable to provide independent information on the ticking bomb's location. Furthermore, torture is notoriously unreliable, not least because its victims sometimes die under torture or fall unconscious. So, to assume that torture will work while other methods of interrogation will

---

[13] This is a version of a list drawn from the Association for the Prevention of Torture's report "Defusing the Ticking Bomb Scenario," available at <http://www.apt.ch/>, combined with some of the factors I discuss in my own chapter "Liberalism, Torture, and the Ticking Bomb," in *The Torture Debate in America*, ed. Karen J. Greenberg.

not is to assume something doubtful. The reader will have little difficulty in seeing the improbability of many of the other assumptions in the TBS. It stipulates that the interrogator knows things that interrogators will seldom know.

Thus, for example, Krauthammer writes, "The principle would be that the level of inhumanity of the measures used ... would be proportional to the need and value of the information. Interrogators would be constrained to use the least inhumane treatment necessary relative to the magnitude and imminence of the evil being prevented and the importance of the knowledge being obtained." The incoherence of this "principle" should be clear: you can't know the need and value of the information unless you already know what it is.

Moreover, it is important to notice that some of the methods of "torture lite" used by American agents—prolonged isolation, sleep deprivation, sexual humiliation—are time-consuming, and incompatible with the imminence requirement of the TBS. Ergo, the TBS implies that "torture heavy," not "torture lite," is the true subject of discussion.

The second point to notice about the TBS, closely related to its unlikelihood, is the lack of documented cases of it. Authentic cases, not myths; I say this, because the subject is drenched in myths. A few examples will illustrate.

1. In 1995, Philippine authorities captured Abdul Hakim Murad, a Pakistani bomb-maker who accidentally detonated chemicals in his Manila apartment and then was foolish enough to come back to try to retrieve his laptop. They tortured him for sixty-seven days with great brutality, and, in the end, Murad revealed details of a plot to blow up eleven U.S. airliners, and another to assassinate the pope. Murad is sometimes cited as the poster-child of the TBS, a real-life argument for the efficacy of torture.

In fact, however, Murad was tortured without his interrogators knowing what his plots were, or even whether there were any imminent plots—they simply had no idea if there was a genuine, time-sensitive, ticking bomb. They were on a fishing expedition, and torture was their first resort, not their last. Furthermore, they themselves expressed surprise that Murad didn't die under their torture, in which case the interrogation would have failed; apparently, they didn't care enough about finding ticking bombs to stop beating him with chairs. Third, Murad did not in fact reveal information under torture, despite beatings that broke most of his ribs, cigarettes ground out on his genitals, and near-drowning by being pumped full of water. He finally talked only when the interrogators threatened to turn him over to the Israelis, who, as one journalist put it, he feared as much as he hated.[14] Last, but far from least: all the information about the plots was in Murad's laptop computer. Darius Rejali, in his magisterial book *Torture and Democracy*, describes the Murad interrogation as a textbook case of "how a police force is progressively deskilled by torture."[15] In other words: when torture is the first resort, decrypting computers becomes only a secondary skill. In that case, torture becomes the A-option; torture breeds more torture. Murad's torture turned out to be unnecessary, as well as insufficient, to discover the life-saving information.

2. In 2005, I gave a talk about torture and the TBS to a large audience of cadets at West Point, the U.S. Military Academy. Talking to the cadets and their instructors, I learned that they were preoccupied with the case of an Army officer in Iraq who discovered that his troops were going to be ambushed. He had a captive who knew the details. When the captive wouldn't talk, the officer fired his pistol into the ground next to the captive's head—which frightened him into revealing all. Having saved his men, the officer then did the honorable thing and turned himself in. He was punished for it. The cadets were understandably upset by the outcome. Isn't this a version of the TBS? And didn't the officer do the right thing? And wasn't it wrong to punish him for doing the right thing?

But the cadets had the facts wrong. The officer—Lieutenant Colonel Allen West—had heard about an assassination plot against himself (not an ambush of his unit), and captured a policeman who may or may not have been a conspirator. West watched while his troops beat the man for an hour, shouting "Who the fuck is trying to kill him?"—to no avail. That was when West told the man "Either you answer the questions, or die tonight," and fired one or two shots next to his head. The man stiffened in terror, but still revealed nothing. According to journalist Tom Ricks, "At that point, the senior sergeant present decided he had seen enough. 'Sir, I

---

[14] Peter Maass, "Torture, Tough or Lite; If a Terror Suspect Won't Talk, Should He Be Made To?" *New York Times*, March 9, 2003; see also Marites Dañguilan Vitug and Glenda M. Gloria, *Under the Crescent Moon: Rebellion in Mindanao* (Quezon City, Philippines: Ateneo Center for Social Policy & Public Affairs, 2000), p. 223. Darius Rejali observes that Murad cannot have been merely afraid of Israeli torture, given what he had already been through, and speculates plausibly that his fear was long-term imprisonment in Israel—both because he hated Jews, and because he may have calculated that his prospects for release were greater in the Philippines; Darius Rejali, *Torture and Democracy* (Princeton, N.J.: Princeton University Press, 2007), p. 507.

[15] Rejali, *Torture and Democracy*, p. 507.

don't think he knows,' he said to West. ('It was something I had never experienced before and don't care to again,' the sergeant first class added in his statement.) 'Put him back in the cell,' West responded."[16] After self-reporting his actions, West was charged with assault, fined, and relieved of his command. The rumor mill did the rest. There was no ticking bomb, and West apparently had the wrong man.[17]

3. In 2006, President Bush revealed the existence of secret CIA prisons, along with "alternative" interrogation procedures which turned out to include stress positions, waterboarding, and other forms of torture.[18] Bush defended these procedures by discussing the case of Abu Zubaydah, a detainee who was interrogated through the alternative procedures. According to the President, Zubaydah was a major Al Qaeda planner, and his "alternative" interrogation revealed important information: the identity of terrorist Ramzi bin al-Shibh, information leading to al-Shibh's capture as well as that of 9/11 mastermind Khalid Sheikh Mohammed, and the plans of an unnamed terrorist who turned out to be Jose Padilla.

However, all the President's assertions are either contested or provably false. Al-Shibh's identity was well known even before Zubaydah's capture.[19] Al-Shibh's capture, according to journalist Ron Suskind, resulted from information provided by the Emir of Qatar, not Zubaydah; the Emir also provided information that helped locate KSM. For that matter, Zubaydah was not an important Al Qaeda figure; he was the equivalent of Al Qaeda's travel agent, and furthermore he was insane. Finally, he did not break under torture, but rather began to talk when a new interrogator discontinued torture and successfully persuaded Zubaydah that revealing information was his religious obligation.[20] At that point Zubaydah did reveal Padilla's identity, but Padilla was not exactly the purveyor of a

---

[16] Tom Ricks, *Fiasco: The American Military Adventure in Iraq* (Harmondsworth, Mddx.: Penguin, 2006), pp. 280–1. Ricks footnotes his version of the story to a document titled "CID Report of Investigation—Final" (Feb. 6, 2004), with exhibits and sworn statements.

[17] West, however, maintains that the more flattering version of the story is true. Gina Cavallaro, "Tarnished Soldier Runs for Congress," *Army Times*, Jan. 5, 2008, available at <http://www.armytimes.com/news/2008/01/army_westcongress_08013w/>.

[18] "President Discusses Creation of Military Commissions to Try Suspected Terrorists," Sept. 6, 2006, available at <http://www.whitehouse.gov/news/releases/2006/09/20060906-3.html>.

[19] My own Lexis/Nexis search on al-Shibh's name turned up eighty-seven hits in major newspapers from before the date of Zubaydah's capture.

[20] Ron Suskind, *The One Percent Doctrine: Deep Inside America's Pursuit of Its Enemies Since 9/11* (New York: Simon & Schuster, 2006), pp. 99–100 (on Bush's mischaracterizations of Abu Zubaydah), pp. 111, 115–18 (on the interrogation of Abu Zubaydah), 136–40 (on the role of the Emir of Qatar in the capture of KSM and Ramzi bin al-Shibh).

ticking bomb. He supposedly hoped to manufacture a radioactive "dirty bomb," but explained that he would centrifuge the radioactive material (which he did not possess) by spinning it in a bucket over his head. (In the interest of fairness, I should note that the value of Zubaydah's interrogation remains a matter of dispute. In December, 2007, former CIA agent John Kiriakou made headlines by conceding that Zubaydah was tortured, but called it torture that "probably saved lives." In the wake of Kiriakou's statements, FBI and CIA sources sharply disagreed with each other, with the FBI backing Suskind's account, and the CIA backing President Bush's.[21])

In other words, there have been no undisputed TBSs in American experience. Perhaps some are unreported. But, given the enormous public-relations advantage that would have accrued to the Bush administration by leaking details of an authentic TBS, the fact that the dog did not bark in seven years seems like a significant basis for doubt. The ready public acceptance of TBS myths may reflect the desire of torture supporters for factual validation of their fantasies.

3. The TBS and the Innocent Victim

Once we set out the conditions assumed in the TBS, we are in a position to notice one of the most important ways it cheats in evoking pro-torture moral intuitions. It assumes that it is the terrorist himself, or someone complicit with the terrorist, who will be tortured for information. But that assumption runs the risk that the real source of the pro-torture intuitions in the TBS is not the "rational moral calculus" Krauthammer speaks of— one person's pain weighed against many people's lives (and pain)—but rather rage at a guilty terrorist and the desire to punish him harshly. It seems quite likely that many people consciously or unconsciously approve of the torture of terrorists for punitive reasons, which they may deceive themselves into repackaging under a consequentialist, intelligence-gathering rationale. (Krauthammer, for example, seems to enjoy writing sentences like this: "Anyone who blows up a car bomb in a market deserves to spend the rest of his life roasting on a spit over an open fire.") One might even speculate that the popularity of the TBS grows out of

---

[21] Dan Eggen and Walter Pincus, "FBI, CIA Debate Significance of Terror Suspect; Agencies Also Disagree On Interrogation Methods," *Washington Post*, Dec. 18, 2007.

frustrated hatred of terrorists, with many citizens relishing the thought of torturing this monster and therefore gravitating to hypotheticals in which it would happen and seem right.

This is critically important, because a great many detainees claim that they are cases of mistaken identity (and this has been proven to be true in the highly publicized case of Mohammed El-Masri, a German cab-driver who was kidnapped and rendered by U.S. agents). A former U.S. contract interrogator explained to me that in Iraq, detainees were brought in whose arrest report stated nothing beyond "Suspected of anti-coalition activity"—and that this often meant only that they were young men in the vicinity of roadside bombs. When interrogators have no facts to go on (he elaborated), they find it harder to use non-coercive means such as persuading the detainee that "we already know everything about him, so he might as well talk." Under these circumstances, interrogators turn to abuse. The upshot is that many innocent men have been wrongly abused by U.S. interrogators. Anyone who uses the TBS to defend torture must, if he is intellectually honest, defend it in cases where it is quite possible that the captive is innocent. Otherwise, the TBS-monger is cheating.

In order to control for this way of cheating, we must make sure that in describing the TBS we build in that the person being tortured for information is completely innocent. Perhaps it is the terrorist's seven-year-old child, who won't reveal her daddy's location out of love and loyalty. Or, to remove even this childish level of complicity, perhaps it will turn out that the only way Jack Bauer can break the terrorist is to torture his child, who knows nothing of intelligence value, in front of him.[22] Or torture someone else's innocent children? (Two can play at the game of hypothetical-mongering.) Will Krauthammer or Elshtain insist that, as a public official, the president lies under a moral obligation to order it? Krauthammer, at any rate, tries to position himself as a hard-headed consequentialist, by using the phrase "rational moral calculus" to explain why torture is morally required in the TBS. But, if he or Elshtain would flinch at answering "yes" in the grotesque hypotheticals I have just posed, they will reveal that it is loathing of the terrorist, not rational moral calculation, that drives their response to the original TBS, where it is the guilty terrorist who is being tortured. Krauthammer might reply that I am doing the same thing by surreptitiously appealing to our protective instincts toward children. Very well. Would Krauthammer or Elshtain

---

[22] This is Samuel Scheffler's hypothetical, in his introduction to *Consequentialism and Its Critics* (Oxford: Oxford University Press, 1988), p. 3.

proclaim a moral obligation to torture a completely innocent adult to locate the ticking bomb?

Perhaps they will bite the bullet and answer "yes." That would be a consistent consequentialist answer, but it would not be an answer that preserves the persuasive force of the TBS. It would be interesting to hear the audience response if the TBS enthusiast—let's suppose it is Alan Dershowitz giving a speech[23]—poses the problem thus: "If the only way to get a terrorist to reveal the location of the ticking bomb is to torture *you*—that's right, you, the audience member, personally, for days on end— do you think the government should do it? You'll be kidnapped, hooded, have your clothes cut off; you'll be diapered and dressed in an orange jump suit, blindfolded, shot up with sedative, flown to Cuba, beaten, stripped naked and mocked by members of the opposite sex, hogtied, blasted with ear-splitting rap music and strobe lights for hours, hosed down and thrown into a frigid cell overnight, then shackled to an eye-bolt in the floor and made to stand up until your ankles double in size and your kidneys start to fail. Then you'll be chained to the ceiling with your arms behind your back, and lastly have sterilized needles thrust under your fingernails. For some reason or other, that's the only thing that will make the terrorist talk. Should we do it?"[24] It seems likely that the audience member would either dismiss the hypothetical as preposterous or answer with a resounding "no."

But instead, Krauthammer or Elshtain might distinguish the torture of the innocent from the torture of the guilty and respond that interrogational torture can be justified only against someone who has forfeited rights against torture by planting the time-bomb. That would be a coherent deontological response to my hypothetical questions, one that might explain why torturing the terrorist is acceptable but torturing the innocent person is not.[25] In that case, however, the notion that public officials must obey a consequentialist dirty-hands public morality has been abandoned. Now the morality turns out to be consequentialism limited by a deontological restriction inexplicable on consequentialist grounds. And,

---

[23] Dershowitz has said that he often raises the TBS to audiences.

[24] All but the last technique have been used by U.S. authorities. The sterile needles idea is Dershowitz's own: *Why Terrorism Works* (New Haven, Conn.: Yale University Press, 2002), p. 144 ("a sterilized needle inserted under the fingernails to produce unbearable pain without any threat to health or life").

[25] So Jeff McMahan argues in "Torture, Morality, and Law," *Case Western Reserve Journal of International Law*, 37 (2006), 241–8 at pp. 244–5. In McMahan's view, if an agent has made it inevitable that somebody is going to be harmed, either the terrorist or the potential victims, fairness requires that it be the terrorist.

having allowed one restriction to consequentialist calculation, Krautham-mer and other advocates of torture must explain why it is the only one. In particular, they must answer the question of whether it really is true that our wrongful actions can waive all rights, even the right against torture. Many of us—including all the governments that joined the Convention Against Torture—disagree. We think that wrongful action can waive some rights but not others, and that the right against torture is bedrock—torture is evil enough that, in the words of CAT, "no exceptional circumstances whatsoever, whether a state of war or a threat of war, internal political instability or any other public emergency, may be invoked as a justification of torture."[26]

4. The Evils of Torture: A *Catalogue Raisonné*

Why the special revulsion for torture? Why is it worse than killing? What, specifically, characterizes the evil of torture?

One might find this a silly question, and answer in the simplest way: it's the pain, stupid! No experience is more horrible than severe pain; and, one might think, nothing more needs to be said. Many people would prefer death to prolonged severe pain. Those who devised Christian doctrines of Hell imagine it as a place of endless torture, not of endless oblivion; for that reason, Bayle argued that a God who tortures eternally is an unjust monster, since the punishment is disproportionate to any imaginable sin.[27] One might melodramatize the point: Find the living being who is enduring the worst pain (physical or mental) at any given moment and you have found, quite literally, the point of greatest horror in the universe at that moment. As you read these words, the locus of greatest horror on Earth may be a hospital bed in Kingston, Jamaica; tomorrow, in a collapsed mineshaft in Szechuan Province; next week, in the house of a man in San Francisco who has accidentally killed his own beloved child; an hour later, in your own house, as your herniated disc leaves you panting in agony on the bathroom floor. Disproportionately often, the point of greatest horror will be in a torture chamber somewhere. Torture is not just one bad thing among many: while it is occurring, it may be, depending on its severity, quite literally the most horrible thing in the world.

---

[26] CAT, Article 2(2).
[27] See Susan Neiman, *Evil in Modern Thought* (Princeton, N.J.: Princeton University Press, 2002), p. 19.

There is indeed more to be said than "it's the pain," however. The awfulness of pain, including physical pain, is deeply connected with its context. The pain of childbirth is undoubtedly comparable to or even worse than many tortures, including severe ones. Men, I'm told, could not bear the pain that birthing mothers endure. Yet millions of women who no one would call irrational have preferred natural childbirth to anesthesia: the connection of birth pangs to a joyful or even ecstatic event transforms the sensations' character without diminishing their painfulness.

In the case of torture, the connection is with fearful, degrading, soul-destroying events. Fear is perhaps the most important evil-maker connected with the pain of torture. The torture victim never knows whether his torturer will do even worse things: the uncertainty is perpetual. Today it may be "torture lite"—sleep deprivation or bombardment with loud cacophonous music; tomorrow, the torturer may beat me or mutilate me or kill me. As the example of Murad (who didn't break under torture, but did under the threat of the Israelis) illustrates, fear may be worse than the torture itself.

The difference fear makes should be obvious, but I have discovered that it isn't. Surprisingly often, especially discussing these issues with soldiers or veterans, I have heard the sneering response, "If that's torture, I got tortured in basic training," as if this were a triumphant reductio of claims that forced prolonged standing, extremes of hot and cold, or sleeplessness amount to torture. Sometimes, the friends of torture point out that these interrogation tactics were devised by the architects of the U.S. military's SERE program, which consists of training in how to resist enemy mistreatment. It can't be torture, they argue, because we do it to our own guys and they don't call it torture.

These arguments are silly, because they focus only on physical sensations and neglect the crucial difference: SERE participants and soldiers in basic training know that those inflicting the treatment on them have no intention of killing or maiming them; they also know that within a short, fixed period of time the treatment will stop. They have none of the fear of a torture victim who knows neither of these things, and whose captors tell him that unless he talks he may be in Guantánamo forever. Torture inevitably intensifies pain with terror.

Many writers have focused as well on the connection between torture and humiliation or degradation. I don't mean only that torturers like to humiliate their victims—they mock their naked bodies, they force them to masturbate or drink their own piss or do dog tricks or beg for mercy. I am referring to two additional facts. First, the experience of acute pain is itself degrading because it reduces us to mere prisoners of our bodies.[28] Second, the relation between the torturer and the victim is one of absolute domination and absolute subordination. The torturer, as Jean Améry remarks, "has control of the other's scream of pain and death; he is master over flesh and spirit, life and death."[29] Améry (a torture victim himself) elaborates:

But in the world of torture man exists only by ruining the other person who stands before him. A slight pressure by the tool-wielding hand is enough to turn the other—along with his head, in which are perhaps stored Kant and Hegel, and all nine symphonies, and the World as Will and Representation—into a shrilly squealing piglet at slaughter. When it has happened and the torturer has expanded into the body of his fellow man and extinguished what was his spirit, he himself can then smoke a cigarette or sit down to breakfast or, if he has the desire, have a look in at the World as Will and Representation.[30]

Like fear, humiliation and degradation are horror-multipliers to the physical sensations of cruel treatment.

In an earlier paper, I argued that liberals "put cruelty first" among the vices—Judith Shklar's famous phrase—precisely because torture is a microcosm of the totalitarian political relationships that liberalism fears the most.[31] David Sussman locates the evil of torture in the fact "that the only thing that matters to [the torture victim] is pleasing this other person who appears infinitely distant, important, inscrutable, powerful, and free."[32] In his 1978 paper, Henry Shue focuses on the defenselessness of the torture victim. Although these diagnoses of torture's evil have significant points of difference, they all call attention to the degrading relational character of torture, in addition to the pain and the fear. Améry's remarks highlight as well the corruption and deformation of the torturer. Seidman

---

[28] This diagnosis of the evil of torture comes from Louis Michael Seidman, "Torture's Truth," *University of Chicago Law Review,* 72 (2005), 905, and Elaine Scarry's famous analysis in *The Body in Pain: The Making and Unmaking of the World* (Oxford: Oxford University Press, 1985), p. 29. See in addition Jean Améry, "Torture," in *At the Mind's Limits: Contemplations By a Survivor on Auschwitz and Its Realities,* trans. Sidney Rosenfeld and Stella P. Rosenfeld (Bloomington: Indiana University Press, 1980), p. 33: "the tortured person is only a body, and nothing else beside that."

[29] Améry, "Torture," p. 35.   [30] Ibid.

[31] Luban, "Liberalism, Torture, and the Ticking Bomb," pp. 37–43; also Améry, "Torture," p. 39.

[32] David Sussman, "What's Wrong with Torture?" *Philosophy & Public Affairs,* 33 (2005), 1–33 at pp. 25–6. Sussman offers a slightly different explanation in "Defining Torture," *Case Western Reserve Journal of International Law,* 37 (2006), 227–30, where he describes the distinctive evil of torture as forced passivity.

and Sussman both point to the destruction of the torture victim's will.[33] And Améry identifies one more evil folded into torture:

with the very first blow that descends on him he loses something we will perhaps temporarily call "trust in the world." ...

The expectation of help, the certainty of help, is indeed one of the fundamental experiences of human beings, and probably also of animals ... The expectation of help is as much a constitutional psychic element as is the struggle for existence. Just a moment, the mother says to her child who is moaning with pain, a hot-water bottle, a cup of tea is coming right away, we won't let you suffer so! I'll prescribe you a medicine, the doctor assures, it will help you. Even on the battlefield, the Red Cross ambulances find their way to the wounded man. In almost all situations in life where there is bodily injury there is also the expectation of help; the former is compensated by the latter. But with the first blow from a policeman's fist, against which there can be no defense and which no helping hand will ward off, a part of our life ends and it can never again be revived.[34]

Those who have spent time in the company of torture victims will have little difficulty understanding how terrible a loss this is.

We need not choose among these explanations of the evil of torture; they augment each other (and all of them are found in Améry's famous essay, the most analytical memoir of a torture survivor I have read). Torture is the union of relational and non-relational evils, which function as horror-multipliers of the raw physical sensations. The pain, the fear, the degradation, the domination combine to make torture the greatest human evil. If there are any limits to what people can do in pursuit of legitimate ends, the prohibition on torture seems like an obvious candidate.

5. Shue's Dictum "Artificial Cases Make Bad Ethics"

The ticking bomb is the subject of Shue's 2005 paper on torture. Like other writers on the TBS, he focuses on its improbability. In his earlier paper, Shue raised a methodological objection to fanciful hypotheticals in moral philosophy: "there is a saying in jurisprudence that hard cases make bad law, and there might well be one in philosophy that artificial cases make bad ethics."[35] If the improbable features are the ones that secure the desired conclusion, then nothing of significance follows: "one cannot

---

[33] Sussman, "What's Wrong with Torture?" p. 4; Seidman, "Torture's Truth," p. 907.
[34] Améry, "Torture," pp. 28–9.   [35] Shue, "Torture," p. 141.

easily draw conclusions for ordinary cases from extraordinary ones."[36] Shue raises the same objection to artificial torture examples in *Basic Rights*.[37]

Before turning to Shue's re-evaluation of this caution in the 2005 paper, let us pause to consider the adage that artificial cases make bad ethics. It might mean one or more of several things; and in the remainder of the chapter I unfold the argument by elaborating on the things it might mean. Here are two:

(1) By focusing on improbable artificial cases, theorists misdirect readers' attention from genuine issues in the real world to specious issues. They illicitly change the subject from important and authentic questions about the limits of legitimate interrogation in non-TBS cases to intuition-mongering about a tendentious hypothetical.

Or it might mean (emphasizing the "hard cases make bad law" trope):

(2) Policies have to do with rules, procedures, protocols, and laws. Lawmakers should build policies and rules around typical cases and ignore the rare hard cases; and moralists should ignore the weird ones. Thus, even if there were rare cases of morally justifiable torture, procedures and laws should not accommodate them by making exceptions for them.

Shue and I both have criticized the TBS on ground (1).[38] Politically, I continue to think this is the crucial point: the TBS has displaced genuine issues in the public forum and substituted a fictitious example stacked in favor of torture-permissiveness. That is a good reason for changing the subject away from the TBS, rather than trying to respond to it.

However, changing the subject will seem to many like mere evasiveness, and someone whose mind is not made up about the torture issue may insist that the torture opponent respond to the hypothetical rather than

---

[36] Ibid.

[37] Henry Shue, *Basic Rights: Subsistence, Affluence, and U.S. Foreign Policy*, 2nd edn. (Princeton, N.J.: Princeton University Press, 1996), pp. 196–7, n. 25. Shue's objection to artificial cases in philosophy turns out to be central to his argument that duties to avoid harming others and duties to protect others are far less different than many philosophers suppose; ibid., p. 59. See also pp. 184–7, n. 13, where Shue rejects a supposed counterexample to one of his theses by demonstrating that the counterexample can be saved only at the cost of making it "contorted and exotic," and "treating this eccentric example as a clear case would be question-begging against my view, I think" (p. 187).

[38] See Luban, "Liberalism, Torture, and the Ticking Bomb," pp. 45–6; Luban, "Torture, American-Style," *Washington Post*, Nov. 27, 2005, p. B1, available at <http://www.washingtonpost.com/wp-dyn/content/article/2005/11/25/AR2005112501552.html>.

dodging it. Interpretation (1) will not help; it says nothing about whether torture would in fact be justifiable in the TBS, assuming that the improbable happened and it actually occurred. In his 1978 paper, Shue concedes that torture would be permissible in a genuine TBS.[39] He recants from that view in the 2005 paper; but before examining the recantation, we must ask what follows from the 1978 concession.

In the 1978 paper, Shue argues that very little follows from it, because all he has conceded is "the permissibility of torture in a case *just like this*"[40]— that is, a case in which all the conditions in the TBS are satisfied.

I am not so sure. The problem is that once one has conceded the permissibility of torture in a TBS case, one has apparently admitted that the prohibition on torture is not moral bedrock. As Krauthammer puts it,

> However rare the cases, there are circumstances in which, by any rational moral calculus, torture not only would be permissible but would be required (to acquire life-saving information). And once you've established the principle, to paraphrase George Bernard Shaw, all that's left to haggle about is the price. In the case of torture, that means that the argument is not whether torture is ever permissible, but when—i.e., under what obviously stringent circumstances: how big, how imminent, how preventable the ticking time bomb.[41]

"Haggling about the price" means haggling about which of the assumptions in the TBS can be relaxed and still suffice to justify torture. What if one knows only that the captive is a high-ranking terrorist who might know something useful, but maybe nothing that prevents any particular ticking bomb—but, on the other hand, the mistreatment is "only" sleep deprivation? After making the initial concession, any prohibition on torture faces significant dialectical pressure toward balancing tests and the consequentialist conclusion that interrogational torture can be justified whenever the expected benefits outweigh the expected costs.

This is where (2) becomes important. Interpretation (2) also concedes the logical possibility of cases of justifiable torture but insists, on roughly rule-consequentialist grounds, that the law (or policies, or protocols) should not carve out exceptions for them. The reason is that by carving out an exception, the prohibition on torture is weakened, or becomes less enforceable, and the result will be too many cases of unjustified torture.

---

[39] Shue, "Torture," p. 141.   [40] Ibid.
[41] Krauthammer, "The Truth About Torture." I made the same point in roughly the same words in "Liberalism, Torture, and the Ticking Bomb," p. 44, in order to explain why torture proponents are so fond of the TBS.

The argument on the other side, of course, is that rigorously enforcing anti-torture laws in all cases without exception will deter officials from engaging in torture even in the rare TBS cases where, by hypothesis, it is the right thing to do. And the counter-argument to this objection is, simply, that the ticking bomb cases are so improbable that the genuine worry about underdeterrence (the result of building exceptions into the anti-torture rule) is far more compelling than the worry about overdeterrence (in a genuine TBS).

Some who agree that the ban on torture must stand may still object to the idea of punishing someone who has, in the rare case of a TBS, done the right thing by violating the ban. That is why most proponents of (2) advocate leaving the anti-torture rule in place but permitting accused torturers to plead necessity in the rare authentic TBS, or, alternatively, to receive a sentencing discount or even a pardon if they are convicted of the crime of torture. The first of these was the strategy adopted by the Israeli Supreme Court in its momentous 1999 decision banning torture. The Court allowed that under Israeli law an accused torturer could plead necessity; but when the Israeli security services argued that in that case the court should create an ex ante permission to torture in ticking bomb cases, the Court refused. An ex ante permission is a "general administrative power"—a rule, not an exception—whereas the necessity defense concerns "an individual reacting to a given set of facts; it is an ad hoc endeavour, in reaction to a event. It is the result of an improvisation given the unpredictable character of the events" and is not to be turned into a rule.[42] The Court perceived the trap it would fall into if it turned the possibility of an ex post defense into an ex ante permission: the ex ante permission would be a rule, not an exception. With or without the necessity defense, interpretation (2) allows us to acknowledge the justifiability of torture in the TBS while maintaining rigid prohibitions against torture and CID.

In his 2005 paper, Shue goes beyond (1) and (2) and renounces his earlier concession that torture would be justifiable even in a genuine TBS case. He now maintains that the true TBS is not merely improbable, it is actually impossible. That is because among the key conditions defining the TBS are the requirement that it is an exceptional emergency measure and not an institutionalized practice, and the related point that the torturer is a

---

[42] Israel Supreme Court, Judgment Concerning the Legality of the General Security Service's Interrogation Methods, 38 I.L.M. 1471 (1999), para. 36. Oren Gross has offered a similar argument; "The Prohibition on Torture and the Limits of the Law," in *Torture: A Collection*, ed. Sanford Levinson (New York: Oxford University Press, 2004), pp. 229–53.

conscientious, reluctant interrogator who uses torture only in the rare cases where all the TBS conditions are met. But a torturer must be competent: he must have training and the opportunity to practice; his training requires teachers, and his equipment must have been acquired in advance. There will be a doctor present, to insure that the subject of interrogation does not die. The torturer is not Jack Bauer but an apparatchik in a torture bureaucracy. A TBS without a torture bureaucracy is impossible.

To try to leave a constrained loophole for the competent "conscientious offender" is in fact to leave an expanding loophole for a bureaucracy of routinized torture, as I misguidedly did in the 1978 article.[43]

The "moderate" position on torture represented by (2) is, in Shue's words, torture in dreamland. "So I now take the most moderate position on torture, the position nearest to the middle of the road, feasible in the real world: never again. Never, ever, exactly as international law indisputably requires."[44]

6. The Costs and Benefits of a Torture Bureaucracy

The trouble is that to those who, like Krauthammer, believe in a "rational moral calculus" of costs and benefits, constructing a bureaucracy of routinized torture may be a price worth paying if the bureaucracy stays small enough and the stakes are large enough. The consequentialist may concede to Shue that you won't be able to succeed in the ticking bomb case without a bureaucracy of torture, and will surely count this as a negative in the cost-benefit analysis. But the consequentialist will not necessarily concede that the costs outweigh the benefits even accounting for this large negative. The consequentialist does not concede that the requirement that torture be an exception and not a practice is an indispensable feature of the TBS.

Shue's response is this: "You cannot be a little bit pregnant, you cannot—if you are an alcoholic—have a drink only on special occasions, and you cannot—if your politicians are not angels—employ torture only on special occasions."[45] Once torture becomes a governmental practice, it inevitably metastasizes, as the evidence of torture-states like France in

---

[43] Shue, "Torture in Dreamland," p. 238. I offer similar arguments in "Liberalism, Torture, and the Ticking Bomb," pp. 47–51.
[44] Shue, ibid.   [45] Shue, ibid.

Algeria, Argentina under the junta, and Israel before the Supreme Court banned "physical pressure" illustrates. There are good reasons based in organizational psychology to explain why torture bureaucracies cannot cabin their work to the exceptional cases.

This argument may not persuade, however, because so far the U.S. torture bureaucracy has managed to stay fairly small. The number of people the CIA has subjected to "enhanced interrogation techniques" has been fewer than thirty, while the notorious special interrogation plans of Guantánamo were apparently used on only two detainees. It is unclear how much brutality there has been in Iraq and Afghanistan—certainly it includes hundreds of victims—but much of it (or so I am told by former interrogators) is unauthorized kicking and beating at the time of arrest rather than authorized interrogational torture. Now, it may be that the unauthorized torture is the causal consequence of officially weakening the prohibitions on detainee abuse, and therefore should be laid at the feet of the torture bureaucracy. And it may also be that only the opposition of anti-torture forces has kept the torture bureaucracy from metastasizing more rapidly than it already has. But whatever the cause, the slow rate of metastasis will be something that emboldens hard-nosed consequential-ists to embrace torture, including its bureaucracy, if it wards off greater evils. The general point is simple: any finite costs to torture can be out-weighed by sufficient expected benefits. The worse the anticipated evil, the more horrible the things we can do to ward it off.

7. Is Morality Hostage to Evil?

This is, indeed, a familiar drawback to consequentialism: it always makes morality hostage to evil. "Would you torture to stop the ticking bomb from detonating?" is no different in form from "Would you set up a torture bureaucracy in order to make sure you could torture effectively in a TBS?"; nor is it different in form from "Would you commit genocide to stop a larger genocide?" or "Would you rape one child to prevent ten children from being raped?" Consequentialism has easy answers to all these questions—Bernard Williams thought that fact is itself a fatal objection to consequentialism—and its answer is that enormous evils can neverthe-less be lesser evils, and lesser evils can be morally obligatory even though they are enormously evil. The worse the world is, the worse the behavior that morality countenances to combat it, with no limit to how low we can sink.

For many of us, however, a system that imposes no intrinsic limits on how low we can sink lacks the essential character of morality—call it the moral attractiveness of acting morally. What would be the point of morality if moral action no longer has any connection with elemental decency?

Here I mean to be making a different point from Williams' well-known argument that consequentialists' insistence that we do something awful to stop something even more awful endangers the agent's integrity. My argument here is not about personal integrity, that is, the special first-personal character of one's own values, but about whether a system in which any atrocity, no matter how vile, can be permitted (or, worse, required) can count as a morality. Consequentialists will not downplay the evils of torture, as I have described them above. They cannot, because their system demands that they assign accurate weights to consequences. But, without knowing what the alternatives are, consequentialists will likewise not believe that any moral conclusions whatever follow from identifying the evils of torture. While their position is not a logical contradiction, it severs the ground of morality—the goodness and evil of states of affairs—from the ground of action.

There may simply be an unbridgeable gulf between the theoretical sensibilities of non-consequentialists, who regard compulsory choice among monstrous evils as morally pointless, the equivalent of rearranging deck chairs on the Titanic, and those of consequentialists, who patiently point out that the rearranged chairs actually would make the doomed passengers a tad more comfortable in their final minutes, and isn't that a good thing?

Another indicator of the unbridgeable gulf is this. To the non-consequentialist, recognizing the surpassing horror of torture provides an iron-clad reason not to engage in it. To the consequentialist, recognizing the surpassing horror of torture provides an iron-clad reason to do anything to prevent it—including committing it in lesser degree. Thus, in a variant of the TBS in which torturing one captive is the only way to learn the location where ten hostages are being held and tortured—not completely fanciful during the Iraqi insurgency—the same revulsion toward torture that underwrites an absolute prohibition on torture also urges us to engage in it.

8. The Limits of Moral Rationality

These reflections on the unbridgeable gulf between consequentialist and non-consequentialist thinking about torture, manifested in the fact that the identical revulsion toward torture can pull in conflicting directions given a suitably contrived hypothetical, suggest a third interpretation of Shue's dictum that "artificial cases make bad ethics."

In an earlier paper, I quoted in connection with the TBS a saying of Williams, that "there are certain situations so monstrous that the idea that the processes of moral rationality could yield an answer in them is insane," and "to spend time thinking about what one would decide if one were in such a situation is also insane, if not merely frivolous."[46]

(3) Ordinary practices of moral rationality fail in cases where all courses of action are monstrous. The artificial cases ethicists cook up to control for monstrosity by isolating the right- and wrong-making characteristics of action are misleading. That is precisely because they cover over the monstrousness with a veneer of rationality.

The thought here is that a genuine TBS, like the hypothetical in which the torture of one is weighed against the torture of ten, or in which committing genocide can avert a slightly larger genocide, represent moral singularities analogous to mathematical singularities: points where otherwise-well-behaved functions misbehave, as $y = 1/x$ has a singularity at $x = 0$.

To explicate this idea, I suggest the following meta-ethical and justificatory picture. Moral systems, including consequentialism and its various alternatives, arise by generalizing and abstracting from prototypical cases in which they make intuitive sense and yield intuitively satisfying answers. By this I mean not only that the answers seem obviously correct, but that they seem correct for just the reason that the system offers. (One might suggest, as a slightly more complex picture, that the systems are not mere generalizations from intuitions about prototypes, but rather the result of a process of achieving reflective equilibrium with those intuitions. For present purposes, the details of the justificatory picture are unimportant.) Moral systems are on this view heuristics, complex rules of thumb, based on a bet that the prototypical cases are sufficiently representative that the moral systems they generate contain principled commitment to which will yield a satisfactory moral life. The three principal secular moral systems that attract allegiance from contemporary philosophers—aretaic, deontological, and consequentialist, focusing respectively on actors, acts, and outcomes—will yield largely identical resolutions of a broad range of cases; and each seems powerfully and intuitively appealing in their prototypical cases. Each, therefore, might lay claim to offering a total

---

[46] Bernard Williams, "A Critique of Utilitarianism," in J. J. C. Smart and Bernard Williams, *Utilitarianism: For and Against* (Cambridge: Cambridge University Press, 1973), p. 92.

system of morality, and adherents will be tempted to roll up their sleeves and get to work showing how the system can accommodate even the apparent counterexamples that are prototypical cases of the rival systems.

But completeness claims are illusory, and the temptation to smooth out the bumps should be resisted. Even the best heuristics can fail in trick cases; and the heuristics represented by the chief moral systems can yield inconsistent results in unusual cases. This should not surprise us: the origin of moral systems suggests that they are good only over certain domains, those in the neighborhoods of their prototypical cases. Hopefully those are large neighborhoods; but there is no reason to suppose the absence of singularities.

On the picture I have just sketched, moral rationality is entitled to be blithely pluralistic, or even theoretically indifferent, over the wide range of cases in which the major systems converge, and monistic in the prototypical cases where the systems are at their strongest. You know them when you see them; what I am describing is intuitionism at the meta-level. When faced with a clear-cut rights violation and no countervailing rights, think in deontological terms; when faced with a clear-cut cost-benefit trade-off, think in consequentialist terms. When the cases aren't so clear-cut, take your best shot at it. But there will be cases, like the genuine TBS, in which the systems, regarded as total systems, yield flatly inconsistent outcomes, with no higher-level principle available to remove the contradiction. On logical grounds, such inconsistency is intolerable. But on pragmatic grounds, one may do better as a theoretical agnostic who has no rational answers in some cases than as a principled monist who purchases consistency at the cost of fanaticism in hard cases.

Put in other words, the real mistake may be in assuming that any moral system is universal, rather than simply a good way of systematizing a large class of cases. It may simply be better to shrug our shoulders in intolerable dilemmas and admit that whatever decision we make will be taken on grounds underdetermined by moral rationality than to insist on using a system that wasn't built for cases like this.

9. Thinking the Unthinkable

Shue began his 1978 paper with a striking observation:

Whatever there is to say about torture, there appear to be moral reasons for not saying it ... Mostly, they add up to a sort of Pandora's Box objection: if practically everyone is opposed to all torture, why bring it up, start people thinking about it, and risk weakening the inhibitions against what is clearly a terrible business?[47]

Unfortunately, he adds, it's too late for silence: Pandora's Box is already open, because the torturers are torturing away.

But are the only alternatives silence and dispassionate debate? Williams suggests that "the *unthinkable* was itself a moral category."[48] Although he does not elaborate, we can spell out this observation along roughly the following lines: There are some abominations that, as a society, we don't have moral debates about because they fall so far below the threshold of the acceptable that we don't need to argue about them. These make up "the unthinkable." Slavoj Zizek illustrates with an example:

a clear sign of progress in Western society is that one does not need to argue against rape: it is "dogmatically" clear to everyone that rape is wrong. If someone were to advocate the legitimacy of rape, he would appear so ridiculous as to disqualify himself from any further consideration.[49]

The prohibition on rape, Zizek suggests, belongs to "the set of unwritten rules that form the background of every individual's activity, telling us what is acceptable and what is unacceptable."[50]

Obviously, we *can* think the unthinkable, and even debate it. But the debate will not be a dispassionate weighing of options. Staying with Zizek's example, suppose we raise a version of the TBS in which the only way to break the terrorist is to rape him. Or suppose that the only way Jack Bauer can prevent ten women from being raped is to rape one woman. You will never see that plot-line on television, for obvious reasons: the audience, which is meant to root for Jack Bauer, would find Jack the rapist viscerally revolting. That's the mark of the unthinkable.

Conversely, if we insist on arguing the costs and benefits of rape with an unblinking accountant's eye, as if it is just one option among others, we run the risk of normalizing it, moving it out of the category of the unthinkable. That is the Pandora's Box argument, which, as Shue says, risks weakening inhibitions.

How else can we think about it? Zizek writes that "most of us can imagine a singular situation in which we might resort to torture—to save a loved one from immediate, unspeakable harm perhaps. I can." In what Zizek calls "the unavoidable brutal urgency of the moment," it's unclear

---

[47] Shue, "Torture," p. 124.   [48] Williams, "A Critique of Utilitarianism," p. 92.
[49] Slavoj Zizek, "Knight of the Living Dead," *New York Times*, March 24, 2007.
[50] Ibid.

what I would do. But if I would torture, that is not a fact about rationality, or justifiability, or, ultimately, about morality. It is a fact about me. The essential thing is that "it cannot become an acceptable standard; I must retain the proper sense of the horror of what I did."[51] Put in other words, torture must remain unthinkable, and that means conversations about it must retain the proper sense of horror.

This is a final reason that artificial cases make bad ethics. They are deeply cartoonish; this is true not only of the TBS, but also of a great many cases populating philosophy journals, with fat men thrown in front of runaway trolleys, blown out of mine-shafts with bazookas, or impaled on pitchforks as they fall from windows. (Fat men fare badly in moral philosophy.) The cartoonishness makes it easy to treat them as brain-teasers, in which case the option-sets they present assume an air of unreality that makes them all equally thinkable. So the fourth interpretation of Shue's dictum might be put thus:

(4) Artificial cases make bad ethics because their very artificiality makes the unthinkable thinkable.

10. Unthinking the Thinkable

Throughout this chapter, I have been struck by an air of paradox involved in the very act of writing it. By analyzing the specific evil of torture, and examining the senses of Shue's dicta that artificial cases make bad ethics and "whatever there is to say about torture, there appear to be moral reasons for not saying it," I have aimed to explain why we should stop talking about the ticking bomb. In saying that, I have talked about it incessantly. This is a reluctant decision, based on the fact that ducking the hypothetical simply seems evasive. But enough is enough.

Whereof one should not speak, thereof one must be silent.

[51] Zizek, "Knight of the Living Dead."

10

Security as a Basic Right (After 9/11)

Jeremy Waldron

Should we give up any of our rights for the sake of security? The world is a dangerous place, more dangerous perhaps than it was when our human or constitutional rights were first defined. Many people think we would be safer if we were to abandon some of our rights or at least cut back on some of our more aggressive claims about the extent and importance of our civil liberties. Or maybe the trade-off should go in the other direction. Maybe we should be a little braver and risk a bit more in the way of security to uphold our precious rights. After all, security is not the be-all and end-all; our rights are what really matter. But this alternative line will not work if it turns out that security is valuable, not just for its own sake, but for the sake of our rights. What if the enjoyment of our rights is possible only when we are already secure against various forms of violent attack? If rights are worth nothing without security, then the brave alternative that I alluded to is misconceived.

I considered some of these issues in an earlier article entitled "Security and Liberty: The Image of Balance."[1] But I did not explicitly address the point that security might be a precondition for enjoying any rights at all. In this chapter, I want to consider that possibility. In doing so, I shall make use of an earlier analysis of the relation between security and rights, set out in Henry Shue's book, *Basic Rights*.

1. Security, Shue, and September 11

Basic Rights makes a vivid and compelling case for regarding security and also subsistence as indispensable conditions for the enjoyment of human

---

[1] Jeremy Waldron, "Security and Liberty: The Image of Balance," *Journal of Political Philosophy*, 11 (2003), 191–210.

rights.[2] "No one," says Shue, "can fully if it all enjoy any right if he or she lacks the essentials for a reasonably healthy and active life" (p. 24). And the same, he says, is true of security: "threats to physical security are among the most serious and—in much of the world—the most widespread hindrances to the enjoyment of any right" (p. 21). Threats of violence and lack of subsistence are standard threats which anyone interested in any rights must be prepared to contend with. The abatement of these standard threats is part of the moral minimum: it represents everyone's minimum reasonable demand upon the rest of humanity (p. 19). No one can expect to be taken seriously in his juridical proclamations about rights, says Shue, if he is not prepared to commit himself to a concern for the security and for the subsistence that are presupposed by the enjoyment of the rights that he proclaims.

Much of the discussion of *Basic Rights* has focused on Shue's thesis as it concerns subsistence.[3] Less has been said about the security side of the argument. I believe there is a lot to learn from Shue's argument about security. But I also think that when it is considered in the light of recent events, Shue's claims may need to be clarified or rethought. Certainly when we compare what Shue said with very similar-sounding claims that have been made more recently, we may see the need to engage more critically with his argument about security.

Shue's claims about the indispensability of security for the enjoyment of human rights were made in 1980. Twenty-one years later, something happened in the United States which gave a different resonance to claims about the importance of security. After the terrorist attacks of September 11, 2001, it was commonly said that security needed much greater emphasis among our political values and that liberty needed to give way to security in the priorities of a modern democratic society. As one commentator observed,

it has become a part of the drinking water in this country that there has been a tradeoff of liberty for security, ... that we have had to encroach upon civil liberty and trade some of that liberty we cherish for some of that security that we cherish even more.[4]

---

[2] Henry Shue, *Basic Rights: Subsistence, Affluence, and U.S. Foreign Policy* (Princeton, N.J.: Princeton University Press, 1980). Page references in parentheses in the text are to this work. (I use the 1980 edition rather than the second edition of *Basic Rights* published by Princeton University Press in 1996, because the latter does not include an important chapter on U.S. foreign policy, Chapter 7 of the original edition.)

[3] See, for example, James W. Nickel and Lizbeth L. Hasse, "Review of *Basic Rights* by Henry Shue," *California Law Review*, 69 (1981), 1569–86 and Tara Smith, "On Deriving Rights to Goods from Rights to Freedom," *Law and Philosophy*, 11 (1992), 217–34.

[4] James B. Comey, "Fighting Terrorism and Preserving Civil Liberties," *University of Richmond Law Review*, 40 (2006), 403–18 at p. 403.

Now, when complaints are made, in opposition to these suggestions—complaints that some of the trade-offs being proposed encroach not just on liberty in general but on certain basic liberties that are valued as human rights—what is said in response sounds remarkably similar to Shue's thesis of twenty-one years earlier. You cannot set up human rights against security, it is said, because security is the precondition for the enjoyment of any rights. If we have to give up or cut back on some of our rights for the sake of security, we need to understand that that sacrifice is necessary in order to be able to enjoy any rights at all. I will refer to this in what follows as the 9/11 argument.

Sometimes the 9/11 argument is put forward disingenuously. There were many people in the Bush administration who responded opportunistically to the crisis of 2001 to limit civil liberties, enhance executive authority, and shake off the shackles of rights-based constraints without any real feeling that what these changes were ultimately about was providing an environment in which rights could flourish. They just wanted to enhance executive authority and the power of the national security apparatus. But many proponents of the 9/11 argument are perfectly sincere. They care about rights, but they say that if we want to continue as a free and rights-upholding society, we cannot ignore the security issue. Security is important for everything including rights. And, they say, we should not rule out the possibility that this greater attention to security might require substantial adjustment in our understanding of the rights we have.

As I have said, the 9/11 argument is reminiscent of Henry Shue's argument from 1980. But appearances are sometimes deceptive. Maybe what Shue was getting at is different from what the 9/11 argument is getting at. Indeed it is possible that Shue's argument might throw into relief—illuminate by contrast—some of the flaws and deficiencies in the 9/11 argument. After all, Shue is not generally regarded as a supporter of the modern security state. If anything, his work has been influential in the opposite direction: I refer particularly to his seminal article on torture.[5] It is possible, of course, that Shue might not want to distinguish his argument from the 9/11 argument. Or even if he wants to, it may be wrong to do this because the logic of his case may fit the 9/11 argument exactly. After all, the case that is made in *Basic Rights* is not Shue's property to do with as he will: it purports to draw our attention to certain objectively important

---

[5] See Henry Shue, "Torture," *Philosophy & Public Affairs*, 7 (1978), 124–43. See also Henry Shue, "Preemption, Prevention, and Predation: Why the Bush Strategy Is Dangerous," *Philosophic Exchange*, No. 35 (2005), 5–17.

connections between security and the rest of our rights, and it is important to see how exactly those connections play out in the post-9/11 world, whatever Shue thinks or hopes.

There are two possible ways in which Shue's argument about security might be distinguished from the 9/11 argument. One way is to distinguish the conceptions of security that are being used in these two arguments. The other is to look a little more closely at what Shue says (and what the 9/11 argument says) about the logic of the relation between security (however it is conceived) and other rights. I will consider the first of these approaches in sections 2 through 4 and the second in sections 5 and 6 of this chapter.

2. The Analysis of Security

Our pursuit of the first possibility is hampered by the sorry state of the discussion of security as a concept in political philosophy. Security has not been properly analyzed.[6] We know that the word is vague and ambiguous and that there is good reason to regard its vagueness as a source of danger when talk of trade-offs is in the air.[7] But few attempts have been made in the literature of legal and political theory to bring any sort of analytic clarity to the concept.[8]

Shue's account in *Basic Rights* is no exception. He provides little in the way of analysis of the concept of security. His use of the term is quite narrow. He talks of "physical security" (p. 20) and says we have a right "not to be subjected to murder, torture, mayhem, rape or assault" (ibid.). The only analytic points he makes are about the distinctions between security and liberty and between a right to security and a right to life. On the first point, Shue is adamant that security is not just a matter of freedom. It is true that one can characterize security in terms of "freedom from" beatings, torture, murder, etc., but this idiom connotes only the absence of an evil, not freedom in any meaningful sense (pp. 181–2 n.).[9] On the second point, despite the prominence of mortal threats in his account of security,

---

[6] See the discussion in Jeremy Waldron, "Safety and Security," *Nebraska Law Review*, 85 (2006), 454–507, at pp. 455–9.

[7] In *United States v. United States District Court*, 407 U.S. 297 (1972), at 320, the Supreme Court spoke of the "inherent vagueness of the domestic security concept ... and the temptation to utilize such surveillance to oversee political dissent."

[8] But see the discussion in Glyn Morgan, *The Idea of a European Superstate: Public Justification and European Integration* (Princeton, N.J.: Princeton University Press, 2005), pp. 97–104.

[9] See also the discussion in Waldron, "Safety and Security," pp. 487–8.

Shue is reluctant to treat the right to security as simply part of the right to life (p. 186 n.). How one individuates rights is probably just a matter of pragmatics, but Shue finds it illuminating to deal separately with security and subsistence (which arguably could also be treated as part of the right to life) and their importance, respectively, for rights in general.

3. Security: Focused and Diffuse

When Shue talks about security as a precondition for rights, he seems to have in mind the absence of physical violence *directed specifically at the right-bearers, considered one by one*. The right to security is "a right ... not to be subjected to murder, torture, mayhem, rape, or assault" (p. 20). He is particularly interested in threats which are intended to have or actually do have the effect of preventing people from making the choices that their other rights are supposed to protect. So Shue has in mind individualized personal security: insecurity on his account just is an individual's being directly subject to evils like rape or murder or the threat of them. It is these evils in their most direct and personalized form that Shue sees as inimical to the securing of other rights.

Maybe this distinguishes Shue's argument from the claims about security and rights that have been made since 9/11. Those who say, in the wake of terrorist attacks, that we must give up some of our rights for the sake of security do not necessarily mean security against physical attack of each and every one of us right-holders. They mean something more diffuse: the general security of the nation against attacks of this kind. If this is so, then maybe the two arguments are quite different since Shue is not interested in the premise of the 9/11 argument.

Certainly Shue is anxious to dissociate his thesis of security as a basic right from claims that are often made about the overriding importance of *national security*. He talks of the "cancerous growth" of the concept of national security and he observes that it is "used with an imprecision that would normally not be tolerated even on many less important concepts" (p. 168).[10] He acknowledges that national security was once supposed to have some connection to what he calls "the physical security of the people in the nation" (p. 169), but he says that the concept has grown to become more or less entirely divorced from this, so that now it mainly

---

[10] See also Nickel and Hasse, "Review of *Basic Rights* by Henry Shue," p. 1586.

connotes the integrity and power of the governmental apparatus and its ability to pursue its policies successfully.[11]

Another term that is sometimes used is "homeland security" and that seems to be tied rather more closely to the incidence of physical attack on American civilians than national security is. But homeland security is still a bit more diffuse than the conception Shue seems to be using. We say that we suffer a loss in homeland security when terrorist attacks take place or when the danger of terrorist attack is heightened, but yet the impact of those attacks—even when they are as devastating as the attacks of September 11—is confined to a tiny fraction of the American people. Almost three thousand people were murdered in the attacks on the World Trade Center in 2001; but out of a population of 300,000,000, that is no more than 0.001 percent. If we were to use Shue's conception focusing on *individuals* being insecure, in the sense of being beaten, hurt, or murdered, then we might be forced to conclude that the actual extent of insecurity resulting from the attacks was very low.[12] Even if we take into account well-grounded fears of death or injury from future such attacks, an objective calculation at the individual level is not going to reveal very much insecurity, since the probability of any of us actually suffering the evil that is threatened is somewhat smaller than the insecurity we all accept when we drive on the freeway or engage in physical labor in a factory or a construction site. Now, it is clear nevertheless that the authorities responsible for homeland security do have to regard any further attacks on the scale of the events of September 11 as catastrophic events, to be avoided at almost any cost. They have to regard such threats to homeland security as matters of the greatest concern, even though their consummation would still leave the average resident of the United States with a vanishingly low probability of suffering death and injury as a result. Security in this "homeland" conception is not detached entirely from the physical well-being of individual men and women in the way that the notion of national security seems to be. But it is not a simple function of individuals' being threatened.

The homeland conception is, I think, the notion of security that is appealed to when people say that it may be necessary to require us to give up some of our civil liberties in order to bring our security up to an acceptable level. As I have said, it is a more diffuse conception of security than Shue's. But I am not sure that Shue can avoid something like it at

---

[11] See Waldron, "Safety and Security," pp. 460–1.

[12] I think this individualistic approach is mistaken; I try to explain why in Jeremy Waldron, "Is this Torture Necessary?" (reviewing David Cole and Jules Lobel, *Less Safe, Less Free: Why America Is Losing the War on Terror*), *New York Review of Books*, October 25, 2007.

some stage in his analysis. And the something-like-it may generate conclusions that are very close to those of the 9/11 argument.

Even if one were to begin with Shue's more concrete conception of individualized security, one might still end up in a place not far from the homeland conception. Though the point of Shue's security is to avoid the situation in which particular individuals face death or violence or the threat of death and violence, as the cost of exercising their rights, the strategy for avoiding this prospect need not be as particularized as the prospect itself. True, we might provide security for each individual right-bearer by assigning him a personal bodyguard. But a more efficient and probably a more effective means is to use police forces to ensure a secure environment for everyone. This sort of provision treats security as something like a public good.[13] And under a regime of this kind, individuals benefit from security (in the enjoyment of their rights) not because their own particular security is attended to on a focused one-by-one basis but because threats to security in general are removed or reduced by less personalized means. The police do not wait till any particular death squad or paramilitary militia threatens a particular right-bearer. They outlaw these death squads and militias in general. The public authorities provide lighting in dark places and reliable police officers on patrol and on the beat. They reduce violence and the threat of violence by a variety of strategies to keep the crime rate down and to diminish the vulnerability of various classes of person. And everyone benefits from these efforts, just because they proceed on such a broad front. Using means like these to guarantee security to anyone means that security is guaranteed for many, for most, and—in the ideal case—for all.[14]

Does it make a difference that Shue wants to present security not just as a background condition for the enjoyment of rights but also as itself a basic right? On some accounts, a right to security is just a right correlative to a negative duty not to actually attack or harm others.[15] But Shue refuses to

---

[13] I mean a "public good" in the sense of a good which is *non-competitive* (one person's enjoyment of it does not diminish the amount of it available for enjoyment by anyone else) and/or *non-excludable* (if it is made available to anyone in a given group, such as a whole society, it is necessarily made available to all members of that group).

[14] I acknowledge that this is a very rosy picture of law enforcement in most countries. Often the police are part of the problem, and often the public goods aspect is diminished or attenuated as certain neighborhoods are neglected and certain classes of individuals are made more vulnerable not less vulnerable as a result of law-enforcement activities. All I am trying to show is that Shue may not be able to avoid this sort of diffuse public-good conception as part of what the security ideal requires.

[15] For the traditional distinction between positive and negative rights (i.e., rights correlative to duties of positive action and duties of omission), see Maurice Cranston, "Human Rights, Real and Supposed," in *Political Theory and the Rights of Man*, ed. D. D. Raphael (London: Macmillan, 1967), pp. 43–54.

accept this view of the right to security. (Indeed his challenge to the simplistic distinction between rights correlative to negative duties and rights correlative to positive duties is one of the great virtues of *Basic Rights*.) He says:

Perhaps if one were dealing with some wilderness situation in which individuals' encounters with each other were infrequent and irregular, there might be some point in noting to someone: I am not asking you to cooperate with a system of guarantees to protect me from third parties, but only to refrain from attacking me yourself. But in an organized society, insofar as there were any such things as rights to physical security that were distinguishable from some other rights-to-be-protected-from-assaults-upon-physical-security, no one would have much interest in the bare rights to physical security. What people want and need ... is protection of their rights. (p. 38)

Once this is accepted, then it is an open question whether the best way to protect security is to concentrate on thwarting possible violations one by one as they present themselves or to try to provide a secure environment as a sort of pubic good.

Joseph Raz has argued convincingly that the goods secured by rights often require the existence or provision of public goods, such as the good of a tolerant society or the good of a society in which certain socially recognized options for the exercise of autonomy exist.[16] And Shue himself recognizes that this may be true in the case of subsistence. One of the examples he gives in *Basic Rights* of insufficient attention to subsistence is the introduction of a macroeconomic policy that encourages the production of cash crops for export. The implication seems to be that the basic contribution a government can make to subsistence is avoiding macroeconomic changes like this, and instead maintaining an economic environment in which people can live and hopefully flourish without being all the time on the edge of starvation. And I think he acknowledges this need for macro-strategies also in the case of security, when he says that

protection of rights to physical security necessitates police forces; criminal courts; penitentiaries; schools for training police, lawyers, and guards; and taxes to support

---

[16] See Joseph Raz, *The Morality of Freedom* (Oxford: Clarendon Press, 1986), pp. 198–207. Raz argues that public goods can't themselves be the subject of rights. But he confines this point to what he calls non-contingent public goods. See also the discussion in Denise Reaume, "Individuals, Groups, and Rights to Public Goods," *University of Toronto Law Journal*, 38 (1988), 1–27 at pp. 9–13 and Jeremy Waldron, "Can Communal Goods be Human Rights?" in *Liberal Rights: Collected Papers 1981–1991* (Cambridge: Cambridge University Press, 1993), pp. 339–69. Security as I am imagining it, under the auspices of good policing, is a contingent public good in the relevant sense. On the other hand, there may be aspects of the idea of security which are non-contingent public goods: see the discussion in Waldron, "Safety and Security," pp. 500–2 and also in Ian Loader and Neil Walker, *Civilizing Security* (New York: Cambridge University Press, 2007).

an enormous system for the prevention, detection, and punishment of violations of personal security. All these activities and institutions are attempts at providing social guarantees for individuals' security so that they are not left to face alone forces that they cannot handle on their own. (pp. 37–8)

Once all this is accepted, then it is an easy step to something like the homeland security conception. If thousands of individuals are threatened by sporadic terrorist attacks which it is difficult for them to guard against on their own, then the community has no choice but to adopt general strategies to combat and reduce the incidence of this evil.

4. Insecurity and Deliberate Threats

Even granting all this, there may be a further distinction to be drawn, to distance Shue's thesis from the 9/11 argument. We might distinguish two ways in which lack of security can impact on one's rights. One—which he seems particularly concerned with—involves something like deliberate and direct intimidation relative to the exercise of one's rights. He writes:

No one can fully enjoy any right that is supposedly protected by society if someone can credibly threaten him or her with murder, rape, beating, etc., when he or she tries to enjoy the alleged right. (p. 21)

The other might be a more generalized fear that, so to speak, keeps people indoors, keeps them away from church or public meetings or polling places, not because they expect to be coerced *in the exercise of their rights*, but just because they are afraid of being mugged, for example, by people who have no interest apart from the particular circumstances of the mugging with the way their victims' rights are exercised. The man who robs me doesn't worry about whether I vote Democrat or worship as an Episcopalian or attend meetings of the ACLU; he just wants my money. And if fear of him or of people like him keeps me away from exercising those rights that is an unintended side-effect of his violence.

I think Shue's thesis about a basic right to security is more plausible when the threat of insecurity is understood in the first way than when it is understood in the second way. In the second way, the threat to the exercise of my civil and political rights posed by the mugger is rather like the threat posed to those rights by bad weather. The rain may keep me away from church or from the ACLU meeting as well. (Of course the mugging itself is deliberate and in that way unlike the weather; but we are talking about its collateral impact on the exercise of rights other than those affected immediately by the mugging itself.) On the other hand, Shue talks in a footnote of "non-human threats to both security and subsistence" (p. 189 n. 17), which seems to imply that it may be the second sense that he is interested in. Certainly the second sense is appropriate for subsistence. For lack of subsistence can block or undermine the meaningful exercise of one's rights whether anyone intends that consequence or not. Shue does not really address the question of whether insecurity might be different from lack of subsistence in this regard.

Which category do terrorist attacks (such as the attacks of September 11) fit into? I am not sure. My inclination is to say that they fit into the second category: they are designed just to cause death and wreak havoc and enrage and humiliate the American government; any further impact on the way Americans exercise their civil and political rights was just a side-effect. But I have heard people say the opposite. The term "terrorism" implies a desire for some effect on the society that is attacked which goes beyond the immediate death and havoc that is caused.[17] President Bush says that the terrorists who threaten us do so precisely because they hate our freedoms and want to frighten us away from the exercise of them.[18] But what if the terrorists' strategy is to provoke those who are supposed to protect us into curtailing or undermining our rights?[19] If the state's reaction to A's attack on B is to curtail B's rights, can we really say that it is A's attack that is the standard threat to rights? I don't think so. We certainly can't use that characterization to justify taking rights away from B for the sake of enhancing the security that B is supposed to need in order to enjoy his rights, for that would be to postulate the very same thing (the taking away of rights by the state in the face of terrorist attack) as both the problem and the solution!

5. The Logic of Indispensability

I said there were two ways in which we might distinguish Shue's argument about security from the post-9/11 argument about security. We have considered whether there might be a distinction between the conceptions of security that are being used in the two arguments. Now we must consider

[17] See also the discussion in Jeremy Waldron, "Terrorism and the Uses of Terror," *The Journal of Ethics*, 8 (2004), 5–35.

[18] See George W. Bush, "Freedom at War with Fear," Address to a Joint Session of Congress (Sept. 20, 2001) available at <http://www.whitehouse.gov/news/releases/2001/09/20010920-8.html>. ("Americans are asking, why do they hate us? They hate what we see right here in this chamber—a democratically elected government. Their leaders are self-appointed. They hate our freedoms—our freedom of religion, our freedom of speech, our freedom to vote and assemble and disagree with each other.")

[19] See Waldron, "Terrorism and the Uses of Terror," p. 32.

as well the relation between security and rights, and see whether the relation that Shue asserts is similar in relevant respects to the relation that has been envisaged in recent homeland security strategies.

The language that Shue uses is the language of indispensability. Security is an indispensable condition for the enjoyment of individual rights:

No one can fully enjoy any right that is supposedly protected by society if someone can credibly threaten him with murder, rape, beating, etc., when he or she tries to enjoy the alleged right. Such threats to physical security are among the most serious and—in much of the world—the most widespread hindrances to the enjoyment of any right ... In the absence of physical security people are unable to use any other rights that society may be said to be protecting without being liable to encounter many of the worst dangers they would encounter if society were not protecting the rights. (p. 21)

Indispensability here conveys one or both of two ideas. One is that an individual's security is a necessary condition for his enjoyment of any right. The other is that an individual's security is actually a part of what any other right is a right *to*. Shue uses the second formulation explicitly when he says that security "is desirable as part of the enjoyment of any other right" (p. 21). And he uses the first formulation when he presents the abstract form of his argument in terms of a syllogism: "If everyone has the right to y, and the enjoyment of x is necessary for the enjoyment of y, then everyone has a right to x" (p. 32). In fact the distinction between the two formulations doesn't really matter, since Shue sees no need to distinguish between, as it were, the essence of a right and what is necessary for its enjoyment. The distinction certainly makes no difference to four points that I would like to make about this indispensability relation.

Saying that one thing, x, is indispensable for or inherently necessary for another thing, y, raises a number of questions about the priority that should be accorded to x over y or vice versa. Some of those questions require us to look a little more closely at the indispensability relation and some require us to look skeptically at the issue of priorities. Let me begin with indispensability.

(i) How tight is the relation of indispensability supposed to be, as between security and rights, on Shue's account? People often seem to exercise (and sometimes even enjoy) their rights under the most adverse circumstances. Is Shue really saying that this *can never happen* in the absence of security? Shue is sensitive to the point and says this:

A person could, of course, always try to enjoy some other right even if no social provision were made to protect his or her physical safety during attempts to exercise the right. Suppose there is a right to peaceful assembly but it is not unusual for peaceful assemblies to be broken up and some of the participants beaten ... People could still try to assemble, and they might sometimes assemble safely. But it would obviously be misleading to say that that they are protected in their right to assemble ... If they are as helpless against physical threats with the right protected as they would have been without the supposed protection, society is not actually protecting their exercise of the right to assembly. (p. 22)

And a little later he says that if people do not have "guarantees" that they can assemble in security, then they have not been provided with assembly as a right (p. 27). But I don't think this settles the issue.

The trouble is that security is not an all-or-nothing matter, but a matter of more or less. I may be provided with a guarantee of protection but not a cast-iron guarantee. The government may sincerely undertake to do its best for my security, but it may not be able to prevent every last gang of thugs from occasionally breaking up a public meeting. In this situation, I am not as helpless against attack as I would be if the government had done nothing at all. If I try, often successfully, to exercise my rights in these circumstances, haven't I refuted at least a very strong version of Shue's claim that my security is absolutely indispensable for the enjoyment of my rights? This point seems particularly important when we consider security in the public good sense (i.e., in the sense discussed, above, in section 3). If the provision of security as a public good is less than perfect, or if it falls short of what might in certain circumstances be reasonably required, is it still plausible to say that the absence of security makes the enjoyment of rights impossible? Obviously not, for we have acknowledged that there might be a failure of something like homeland security and yet many individuals may face no actual threat at all.

I think this shows that there is a considerable gap in the 9/11 argument. When the avatars of homeland security justify curtailing a right for the sake of security, they do not usually mean that once this right is curtailed then everyone can be made perfectly secure. Instead they have in mind at best an incremental enhancement of security as a public good as a result of the curtailment: curtailing the right may allow us to move from (say) 51 to 52 percent of the provision of security at an optimal level. Perhaps the curtailment is justified, but if it is, it is not because we need this curtailment in order to enjoy the rest of our rights. The rest of our rights, which we are going to have to exercise *anyway* in something less than perfect security, may not be much affected.

(ii) This leads to my second point. In a dangerous world, the provision of security is a voracious ideal. If we are looking for absolute security, there is no end to the resources that might have to be devoted to it. We could station a police officer every few yards and devote enormous resources to homeland security.[20] Maybe if we devoted the whole of the GDP, we might reduce to something approaching zero the threat of the sort of violence that undermines the enjoyment of rights. But then there would be nothing left for any other social program, let alone for any other program associated with rights. Since, on Shue's account, there are a number of necessary conditions for the enjoyment of rights (subsistence is another), it is not clear how we can or should proceed with this calculation.

(iii) One thing is sure: we must not regard the necessary conditions of the enjoyment of rights as having absolute priority over all other goals. Certainly we should not assign it lexical priority, in the Rawlsian sense.[21] Surely we do not want to devote all our resources and energy to fulfilling a necessary condition for rights, and nothing at all to the rights themselves. We need to find some balance here. Robert Goodin makes a similar point about national defense.[22] Defense, he notes, is sometimes presented as "an indispensable prerequisite to everything else the nation might do" or as a "precondition for pursuing other desirable goals." But if that is how we understand it, we must occasionally allow those other goals to surface in public policy and to stake their claim to some of society's resources. We cannot infinitely postpone their enjoyment to the establishment of what is valued only as a necessary condition for their enjoyment.

When he introduced the notion of lexical priority, John Rawls observed that the idea should only be used in circumstances where the item accorded priority is limited in its demandingness and there is some reasonable prospect of its being satisfied, so that other items further down the list can be attended to: "unless the earlier principles have but a limited application and establish definite requirements which can be fulfilled, later principles will never come into play."[23] Where this condition is not satisfied, we have to proceed on the basis of some sort of balancing, messy though that may seem. This may involve sometimes balancing the costs of rights against other social costs unconnected with rights. It will certainly sometimes require balancing costs associated with the security that is necessary for rights against costs associated with other aspects of the upholding of rights (including, no doubt, other necessary conditions).

---

[20] See Michael Walzer, *Spheres of Justice: A Defense of Pluralism and Equality* (New York: Basic Books, 1983), p. 67.

[21] See John Rawls, *A Theory of Justice*, rev. edn. (Cambridge, Mass.: Harvard University Press, 1999), pp. 37–8.

[22] Robert Goodin, *Political Theory and Public Policy* (Chicago: University of Chicago Press, 1982), p. 232–3.

[23] Rawls, *Theory of Justice*, p. 38.

(iv) In any case, lexical priority may not be appropriate as a way of operationalizing the importance of things which are valued *only* as necessary conditions for other values. A necessary condition for something desirable is *not worth supplying at all* unless there is a practicable possibility of also securing sufficient conditions for that desirable thing; if there is no such possibility, then we should just forget about the necessary conditions.[24] A necessary condition for me to visit the moon is that I should begin astronaut training right now, but even assuming that my visiting the moon is highly desirable, the necessary condition for it is simply of no interest since my visiting the moon is not going to happen. The effect of this point on the deontic logic of necessity and obligation is quite interesting. Suppose I have an obligation to ensure that person P enjoys a certain good, y. We cannot automatically infer that I have an obligation to bring about something else (x) which is a necessary conditions of P's enjoying y. If y cannot in fact be supplied to P under any circumstances (because sufficient conditions are not available), then I do not have an obligation to bring about x even if x itself *can* be brought about by me. The only ground for bringing about x in these circumstances would be if there were some reasonable prospect of sufficient conditions for y being available in the future, in which case bringing about x now would be a sort of advance preparation. Accordingly, if there are other insuperable obstacles to people's enjoyment of their rights, we may not be able to infer from the fact that security is a necessary condition for the enjoyment of their rights that therefore they have a right to security.

This point may be very important further down the line of the chain of necessary conditions. Shue's claim is that the enjoyment of individual rights among a given population depends on the individuals in question enjoying security. Their individual security is a necessary condition for their effective enjoyment of their rights. But as we have seen, it may be a necessary condition for all these individuals' enjoying individual security in the relevant sense that the government provide a secure environment (by its homeland security strategy) in the sense discussed in section 3. And a case may be made that it is a necessary condition for *that* that (say) certain terrorist suspects be detained indefinitely. So we have a chain of necessary conditions:

detention of terrorist suspects
is necessary for
homeland security,
which is necessary for

---

[24] See Waldron, "Security and Liberty," pp. 208–9.

individual security for individual right-bearers,
which is necessary for
individual right-bearers' enjoyment of their rights

But if sufficient conditions are not available for any of these elements then we cannot infer that terrorists ought to be detained. Suppose the terrorist threat is so great that there is no reasonable prospect for the time being of establishing a secure environment for the enjoyment of rights. Then even though detaining the suspects is a necessary condition for a secure environment, it is like my going to astronaut school: it is a necessary condition for something that is not going to happen. It doesn't follow that we should not detain the suspects, but we cannot infer that they should be detained from the fact that their detention is necessary for something which is necessary for something which is necessary for the enjoyment of rights.

6. Rights as the Price of Rights

I have pursued these points about necessary conditions, priorities, and indispensability perhaps too fussily. But I did not do so for the sake of fiscal prudence or out of a concern about the cost overruns that Shue's program might incur. My interest in this chapter is to see what, if anything, there is in common between Shue's argument about the relation between rights and security, and what I have called the 9/11 argument, namely, the argument that it may sometimes be necessary to sacrifice or limit certain rights in order to provide the security that rights in general presuppose. In the previous section, under heading (ii), I said that security was a voracious ideal. But the things that it might eat up are not just resources but rights, and if we give security too great a priority (or indeed lexical priority) over the rights that it is supposed to be a necessary condition for, we may find that much of what we are ultimately aiming to secure has been jettisoned for the sake of that security.

Abraham Lincoln famously asked, in regard to his unlawful presidential suspension of *habeas corpus* in 1861, whether he was to let all the laws but one collapse and go unexecuted for the sake of upholding some particular law "made in such extreme tenderness of the citizen's liberty, that practically it relieves more of the guilty than the innocent."[25] Proponents of

---

[25] Abraham Lincoln, "Message to Congress in Special Session," July 4, 1861, quoted by Sherrill Halbert, "The Suspension of the Writ of Habeas Corpus by President Lincoln," *American Journal of Legal History*, 2 (1958), 95–116 at p. 100.

the 9/11 argument ask something similar about rights: are all the rights but a few to go unprotected, unsupported by the security that rights require, for the sake of protecting those few rights that might actually stand in the way of our providing the requisite security?

Where does Shue stand on this? I believe that Shue is not in a position to rule out the possibility that the post-9/11 argument envisages. There are two ways of reaching this conclusion. One is via the idea of the systematicity of rights. The other is via the exigencies of particular circumstances.

On the systematicity account, we might want to consider whether the right whose sacrifice seems to be required for the sake of security should really ever have been regarded as a right at all. (Or, if it is the limitation, rather than the wholesale sacrifice, of the right that seems to be called for in the name of security, we may want to consider whether the right should ever have been recognized in its unlimited form.) We might want to say that the importance of security represents a constraint on what counts as an acceptable set of individual rights. Just as we would not recognize a right that permitted a person to interfere with or undermine the rights of others, so (it might be argued), we should not recognize a right that is incompatible with conditions required for the security of others. This is analogous to the way in which Shue thinks about subsistence. Some people complain that securing subsistence for everyone might be incompatible with respecting property rights or rights to market freedom. But Shue's position seems to be that no such rights exist if they are incompatible with what is necessary for subsistence: "property laws can be morally justified only if subsistence rights are fulfilled" (p. 124).[26]

Of course there is immense room for argument here—not only argument about the logic of necessity and indispensability considered in the previous section, but also argument about the difference between qualifying property rights for the sake of immediate requirements of individual subsistence and qualifying property rights for the sake of a particular macroeconomic strategy calculated to enhance subsistence in the medium or long term. Analogously, there is considerable room for argument in the space between qualifying a right whose exercise poses a direct threat to security and qualifying a right whose exercise or enjoyment may be incompatible with the particular homeland security strategy that we happen to be pursuing.

The systematicity approach assumes that, in some sense, we can settle in advance on a set of rights that are compossible *inter se* and compatible with

---

[26] See also the discussion at the beginning of the "Afterword" in *Basic Rights*, 2nd edn. (Princeton, N.J.: Princeton University Press, 1999), p. 153.

the requirements of security.[27] Of course we have to do the figuring in real time, but the systematicity approach assumes that there is, objectively, a solution—something available to be figured out. The exigency approach is more skeptical about that. It does not assume that we have access to an objective set of rights whose natural-law provenance ensures that they fit together rationally or coherently (p. 93). Instead we have to calculate and recalculate the effect on one another of the exercise of various rights in various circumstances. It assumes that no right is absolute, and that occasionally rights might have to be overridden or our sense of what rights we are entitled to rely on in particular circumstances may have to be revised. This is a troubling possibility, but Shue refuses to rule it out (p. 94).

A particularly troubling consequence of the exigency approach is that it might allow for the rights of *some people* to be overridden even when the similar rights of others are not. (This is unlikely on the systematicity approach since some sort of guarantee of equality of rights will operate alongside security and subsistence as an adequacy condition on any acceptable set of human rights.) So, for example, provision may be made for the detention without trial of people whose ethnicity and appearance are similar to those of a certain category of terrorists, even though it would be unthinkable to permit such detention in the case of citizens generally. Some of us have argued that this has been characteristic of the Bush administration's homeland security strategy.[28] Though there is talk of a general trade-off of (say) liberty for security as though everyone were giving up a certain amount of liberty so that everyone could achieve greater security, in fact the trade-off has often been a matter of them-and-us—*their* liberty for *our* security. As Ronald Dworkin has pointed out:

None of the administration's decisions and proposals will affect more than a tiny number of American citizens: almost none of us will be indefinitely detained for minor violations or offenses, or have our houses searched without our knowledge, or find ourselves brought before military tribunals on grave charges carrying the death penalty. Most of us pay almost nothing in personal freedom when such measures are used against those the President suspects of terrorism.[29]

Still, nothing in Shue's account affords any basis for ruling this sort of thing out as a matter of principle, at least on the exigency approach.

---

[27] On compossibility, see Hillel Steiner, "The Structure of a Set of Compossible Rights," *Journal of Philosophy*, 74 (1977), 767–75.

[28] See, e.g., David Cole, "Their Liberties, Our Security," *Boston Review*, December 2002/ January 2003 and Waldron, "Is this Torture Necessary?"

[29] See Ronald Dworkin, "The Threat to Patriotism," *New York Review of Books*, February 28, 2002.

Everything will depend on the particular dimensions of what is proposed and the case that can be made—subject to all the caveats of section 5—as to its necessity.

Elsewhere I have argued that if we are in the business of sacrificing or limiting rights for the sake of rights, we are required to pay particular attention to the logic of rights.[30] When Lincoln spoke of preserving "all the laws but one," he seemed to be using a simple maximizing approach: if not all the laws can be upheld, then we should uphold as many as possible. That may or may not be plausible in the case of laws. But when the currency of our calculation is rights, maximization is certainly not appropriate. Rights are inherently equal, and the only justification for the sort of unequal upholding of rights envisaged in the previous paragraph is that it is necessary to avoid even greater or more extensive inequality. So, for example, if we have to choose between two strategies for security, one that requires everyone in a community of (say) a quarter of a billion people to give up one right (for the sake of security) and one that requires ten thousand people in that same community to give up ten rights each (for the sake of security) while all the others enjoy their rights intact, we should prefer the former strategy even though incomparably more rights in the aggregate are safeguarded by the latter strategy. There is not space here to pursue this matter further and, in any case, the philosophical study of such calculations remains fairly rudimentary. But it needs to be emphasized again and again that the mere fact that it is appropriate to contemplate trade-offs between rights and security does not license a more general move away from the egalitarian domain of rights to the more brutal logic of maximization. Trade-offs may seem to be the exclusive domain of the Benthamite economist; but the fact that trade-offs among rights are sometimes necessary shows that, in at least some cases, trade-offs need to be handled more carefully than one can expect economists to handle them.

For my money, these questions are much more likely to be handled with the appropriate care by someone like Henry Shue than by the latter-day proponents of the 9/11 argument. Shue does not discuss the issues about security exactly as I have posed them. But he does talk about trade-offs of similar kinds in other contexts, and this gives us an indication I think of how he would respond to the 9/11 argument. Shue does not deny the possibility that sometimes some rights, or some things that we thought were rights, might have to be sacrificed to secure other rights. But, in a

---

[30] Waldron, "Security and Liberty," pp. 198–200.

discussion in *Basic Rights* of the limits on what we are required to do or to put up with for others, he draws the line at the sacrifice of anyone's *basic* rights. "One is required," says Shue, "to sacrifice anything but one's basic rights in order to honor the basic rights of others" (p. 114). Why this line? As I understand it, Shue's position is that the sacrifice of anyone's basic rights means the sacrifice of the conditions that make it possible for that person meaningfully to enjoy and exercise any rights at all. And it is a consequence of what I believe is his acute sensitivity to the logic of the distribution of rights that he rules out this possibility. Even if innumerably more rights could be secured by this means, sacrificing some person as a rights-bearer—reducing him in effect to a non-person, a being who has no rights at all—is out of the question. Our responsibility with rights is to recognize everyone as a rights-bearer and to adjust our sense of what rights each person is to have under the discipline of this fundamental recognition.

What if the basic rights of some have to be sacrificed not just for the sake of rights but for the *basic* rights of others? In this case, Shue says, "it is certainly not obvious which set of rights ought to be sacrificed" (pp. 166–7). One possibility he considers is that, in such a trade-off, a government (such as the U.S. government) is entitled to prefer the basic rights of its own citizens to the basic rights of foreigners. The most he is prepared to say in regard to this proposal is that government may elect to give priority to securing the basic rights of its own citizens to securing the basic rights of foreigners, but that this does not imply that it is entitled to violate the basic rights of foreigners—that is, act deliberately to undermine them—as a means to securing its own citizens' basic rights (p. 166).[31]

This sense of constraint is very important, both for what it represents about Shue's commitment to the logic of rights, and for its actual impact on the post-9/11 proposals. It is important to remember, in evaluating various proposals for trade-offs that might enhance our security in a post-9/11 world, that at times of national panic the deprivations imposed on (or proposed for) members of vulnerable and identifiable minorities are often deprivations of security, not just deprivations of civil liberties or other ordinary rights. For example, those who have been beaten and tortured—some beaten and tortured to death[32]—by American

---

[31] Shue argues in an endnote (219 n.) that this does not involve reintroducing the distinction between positive and negative rights that, as we saw in section 3, he rejects. (See above, text accompanying note 15.)

[32] "In U.S. Report, Brutal Details of Two Afghan Inmates' Deaths," *New York Times*, May 20, 2005.

intelligence operatives in the war against terrorism have suffered not just the loss of rights, but the radical loss of security. As I argued in section 3, the infliction of pain during interrogation renders a person not just less free—though he has to be made unfree (*held down*) in order to be tortured—but less safe, less secure in a very straightforward sense.[33] The security that we all crave is security against violent attack, but that is exactly what many people lose when they are imprisoned in Guantánamo Bay or in "black" U.S. prisons in Eastern Europe, or when they are "rendered" by U.S. agents to foreign countries like Syria for torture by their authorities. Their security is sacrificed in order to make the rest of us more safe.[34] That is an appalling prospect to contemplate on any account. But on Shue's account, it is particularly troubling, since he understands their security as not just a good to be enjoyed, but as a basic right, a condition for their having any other rights at all.

Elsewhere I have argued that we should not treat security as a good to be maximized in society, but as something to be achieved, as far as possible, at an equal level for everyone.[35] But that was not an easy argument to make.[36] Shue makes it much easier, however, by conceiving of security as a basic right. If security is the condition of the effective enjoyment of rights, then sacrificing anyone's security for the sake of others' is absolutely ruled out. What is commanded here by the logic of rights is peremptory and deafening: we are to do everything possible to avoid the situation in which anyone's security is comprehensively sacrificed, for to do so is to act as though none of that person's rights matter, ultimately as though his personhood doesn't matter. Obviously there is still a little room for argument inasmuch as even the sacrifice of security can be conceived as a matter of more or less. But it is a sign of the importance of Shue's analysis that it locates the issue firmly on this ground of basic rights.

---

[33] See above, note 9 and accompanying text.

[34] See the discussion in Waldron, "Is this Torture Necessary?"

[35] Waldron, "Safety and Security," pp. 491–4.

[36] See also the argument about security in Bernard Williams, *In the Beginning was the Deed: Realism and Moralism in Political Argument* (Cambridge: Cambridge University Press, 2005), pp. 4 ff.

11

Human Rights, Responsibilities, and Climate Change*

Simon Caney

There is no longer any doubt that human activity is bringing about serious and accelerating deterioration in the earth's climate. The most recent assessment report of the authoritative Intergovernmental Panel on Climate Change (IPCC) finds that global average surface temperatures have increased by $0.74°C \pm 0.18°C$ in the period from 1996 to 2005.[1] The IPCC employs six different scenarios—all of which find that temperatures will increase and sea levels will rise. Using the "best estimates" of the likely temperature increase from each of these scenarios it concludes that by 2090–2099 temperatures will increase by between 1.8°C and 4.0°C. Sea levels are projected to increase by between 0.18 and 0.59 meters (and this excludes "future rapid dynamical changes in ice flow").[2]

Climate change raises a host of ethical questions. In virtue of what is climate change wrong? What responsibilities do current generations owe to future generations who will bear the brunt of the changes? Should the resources that some think should be spent on climate change be spent on other objectives instead? If humanity should seek to prevent dangerous climate change, who should bear the burden of combating climate change? What ethical constraints are there on the policy instruments that might be employed to tackle climate change (geo-engineering, nuclear energy)?

* I am grateful to Charles Beitz and Robert Goodin for their many helpful comments on an earlier draft of this chapter.

[1] S. Solomon et al., "Technical Summary," in *Climate Change 2007: The Physical Science Basis. Contribution of Working Group I to the Fourth Assessment Report of the Intergovernmental Panel on Climate Change*, ed. S. Solomon, D. Qin, M. Manning, Z. Chen, M. Marquis, K. B. Averyt, M. Tignor, and H. L. Miller (Cambridge: Cambridge University Press, 2007), p. 36.

[2] Ibid., p. 70. The baseline for all these projections is the global average temperatures and sea levels in 1980–1999.

These questions have been largely ignored by moral and political philosophers until very recently. Henry Shue is one notable exception to this rule. Since the early 1990s he has published a series of penetrating papers identifying the challenges raised by climate change. He has, moreover, persuasively argued that developing countries are entitled to make "subsistence emissions" and that this requires the affluent and industrialized countries to make radical cuts in their greenhouse gas emissions.[3] In addition to this, he has made powerful objections to some of the policy instruments proposed, including most notably the Clean Development Mechanism.[4]

There is, however, one puzzling feature of Shue's analysis of climate change—namely that it makes very little use of the concept of rights in general, and basic rights in particular.[5] One might expect that the author of *Basic Rights* would see climate change through the lens of the notion of "basic rights." Shue, however, makes very little use of this framework in his treatment of climate change. With one exception he does not draw on the concept of rights to approach the ethical issues raised by climate change.[6] In this chapter I suggest that a rights-centered approach provides a fruitful way of thinking about climate change. Anthropogenic climate change, so I argue, jeopardizes fundamental human rights (section 1). This prompts the question "who is duty-bound to uphold these rights?" In the second section of the chapter I develop an account of the responsibilities generated by the rights identified in section 1, contrasting my account with that defended by Shue.

1. The Role of Rights

1.1. Evaluating Impacts

Climate change has been analyzed using a variety of different frameworks. Some approach it using cost-benefit analysis (CBA). For example, though

---

[3] This is a constant theme of Shue's work. See, for example: "Subsistence Emissions and Luxury Emissions," *Law and Policy*, 15 (1993), 39–59; "After You: May Action by the Rich be Contingent upon Action by the Poor?" *Indiana Journal of Global Legal Studies*, 1 (1994), 343–66; "Avoidable Necessity: Global Warming, International Fairness, and Alternative Energy," in *Theory and Practice: Nomos XXXVII*, ed. Judith Wagner DeCew and Ian Shapiro (New York: New York University Press, 1995), pp. 239–64; and "Global Environment and International Inequality," *International Affairs*, 75 (1999), 531–45.

[4] "A Legacy of Danger: The *Kyoto Protocol* and Future Generations," in *Globalisation and Equality*, ed. Keith Horton and Haig Patapan (London: Routledge, 2004), pp. 164–78.

[5] This point is made in the Introduction to this volume by Charles Beitz and Robert Goodin.

[6] The exception is "Bequeathing Hazards: Security Rights and Property Rights of Future Humans," in *Global Environmental Economics: Equity and the Limits to Markets*, ed. Mohammed H. I. Dore and Timothy D. Mount (Malden, Mass.: Blackwell Publishers, 1999), pp. 38–53.

they differ in many ways, both William Nordhaus and Sir Nicholas Stern evaluate the impacts of climate change and whether it is appropriate to engage in a program of mitigation and adaptation by comparing the costs and benefits of climate change with the costs and benefits of mitigating and adapting to climate change.[7] They differ in the pure time discount rate that they employ and in the conclusions they arrive at but they share a common commitment to CBA.[8]

Others have evaluated climate change by considering its impact on security. To take one well-known example, a group of retired U.S. generals and admirals prepared a report on *National Security and the Threat of Climate Change*. This contends that climate change leads, through a variety of different mechanisms, to threats to U.S. security.[9] Another example is the United Nations Environment Programme's report on conflict in Sudan which maintains that: "there is mounting evidence that the decline in precipitation due to regional climate change has been a significant stress factor on pastoralist societies—particularly in Darfur and Kordofan—and has thereby contributed to conflict."[10]

In this chapter I wish to argue that, whatever merits these existing normative frameworks possess, they are incomplete. They omit an important dimension. Climate change, I argue, poses a threat to human rights.

1.2. Three Human Rights

There is not space to provide a full defense of human rights. In what follows I shall therefore posit several key human rights and then show how climate change threatens each of them.[11] In doing so, I focus on what I take to be fairly uncontroversial human rights and, moreover, I select the most minimal interpretations of these rights.[12] The aim is to show that

---

[7] See William Nordhaus, *A Question of Balance: Weighing the Options on Global Warming Policies* (New Haven, Conn.: Yale University Press, 2008) and Sir Nicholas Stern, *The Economics of Climate Change: the Stern Review* (Cambridge: Cambridge University Press, 2007).

[8] For their disagreements about the pure time discount rate see: Stern, *The Economics of Climate Change*, pp. 35, 51; Stern, "The Economics of Climate Change," *American Economic Review*, 98 (2008), 12–15; and Nordhaus, "A Review of the *Stern Review* on the Economics of Climate Change," *Journal of Economic Literature*, 45 (2007), 686–702 at p. 689.

[9] *National Security and the Threat of Climate Change* (Alexandria, Va.: CNA Corporation, 2007).

[10] United Nations Environment Programme, *Sudan Post-Conflict Environmental Assessment* (Nairobi, Kenya: United Nations Environment Programme, 2007), p. 9.

[11] I am grateful to Kate Raworth for helpful discussions of the nature of the rights jeopardized by climate change.

[12] My strategy here is much influenced by the work of Thomas Pogge. See, in particular, his important work *World Poverty and Human Rights: Cosmopolitan Responsibilities and Reforms*, 2nd edn. (Cambridge: Polity Press, 2008).

even on a minimal set of human rights anthropogenic climate change violates human rights. I shall focus on four such rights.

(i) The first is the human right to life. This right appears in Article 3 of the Universal Declaration of Human Rights (1948) as well as many subsequent declarations and conventions. According to the minimalist conception of the human right to life that I shall posit, *persons have a human right that others do not act so that they "arbitrarily" deprive them of their life.*[13] This right is clearly a "basic right" in the sense that Shue gives that term. For Shue basic rights are rights that one must possess if one is to exercise other rights.[14] And it is evident that without the human right to life one is unable to enjoy other rights.

The human right to life as I have characterized it is clearly jeopardized by the current anthropogenic climate change. First, climate change will lead some to die because of an increase in the frequency and in the intensity of freak weather events. In particular, hurricanes, storm surges, and extreme precipitation will lead to direct loss of life. Storm surges can have a particularly devastating impact and have in the past led to the loss of thousands of lives. Second, climate change will also lead some to die because of heat stress. The IPCC reports, for example, that "in August 2003, a heatwave in France caused more than 14,800 deaths ... Belgium, the Czech Republic, Germany, Italy, Portugal, Spain, Switzerland, the Netherlands and the UK all reported excess mortality during the heatwave period, with total deaths in the range of 35,000."[15] European cities may be able to adapt to increased temperatures. It bears noting, therefore, that heatwaves can have disastrous effects in less developed countries. The IPCC also writes that "eighteen heatwaves were reported in India between 1980 and 1998, with a heatwave in 1988 affecting ten states and causing 1,300 deaths ... Heatwaves in Orissa, India, in 1998, 1999 and 2000 caused an estimated 2,000, 91 and 29 deaths, respectively ...

---

[13] This formulation follows the way that the right to life is framed in the International Covenant on Civil and Political Rights (ICCPR) (1966) where Article 6.1 states that "[n]o one shall be arbitrarily deprived of his life." By making reference to the "arbitrary" loss of life this formulation allows the possibility that loss of life can in some cases be compatible with this right so long as a non-arbitrary reason can be given. This permits us to set some controversies aside (concerning its implications for fetuses, capital punishment, euthanasia, killing in war, and so on) for they can be discussed under the heading of whether they are arbitrary or not, and it thereby enables us to focus on the very many cases where it is absolutely clear that depriving others of their life is a human rights violation.

[14] Henry Shue, *Basic Rights: Subsistence, Affluence, and U. S. Foreign Policy*, 2nd edn. (Princeton, N.J.: Princeton University Press, 1996), pp. 19–20; cf. also pp. 26–7.

[15] Ulisses Confalonieri and Bettina Menne, "Human Health," in *Climate Change 2007: Impacts, Adaptation and Vulnerability. Contribution of Working Group II to the Fourth Assessment Report of the Intergovernmental Panel on Climate Change*, ed. Martin Parry, Osvaldo Canziani, Jean Palutikof, Paul van der Linden, and Clair Hanson (Cambridge: Cambridge University Press, 2007), p. 397.

and heatwaves in 2003 in Andhra Pradesh, India, caused more than 3000 deaths."[16] Anthropogenic climate change thus arbitrarily deprives people of their life and thereby undermines the human right to life.[17]

(ii) Consider now a second proposed human right—the right to health. Again, this can be construed in controversial ways. For example, when the International Covenant on Economic, Social and Cultural Rights (ICESCR) (1966) affirms "the right of everyone to the enjoyment of the highest attainable standard of physical and mental health" (Art 12.1) this might be criticized on the grounds that to maximize attainable levels of health would consume all available resources even though they might be needed for other equally important rights or goals. In order to avoid such controversies I shall posit a much more minimal version of the human right to health, namely: *persons have a human right that others do not create serious threats to their health.*[18]

Now when formulated in this way, it is clear that anthropogenic climate change jeopardizes the human right to health in (at least) four ways. First, climate change will result in greater exposure to vector-borne diseases such as malaria and dengue. In addition to this, some will suffer from water-borne diseases. Furthermore, there will be an increase in cardio-respiratory problems. Fourth, and finally, it is projected to lead to an increase in the incidence of diarrhea.[19] Those responsible for causing climate change are, thus, jointly acting in such a way as to seriously threaten the health of many others. As such they violate the minimal version of the human right to health posited above.

[16] Ibid., p. 396.

[17] A comparison with Shue's work is appropriate here. In his paper "Bequeathing Hazards: Security Rights and Property Rights of Future Humans," Shue maintains that climate change violates the "basic right to physical security" (p. 39). The right to physical security might be thought to be similar, at least in part, to the right to life that I have discussed. It is not clear to me, however, that the malign effects of climate change that Shue describes in support of this claim are in fact all threats to physical integrity. He points out that climate change leads to (a) an increase in diseases transmitted by mosquitoes, (b) saline intrusion of freshwater sources, and (c) threats to agriculture, and concludes that they violate the right to physical security ("Bequeathing Hazards," p. 50.). Saline intrusion and poor crops are without a doubt harmful but they do not constitute an attack on a person's bodily integrity. They are not threats to "physical security" as Shue defines that term in *Basic Rights*, for there he describes "a basic right to physical security" as "a right that is basic not to be subjected to murder, torture, mayhem, rape, or assault" (*Basic Rights*, p. 20).

[18] This claim is presupposed by the ICESCR's conception of the right to health (see ICESCR Art 12.2 (b) and (c)), but it does not commit itself to the ICESCR's ambitious goals.

[19] Confalonieri and Menne, "Human Health," especially p. 393. On the health effects of climate change see further A. J. McMichael et al., eds., *Climate Change and Human Health: Risks and Responses* (Geneva: World Health Organization, 2003) and Anthony J. McMichael et al., "Global Climate Change," in *Comparative Quantification of Health Risks: Global and Regional Burden of Disease Attribution to Selected Major Risk Factors*, ed. Majid Ezzati, Alan D. Lopez, Anthony Rodgers, and Christopher J. L. Murray (Geneva: World Health Organization, 2004), ch. 20, pp.1543–649 esp. pp.1562–605.

(iii) Consider now a third fundamental human right—the right to subsistence (where this is defined as the right to the food and water necessary for subsistence). As is well known, Shue argues in *Basic Rights* that persons have a basic right to "minimal economic security," which he defines as involving "unpolluted air, unpolluted water, adequate food, adequate clothing, adequate shelter, and minimal preventive public health care."[20] This includes the right to subsistence as I am defining it, as well as other components (such as access to shelter and health care). Now Shue interprets this right to entail not simply that persons are entitled that others do not deprive them of food and water, but also that they have a right that others provide them with adequate food and water if their ability to subsist is undermined by wholly natural causes.[21] This, however, might be contested by some who would argue that persons do not have a claim to aid to meet subsistence needs that arise not because of any wrongdoing of others but simply because of natural calamities.[22] To accommodate those with such concerns, I shall posit a minimalist conception of the human right to subsistence, namely: *all persons have a human right that other people do not act so as to deprive them of the means of subsistence.*[23]

Even if we adopt this minimalist conception of the human right to subsistence, it is clear that anthropogenic climate change undermines it. Four different mechanisms may all jeopardize the enjoyment of this right. First, temperature and decreased precipitation in some areas will lead to drought. In addition to this, increased precipitation in other areas may lead to flooding and this too can cause crop failure. Third, sea-level rise (in countries like Bangladesh and in the Nile Delta) can lead to the loss of fertile land to the sea and to the spread of salt water to existing fresh water. Finally, severe weather events (like hurricanes and storm surges) can destroy agriculture. All of these processes thus undermine the enjoyment of the right to subsistence. The magnitude of this issue is conveyed by Anthony Nyong and Isabelle Niang-Diop, who report that "climate change will place an additional 80–125 million people (plus or minus 10 million) at risk of hunger by the 2080s, 70–80% of whom will be in Africa."[24]

---

[20] See Shue, *Basic Rights*, p. 23.   [21] Ibid., pp. 57, 60.

[22] See, for example, Thomas Pogge's chapter in this volume.

[23] This formulation is similar to that found in Article 1.2 of the International Covenant on Civil and Political Rights (1976).

[24] Anthony Nyong and Isabelle Niang-Diop, "Impacts of Climate Change in the Tropics: the African Experience," in *Avoiding Dangerous Climate Change*, ed. Hans Joachim Schellnhuber, Wolfgang Cramer, Nebojsa Nakicenovic, Tom Wigley, and Gary Yohe (Cambridge: Cambridge University Press, 2006), pp. 235–42 at pp. 237–8.

(iv) Thus far I have drawn attention to the relationship between climate change and some well-known human rights. The fourth human right that I wish to posit is much less familiar, the human right not to be subject to enforced relocation: *all persons have a human right not to be forcibly evicted.* The thought is that persons are entitled not to be forcibly evicted from their place of residence because of the actions of others. The underlying principle is not wholly unknown to human rights documents. For example, the Guiding Principles on Internal Displacement (1997) state in Article 6.1 that "[e]very human being shall have the right to be protected against being arbitrarily displaced from his or her home or place of habitual residence."[25]

It is clear that this right, too, is jeopardized by anthropogenic climate change. Rising sea levels and drought will both lead to displacement and, as such, jeopardize this right. Rising sea levels, for example, will force people to migrate from many small island states such as Tuvalu, Kiribati, and the Maldives. Moreover, the 2007/2008 Human Development Report of the UNDP argues that "[g]lobal temperature increases of 3–4°C could result in 330 million people being permanently or temporarily displaced through flooding. Over 70 million people in Bangladesh, 6 million in Lower Egypt and 22 million in Viet Nam would be affected."[26]

1.3. The Road not Taken

In short, then, anthropogenic climate change jeopardizes the human rights to life, health, subsistence, and not to be forcibly evicted. Notably it violates two of the basic rights that Shue affirms—the right to "physical security" and the right to "economic security." So why has Shue not made more of the links between climate change, on the one hand, and rights (especially basic rights), on the other?

I believe that the answer lies in his concern to eschew needlessly controversial assumptions to make his argument. The arguments for basic rights are contested by some[27] and given this there is a case for eschewing such contentious considerations if possible. The concern to avoid unduly contentious assumptions is understandable. This concern can be accommodated in another way, however.

---

[25] These can be found in Ian Brownlie and Guy S. Goodwin-Gill, eds., *Basic Documents on Human Rights,* 5th edn. (Oxford: Oxford University Press, 2006), pp. 220–9.

[26] The United Nations Development Programme, *Human Development Report 2007/2008 Fighting Climate Change: Human Solidarity in a Divided World* (New York: Palgrave Macmillan, 2007), p. 9.

[27] See, for example, the arguments discussed in the chapters by Ashford and Pogge, this volume.

Rather than avoid reference to rights in general, and basic rights in particular, one can instead present both rights-oriented analyses of climate change and other arguments which do not rely upon rights. To put it in Rawlsian terms, one may seek to develop an "overlapping consensus," in which there are several distinct rationales for endorsing a strong program of mitigation and adaptation, one of which is a rights-centered rationale of the kind defended above.[28] By adopting this approach, one would not forfeit the virtues of a rights-centered approach but could avoid the disadvantages of relying solely on a rights-centered analysis (namely the burden of persuading those who reject Shue's arguments for basic rights or who generally reject the language of rights).

Some may, however, argue that what I am terming a rights-centered approach is highly problematic and for that reason ought to be rejected altogether. In the rest of this section I therefore consider two such objections.

1.4. Human Rights and the Future

One commonly expressed doubt is prompted by the fact that climate change is an intergenerational phenomenon. Molecules of carbon dioxide can last for hundreds of years—the average is 100 years.[29] Some, though, deny that future generations possess rights and therefore hold that the emissions of current generations cannot violate the rights of future generations. Consequently, it is held that a rights-centered analysis cannot provide an adequate analysis of climate change. Wilfred Beckerman and Joanna Pasek, have, for example, argued in this way. Their argument is very simple and straightforward. On their view, to possess a right one must be in existence. One cannot possess anything, including a right, unless one is alive. Therefore the idea that people who are not born have rights is nonsense.[30]

One obvious response is to note that climate change will affect not simply future people but also those who are currently alive. A rights-oriented approach to climate change thus has much to offer. This response

[28] As we shall see in section 2, Shue himself takes an "overlapping consensus" approach when discussing who should bear the burdens of combating climate change. The concept of an "overlapping consensus" can be found in John Rawls, *Political Liberalism* (New York: Columbia University Press, 1993), Lecture IV.

[29] Sir John Houghton, *Global Warming: The Complete Briefing*, 3rd edn. (Cambridge: Cambridge University Press, 2004), pp. 30–1.

[30] Wilfred Beckerman and Joanna Pasek, *Justice, Posterity, and the Environment* (Oxford: Oxford University Press, 2001), pp. 11–28, esp. pp. 15–16, 19.

is correct as far as it goes but I believe we can go further and need not acquiesce in the charge that climate change will not harm the rights of future people. In particular, two points can be made in reply. First, it is helpful to employ a distinction invoked by Robert Elliott. Elliott distinguishes between the claim that future people possess rights now (what he terms the "Non-concessional View") and the claim that future people will possess rights when they are born (what he terms the "Concessional View").[31] Now the Concessional View is not vulnerable to Beckerman and Pasek's objection because it does not affirm what they deny (namely the claim that future people have rights now).[32] As such one can accept their claim and still hold that future people will have rights and that what we do now can jeopardize those rights. Furthermore, the Concessional View is supported by the following line of reasoning: When future people are born they will have a full moral status and a set of interests which should be respected. As such, these interests generate duties on other people—duties not to harm (and perhaps also to aid). Now these interests can, of course, be jeopardized by their contemporaries but they can also be jeopardized by members of previous generations. And it would seem odd to say that the contemporaries are duty-bound to honor these vital interests but that members of earlier generations are not subject to exactly the same duty. If the interests are so fundamental that they generate duties they surely generate duties on all who can jeopardize them. Thus those who are alive at t_1 are under an obligation not to act in ways that will threaten the rights that persons at t_{200} will hold. Given this, one can say that future people will have rights and their doing so entails obligations on earlier generations.[33]

A second point bears noting. Many of those who deny that future people have rights soften the blow by making conciliatory statements. They often claim, for instance, that persons have duties to future generations.[34] Now

---

[31] See Robert Elliott, "The Rights of Future People," *Journal of Applied Philosophy*, 6 (1989), 159–69, especially pp. 160–2.

[32] Shue does not make this distinction and so not too much should be read into any of his formulations of the rights of future people. However, his statements about the rights of future humans are closer in tenor to the Non-concessional View; see Shue, "Bequeathing Hazards," p. 48.

[33] See Elliott, "The Rights of Future People," p. 162. See also Joel Feinberg, "The Rights of Animals and Unborn Generations," in *Rights, Justice, and the Bounds of Liberty: Essays in Social Philosophy* (Princeton, N.J.: Princeton University Press, 1980), pp. 181–2 and Lukas H. Meyer, "Past and Future: The Case for a Threshold Notion of Harm," in *Rights, Culture, and the Law: Themes from the Legal and Political Philosophy of Joseph Raz*, ed. Lukas H. Meyer, Stanley L. Paulson, and Thomas W. Pogge (Oxford: Oxford University Press, 2003), pp. 143–59 at p. 145.

[34] See, for example, Beckerman and Pasek, *Justice, Posterity, and the Environment*, pp. 18, 25, 28, 107–24.

it is, of course, true that one can have duties to persons which do not entail that those persons have corresponding rights. It is, however, difficult to advance the "argument from non-existence" to undermine the claim that future people have rights *whilst still holding that there are duties to future people*.[35] If the current non-existence of future people entails that they cannot *have* rights then it also undermines any claim that they *have* a moral status which should be respected or they *have* interests which should not be jeopardized.[36] Put another way: the "argument from non-existence" fails to show why there is anything particularly problematic about ascribing rights to future generations and why it does not also undermine the application of all other approaches (including welfare economics and the duty-based approach that Beckerman and Pasek affirm).

Beckerman and Pasek might reply that future people will have fundamental interests and this fact can generate duties on current generations.[37] But if future people will have fundamental interests then it follows that they will have rights and so this response leaves no room for them to reject the Concessional View. Thus, either one holds that future people cannot have anything (but this both has no force against the Concessional View and also rules out duty-based approaches as well); or else one holds that future people will have interests and thus we now have duties to them (but this leaves the Concessional View intact).

1.5. Human Rights and the Non-Identity Problem

Consider now a second challenge. Someone might invoke Derek Parfit's "non-identity problem." Does this not undermine the claim that I am advancing that future people possess the right not to suffer from dangerous climate change? Let us consider Parfit's well-known problem. Parfit points out that the decisions that people make—including whether to use

---

[35] Any attempt to do so would have to give an argument for why there are duties (to future people) which does not appeal in any way to how these will serve important interests. Even if one could give an argument for duties that eschews any reference to the need to protect important interests it seems to me highly implausible that such an account could *fully* explain our understanding of our responsibilities to future people. A large part (if not the entirety) of the appeal of such duties is that they are needed to protect the vital interests of future people.

[36] Joerg Chet Tremmel, "Establishing Intergenerational Justice in National Constitutions," in *Handbook of Intergenerational Justice*, ed. Tremmel (Cheltenham: Edward Elgar, 2006), pp. 187–214 at p. 200.

[37] They say, for example, that "we are under a moral obligation to take account of the interests that they [future generations] will have"; *Justice, Posterity, and the Environment*, p. 25, cf. p. 28.

up natural resources or not—affect who gets born in the future. If people make different choices now different people will get born. It follows from this that if we emit high levels of greenhouse gases now, it is not true that we are making those in the far future worse off than they would otherwise have been since without our actions they (very probably) would not have been born.[38]

Does this undermine the rights-oriented view defended above? Not necessarily. Parfit's argument poses a strong challenge to what he terms "person-affecting" views.[39] These hold that actions are wrong because they make people worse off and Parfit's argument calls such views into question. This, however, gives us reason to reject the claim that future people have rights only if the latter is necessarily a "person-affecting" claim. There are, though, other ways of thinking about the rights of future people.

Consider Amartya Sen's concept of a "goal rights system." Sen defines this as follows: "A moral system in which fulfilment and nonrealization of rights are included among the goals, incorporated in the evaluation of states of affairs, and then applied to the choice of actions through consequential links will be called a goal rights system."[40] On this view, a commitment to rights requires that we bring about states of affairs in which people are able to exercise their fundamental rights. The key point is that this is not a "person-affecting" approach but what Parfit terms an "impersonal" one.[41] As such, it is not undermined by Parfit's non-identity problem.

If we use Sen's approach it follows that a rights-centered analysis does not claim, and is not committed to claiming, that an action committed now violates a particular (future) person's right in the sense that it prevents a person from enjoying a right that he or she would otherwise be able to enjoy.[42] Rather, what it entails is that persons should not act in such a way that those who are born in the future are unable to enjoy certain rights.[43]

---

[38] Derek Parfit, *Reasons and Persons* (Oxford: Oxford University Press, 1986), pp. 351–79.

[39] *Reasons and Persons*, p. 370.

[40] Amartya Sen, "Rights and Agency," *Philosophy and Public Affairs*, 11 (1982), 3–39 at p. 15.

[41] *Reasons and Persons*, p. 386.

[42] Shue appears to endorse this Sen-like way of conceiving of rights. He writes that "rights ... are goals to be attained. The provision of adequate security for basic rights is a goal"; "Bequeathing Hazards," p. 51 n. 12. He does not, however, employ this claim in order to explain the rights of future people.

[43] Shue himself does not devote much attention to the non-identity problem. He mentions it in two places. In the first he states that it does not have any bearing on the "shape and character of our responsibilities"; Shue, "Responsibility to Future Generations and the Technological Transition," in *Perspectives on Climate Change: Science, Economics, Politics, Ethics,*

2. Responsibilities

2.1. Shue's Three Principles

Having drawn attention to the ways in which climate change jeopardizes a set of human rights and defended the intergenerational application of this claim, I now turn to the question of who is duty-bound to uphold these rights. In "Global Environment and International Inequality," Shue identifies three distinct but familiar principles and argues that they all converge on the same conclusion. In what follows, I want to argue that his principles need to be modified and the relationship between them reconceived. Instead of supposing that three separate principles all lead to the same conclusion, we should, I argue, adhere to a hybrid model that combines revised versions of two of the principles.

Let us consider Shue's three principles. His first principle reads as follows:

Principle I
When a party has in the past taken an unfair advantage of others by imposing costs upon them without their consent, those who have been unilaterally put at a disadvantage are entitled to demand that in the future the offending party shoulder burdens that are unequal at least to the extent of the unfair advantage previously taken in order to restore equality.[44]

Principle I allocates duties in line with agents' "contribution to the problem" so I shall term it the Contribution Principle.[45] Shue follows his defense of this first principle with a second:

Principle II
Among a number of parties, all of whom are bound to contribute to some common endeavour, the parties who have the most resources normally should contribute most to the endeavour.[46]

---

ed. Walter Sinnott-Armstrong and Richard B. Howarth (Amsterdam: Elsevier, 2005), pp. 265–84 at p. 271. In the second he says that it "has no implications at all for what we ought to do. At most, it has some implications for how we explain our moral judgements"; Shue, "Deadly Delays, Saving Opportunities: Creating a More Dangerous World?" in *Energy and Responsibility*, ed. Denis Arnold (forthcoming), footnote 5. The first strikes me as rather sweeping: Parfit has issued a powerful challenge to person-affecting principles and this at least bears on the "character" of our responsibilities, by which I mean what kind of responsibility we have. The second strikes me as more plausible. What I have sought to do is "explain" how the concept of rights applies even in cases where the actions of some affect the identities of others.

[44] "Global Environment and International Inequality," p. 534; cf. also pp. 534–7.

[45] The phrase comes from ibid., p. 533.

[46] Ibid., p. 537; cf. also pp. 537–40. Shue also plausibly suggests that on this conception the amount required should correspond to the party's wealth (p. 537).

This is an "Ability to Pay" principle. Shue's final principle makes the following claim:

Principle III
When some people have less than enough for a decent human life, other people have far more than enough, and the total resources available are so great that everyone could have at least enough without preventing some people from still retaining considerably more than others have, it is unfair not to guarantee everyone at least an adequate minimum.[47]

This might be termed the "Guaranteed Minimum" Principle.[48]

As noted above, Shue's own conclusion is that "they all converge upon the same practical conclusion ... the costs should initially be borne by the wealthy industrialized states."[49] It does not matter which of these principles one adopts: they all lead to the same conclusion. All roads, so to speak, lead to Rome.

2.2. Examining Principle I

Shue's first principle has considerable intuitive appeal. It is a fixed conviction that if an agent causes some pollution then, other things being equal, that agent is duty-bound to clear it up. Two further points should, however, be noted.

First, it is important to observe that Shue's first principle states that if a party has taken "an *unfair* advantage of others by imposing costs upon them without their consent" (emphasis added)[50] then that party should bear a commensurate burden. Shue does not tell us what would count as taking a "fair" advantage. His point, though, is that we should distinguish between different kinds of contribution to a problem—some are "unfair" (and perpetrators of these should therefore pay for that) but others are "fair." Drawing on what Shue has said elsewhere it is clear that he would think that those emissions that are required for subsistence are "fair" and so those who emit them should not be bound to pay for those emissions.[51] This is highly relevant to the case of climate change given the rising emissions of developing countries.

Note, though, that if we make this move we are effectively incorporating Shue's third principle into the first. At its simplest, the third principle holds that the very poor should not have to pay for their emissions if doing so would push them to a sub-subsistence level (and if the wealthy

---

[47] Ibid., p. 541. [48] Ibid., pp. 540–4. [49] Ibid., p. 545. [50] Ibid., p. 534.
[51] See, among many other places, his "Subsistence Emissions and Luxury Emissions."

could pay and there would still be enough wealth for all to have enough and for some to have much more than enough). However, if "fair" emissions include "subsistence emissions" then the revised version of the first principle swallows up the third principle.[52] If, moreover, we tailor PI to address climate change, we would arrive at something like the following principle:

Principle I*
Parties who contribute to dangerous climate change should bear the burden of combating it unless doing so would push them below a decent minimal standard of living.

If the argument of this paragraph is correct it then follows that there are two principles on the table—the revised version of the Contribution Principle and the Ability to Pay Principle—and not three.

Second, it is worth noting that the application of the Contribution Principle to climate change is necessarily incomplete. As was noted above, climate change has an intergenerational aspect to it. Many of those who have contributed to the problem by emitting high levels of greenhouse gases are no longer alive. Given this, the first principle is insufficient: the doctrine that the contributor to a problem should pay obviously cannot be applied if the contributor is no longer alive. The Contribution Principle on its own is therefore inadequate.[53]

2.3. Examining Principle II

Consider now the second principle that Shue affirms. This is vulnerable to two objections. First, it is questionable whether it can stand on all fours with the first principle. The reasoning for Principle I and Principle II compete for the same space. Of course, the two principles might, as Shue says, coincide in their conclusions as to who should pay and how much they should pay. Nonetheless they operate according to competing

---

[52] It should be noted here that if affluent persons continue to emit far in excess of their subsistence emissions then there might be a point at which even subsistence emissions will, given the extent of greenhouse gases already emitted, result in threats to others' human rights. However, even here it is arguable that people are entitled to take steps to ensure their very survival and hence are entitled to emit subsistence emissions.

[53] One response to this might be that later generations will enjoy goods produced by the acts of earlier generations and are therefore under a duty of restitution. I agree and defend a version of this later (section 2.3) but believe that this introduces a new principle. It is no longer a claim about the *contributors* to a problem paying (and so should not be treated as a version of, or corollary of, the Contribution Principle). It ascribes responsibilities to *non-contributors* and so it is appropriate to treat it under a different principle.

logics—one forward-looking and unconcerned with who created the problem and the other backward-looking in just those terms. In cases where
both principles can be applied the affirmation of the logic underlying the
one thus requires a rejection of the logic of another. Hence insofar as we
think that polluters should pay we are committed to rejecting Shue's
second principle.

Two considerations speak in favor of according primacy to Principle I
over Principle II. First, it fits best with our fixed intuitions about specific
cases. If, for example, a firm spills oil at sea then we think that it—the
polluter—should pay, not that a wealthier firm should pay. Or if someone
knocks over a rubbish bin in the street then we expect that person to clear
it up and not someone else who happens to have a greater ability to lift or
to pay or whatever. Second, the claim that polluters should pay follows
from the principle, articulated by Rawls and others, that persons should
take responsibility for their actions and their ends.[54] If we grant an agent
autonomy then it is appropriate to hold it responsible for the decisions
that it makes, including burdens it creates for others. The deeply
entrenched principle that persons should be accountable for their ends
can thus provide a philosophical underpinning for giving the doctrine
that the polluter should pay the pre-eminent role in allocating responsibilities.

This is not to say that Ability to Pay considerations should be rejected
entirely. My suggestion is that they should play a supplementary role and
should address the emissions that the first principle cannot cover. There
are two kinds of emissions that fall into this category. First, as noted
above, there are (i) the emissions of previous people. They obviously
cannot pay and yet their emissions contribute to the problem. Second,
there are (ii) the emissions of the current global poor. They might be
able to pay but only by living at a below-acceptable standard of living
and it is therefore unfair to require them to pay. The Ability to Pay
Principle should thus cover categories (i) and (ii)—what I shall hereafter
call the Remainder. We need some principle to govern who should bear
the burden of these kinds of emissions and an Ability to Pay Principle
seems well-suited to doing so.

Principle II, as it stands, is needlessly vulnerable to a troubling objection. Someone might criticize a pure Ability to Pay Principle on the
grounds that it completely disregards the historical record. Principle II,

---

[54] John Rawls, *Collected Papers*, ed. Samuel Freeman (Cambridge, Mass.: Harvard University
Press, 1999), pp. 241–2, 261–2, 269–70, 284.

she objects, is counter-intuitive because it ignores morally relevant considerations such as who brought about the unjust state of affairs. She might reason as follows: Consider two parties who both have an equal ability to pay. In the case of one of them, John, his current wealth stems in part from his inheritance from his parents and grandparents—all of whom, say, emitted an unfair amount of greenhouse gases. Compare him now with Apu. Apu has the same amount of wealth. However, Apu's wealth did not come about in a climate-endangering way. Suppose we now approach John and Apu and argue, following Principle II, that those with the ability to pay should pay in accordance with their wealth. They will no doubt seek to persuade us otherwise and present reasons why they may retain their wealth. Now one common argument they may adduce (perhaps the most powerful that might be deployed in their defense) is to argue that their wealth came about in a fair way and that they are therefore entitled to keep it. But this argument, note, is not available to John. He has less cause for complaint because of the historical process. A pure Ability to Pay Principle, however, fails to recognize this and is defective because it pays no attention to the historical genesis of a problem.

One lesson that one might seek to draw from this is that we should distinguish between two categories—(i) those whose wealth came about in a climate-endangering way and (ii) those whose wealth came about in a "clean" way. One would then argue that when applying the Ability to Pay principle we should distinguish between these two categories of people and should then ascribe greater responsibilities to those in category (i) over those in category (ii).[55]

Two points, however, tell against this. First, it would be highly impractical to propose separating people into categories (i) and (ii). It would be next to impossible to ascertain the exact level of emissions of earlier generations that led to current individuals' holdings. Furthermore, and more crucially, no currently wealthy economies have developed in a clean way. Such is the extent of our dependence on fossil fuels—for heating, road transportation, industry, aviation, cooking, and construction—that it is hard to think of anyone who is wealthy whose current holdings did not come about in any way at all through the heavy use of fossil fuels. Even enterprises, such as service industries, that one might think would involve low emissions will involve emissions for construction, heating, transporting people, using computers, and so on. This, however, suggests a second

[55] See on this Simon Caney, "Climate Change, Justice and the Duties of the Advantaged," *Critical Review of International Social and Political Philosophy*, 12.2 (2009).

way of responding to the point about the historical record. Rather than adopt an Ability to Pay Principle and then ascribe greater responsibilities to those whose wealth came about in a climate-endangering way, we might adopt:

Principle II* (hereafter PII*)
The duty to bear the burden of the Remainder should be borne by the wealthy (proportionately to their wealth) because (a) they can bear the burden most easily and also (b) the wealth that they hold came about in climate-endangering ways.[56]

The central point here is that the claim "You should pay because, and to the extent that, you are wealthy and your wealth is built in part on unjustly high emissions" (PII*) is a more persuasive argument than the bald statement "You should pay because, and to the extent that, you are wealthy" (PII). The revised principle is superior to a pure Ability to Pay Principle because it is sensitive to the historical pedigree of the creation of people's wealth. It allows that it might be unfair to require people to pay for problems just because they happen to be wealthy but it adds that the process by which the wealthy under consideration acquired that wealth has been unjust.

Two further points bear noting about the history-sensitive Ability to Pay Principle. First, I have worded it carefully so as to avoid the "non-identity problem." PII* does not claim that, say, a current wealthy person has benefited from industrialization in the sense that the industrial revolution left him or her better off than he or she would otherwise have been. As such it is immune to the (correct) rejoinder that it is false to assert that industrialization has rendered them better off than they would otherwise have been because if industrialization had never occurred then they might

---

[56] For a similar, but distinct, line of reasoning see Edward Page's instructive discussion in *Climate Change, Justice and Future Generations* (Cheltenham: Edward Elgar, 2006), pp. 172–3. Page suggests that there should "be some 'discount' in what is required of the better off when their behaviour is not cause of the problem" (p. 172). The view considered in the text departs from Page's in two fundamental ways. First, Page applies his principle to all emissions, whereas the revised Ability to Pay Principle (PII*) applies only to the emissions of past generations and the global poor (the Remainder). Second, Page writes that " 'ability to pay' arguments gain at least some of their plausibility from the implicit assumption that those who have the ability to solve environmental problems are generally those responsible for them" (p. 173). This though is not the view affirmed by PII*. The latter does not ascribe duties "to solve environmental problems" to those with the ability to pay on the grounds that they are also "responsible for them" (p. 172). That would be to combine an Ability to Pay Principle with the Contribution Principle. Rather PII* says that the duties fall on the wealthy because they have the greatest ability to pay and their wealth came about in a climate-endangering way (even if they themselves do not emit and have not emitted high levels of greenhouse gases). PII* will make demands of the wealthy even if they themselves emit very low levels because they have inherited wealth that is founded on an excessively high level of emissions.

never have been born. (Their parents might never have met, and even if they did they might not have mated at the time they did. Indeed, their parents might never have been born.) PII* acknowledges that without industrialization many people who are wealthy might never have been born. Its claim, to repeat, is that the current holdings of those who are wealthy are almost certainly built on a history that includes very high emissions.[57] Second, we might note that the revised Ability to Pay Principle has two virtues. As has been mentioned already, it can cope with the objection invoking the relevance of the historic record. An additional virtue is that it has benign incentive effects. Since PII* makes greater demands on those whose wealth came about in a climate-endangering way it gives people an incentive to amass their wealth in ways which do not involve high greenhouse gas emissions.

Someone might ask why PII* refers to "wealth that came about in a climate-endangering way" as opposed to "wealth that came about in an unjust way." Recall that the point about John in the John/Apu example is that he could not say that his wealth had come about in a just way. In the case as described, it had not come about in a just way because it had involved unduly high emissions. But John would have had as weak a claim to his current wealth if it had come about in any other kind of unjust way. Suppose, for example, that his ancestors stole land from indigenous peoples.

Given this it makes sense to revise PII* to reflect this point, and to ascribe the duty to combat climate change to the wealthy because (a) they have the greatest ability to pay and also (b) their wealth came about in climate-endangering or other unjust ways. Hence:

Principle II** (hereafter PII**)
The duty to bear the burden of the Remainder should be borne by the wealthy (proportionately to their wealth) because (a) they can bear the burden most easily and also (b) the wealth that they hold came about in climate-endangering or other unjust ways.

---

[57] As such I am making good the claim made in footnote 53. The point being made here also corresponds to what Shue himself says in "Global Environment and International Inequality." He writes there that those living in affluent industrialized countries are not "completely unrelated" to the emissions of past generations (p. 536) for they inherit many goods resulting from the emissions of the past (pp. 536–7). Shue includes this in his discussion of what I have termed the Contribution Principle but for the reasons set out in footnote 53 I think it is misleading to treat it as a part of, or as a corollary of, the Contribution Principle. It attributes responsibilities to people not in virtue of their contribution to the problem but in virtue of their acquiring goods produced by others. The Contribution Principle, as Shue himself formulates it, attributes the duties *only* to those parties who have imposed the costs on others ("Global Environment and International Inequality," p. 534).

2.4. A Summary

To summarize: I have defended a version of Shue's first principle:

Principle I*
Parties who contribute to dangerous climate change should bear the burden of combating it unless doing so would push them below a decent minimal standard of living.

But what of the emissions of those who are no longer alive (and cannot therefore pay) and the emissions of those who are poor (and therefore should not have to pay)? How should we deal with what I termed the Remainder? This is where the second principle comes in:

Principle II**
The duty to bear the burden of the Remainder should be borne by the wealthy (proportionately to their wealth) because (a) they can bear the burden most easily and also (b) the wealth that they hold came about in climate-endangering or other unjust ways.[58]

2.5. Who are the Duty-Bearers?

This leaves a number of questions unresolved. One pressing question concerns what kind of entity or entities (individual, firm, state, nation, international organization) are the relevant duty-bearers. Many focus almost exclusively on states. This, however, can be misleading. Take, for example, the Contribution Principle. Some states (such as India, for example) have low per capita emissions overall and yet contain some wealthy people with very high emissions. An approach which says that the only duty-bearers are states would fail to pick this up. At the same time some states have high per capita emissions overall and yet within that state there might be very unequal emission levels, with some emitting very little indeed. Yet under a statist framework they might be required to pay. Applying the Contribution Principle to states might then have the effect of requiring a UK citizen to pay and an Indian citizen not to pay when the emissions of the latter dwarf those of the former. This is clearly unfair and contradicts the logic of the Contribution Principle. Exactly the same kind of argument could also be made about the Ability to Pay Principle. Some wealthy countries contain exceptionally poor people and some developing countries contain people who are wealthy.

---

[58] For further discussion see my "Climate Change, Justice and the Duties of the Advantaged."

It might be suggested that as a matter of practicality we should focus on states since the international negotiations are the main determinant of the distribution of emissions. Concerns about feasibility, it might be claimed, entail that we should focus on the allocation of emission rights between states. This reply is, however, misleading. Recognizing the centrality of states does not entail that one cannot apply these principles to individuals or sub-state actors (like commercial enterprises) for two reasons.

First, one can accept the significance of states but then insist that states should apply the two principles to individuals within their own jurisdiction. They can employ carbon taxes and/or carbon quotas in a rough and ready way to ensure that their citizens pay in proportion to their emissions and that the wealthy pay for what I have termed the Remainder. Even if the policy instruments at their disposal cannot precisely capture the two principles defended above, they can approximate them and this is better than simply ignoring the differing emission levels and differing levels of wealth within states.

Second, it bears noting that international carbon trading schemes do not, of necessity, have to allocate emission rights to states. The EU Emissions Trading Scheme is moving towards a scheme that auctions emission rights to firms in a competitive auction. A more radical proposal would be to have a global scheme of the kind employed by the EU and which would spend all the revenues raised on adaptation and funding research and development into clean technology.[59] The key point to note about this kind of scheme is that even if its creation depends on the actions of states, the scheme itself does not allocate emission rights to states. Under the auction scheme, firms pay for emission rights and then will seek to pass the burden on to consumers. As such individual consumers will pay in accordance with their emissions (barring the case of the disadvantaged who, in accordance with Principle I*, will be reimbursed by the revenues produced by the auction). Feasibility considerations do not require that we treat states as the sole moral entities to which the two principles apply.

3. Concluding Remarks

This chapter has sought to defend two claims. First, I have argued that anthropogenic climate change undermines several key human rights. This

---

[59] For my defense of such a scheme see Caney, "Climate Change, Energy Rights and Equality," in *Energy and Responsibility*, ed. Denis Arnold (forthcoming). See also the much fuller and thorough defense given by Oliver Tickell in *Kyoto2: How to Manage the Global Greenhouse* (London: Zed Books, 2008).

raises the question of who is duty-bound to uphold these rights. It would be convenient if either there was one compelling principle or if (as Shue argues) there were a plurality of equally compelling principles that yield the same conclusion and which do not rely on incompatible lines of reasoning. I have argued, however, that no such convenient solution exists. Instead (and this is my second claim) the responsibility to uphold the human rights jeopardized by climate change should be determined by a hybrid approach which combines a version of the Contribution Principle with a version of the Ability to Pay Principle. Much more work needs to be done—both in developing further the links between climate change and rights and in exploring what the principles of responsibility would imply in practice. What I hope to have provided is the beginnings of an account of why climate change is unjust and who is duty-bound to do something about it.

Index